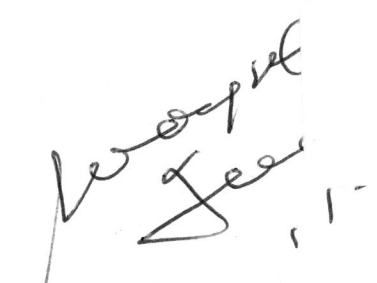

THE TRIUMPH OF DEMOCRACY OVER MILITANT ISLAMISM

Colonel B. Wayne Quist
and Dr. David F. Drake

PublishAmerica
Baltimore

© 2006 by Colonel B. Wayne Quist and Dr. David F. Drake.
All rights reserved. No part of this book may be reproduced, stored in a retrieval system or transmitted in any form or by any means without the prior written permission of the publishers, except by a reviewer who may quote brief passages in a review to be printed in a newspaper, magazine or journal.

First printing

ISBN: 1-4241-4349-7
PUBLISHED BY PUBLISHAMERICA, LLLP
www.publishamerica.com
Baltimore

Printed in the United States of America

To Charlie Nelson—"Rawhide"

for bringing us together and for his significant contributions,

and to Christian Quist and Ethan and Abby Drake

because your generation has been elected to take up the challenge.

What Reviewers Said About
THE TRIUMPH OF DEMOCRACY
OVER MILITANT ISLAMISM

Lieutenant General Thomas G. McInerney, USAF Retired
FOX NEWS Military Analyst and author of
"Endgame—A Blueprint for Victory in the War on Terror"

"The Triumph of Democracy Over Militant Islamism is must reading for everyone who believes in freedom and desires to understand the origins of the ideology of al Qaeda and its relationship to Saudi Arabian Wahhabi-Salafism, the virulent and obscure form of Sunni Islam that inspired Osama bin Laden and al Qaeda and is the state religion of Saudi Arabia. Colonel Quist and Dr. Drake have produced another significant volume that traces the origins of Wahhabi-Salafism and the threat the West faces from radical militant Islamism. The authors have developed a unique thesis regarding the war in Iraq that people need to understand because of the dire threat posed by Saudi Arabian 'Bin Ladenism.' Everyone should read this book!"

Dr. James Forest
Director of Terrorism Studies, Combating Terrorism Center
U.S. Military Academy at West Point

"Colonel Quist and Dr. Drake have compiled an impressive analysis of the threat posed by al Qaeda and other ideologically-affiliated organizations. Their policy recommendations address several important religious, political and economic dimensions of the war on terror. I recommend this useful contribution to the literature for anyone seeking a better understanding of the current global security environment."

Dr. Ali Alyami
Executive Director
Center for Democracy and Human Rights in Saudi Arabia
(www.cdhr.info)

"The Triumph of Democracy over Militant Islamism by Colonel B. Wayne Quist and Dr. David F. Drake is a very readable, comprehensive, and thought-provoking work. The authors clearly outline the looming threat posed by radical, militant, religious extremists and tyrannical regimes such as Saudi Arabia that adamantly reject democracy, non-Muslims, and the rule of law. The Triumph of Democracy over Militant Islamism provides readers with a thorough understanding of a dysfunctional region of the world that is on the verge of religious, economic, political, and social collapse with dire consequences for the entire world. This book provides the American public and U.S. decision-makers with needed tools to enunciate and implement lasting policies that will not only empower the people of the Middle East but will also serve to construct a frontline defense for U.S. national interests globally. This book is required reading for people who desire to understand the mindset of dangerous Islamist ideologues determined to destroy those who do not see the world through their dark vision."

CONTENTS

Authors' Preface	9
Chapter One	
The Saudi Kingdom and Its Unwholesome Alliance	15
Islam and Its Radical Element	16
The Founding of Saudi Arabia	21
The Founder of the Kingdom	21
The Desert Kingdom	26
Discovery of Oil	28
The Kingdom of Oil and Allah	30
Modern Saudi Arabia	37
American Imprint	38
The Bedouin/Islamic Influence	39
The Al Saud-Wahhab Partnership Continues	42
Saudi Relations with the World	45
Ibn Saud's Successors	46
The Board of Directors	50
Crisis in the Kingdom	54
Chapter Two	
Al Qaeda's Origins, Plans, Next of Kin, and Arab-Muslim Problems	58
Bin Ladenism	59
Osama bin Laden's Story	61

Bin Laden's Mentors and Colleagues	62
Al Qaeda's Goals and Objectives	69
Al Qaeda's Antecedents and Allies	71
The Muslim Brotherhood	71
The Brotherhood Spreads to Saudi Arabia	74
Al Qaeda's Next of Kin—Takfir wal Hijra	77
The Concept of Islamist Jihad	79
Modern Wahhabi-Salafism or "Bin Ladenism"	80
Problems in the Modern Muslim World	82
Radicalism Only Part of the Problem	82
Other Contemporary Arab-Muslim Problems	84

Chapter Three
The Worldwide Threat of Saudi Arabian Wahhabism and America's Response — 96

Wahhabism in the West	98
Wahhabism in America	98
The European Problem	104
America's Response to the Saudis and Wahhabism	114
America, the Paper Tiger	116
The Saudi Perspective on America	122
Inscrutable Saudis—Gullible Americans	127
The "Gulling" of America	131
Deteriorating Saudi-American Relations	135

Chapter Four
The Bush Doctrine: Raising the Cost of Terrorism and Providing an Antidote — 136

Formulating and Initiating a New Foreign Policy	138
The Extension of Sovereignty	138
Application in Afghanistan—A Learning Experience	141
Completing the Bush Doctrine and Continuing the Pursuit	146

Expanding the Definition of Hostile Action	147
Application to "Allied" Enemy Governments	149
America's Dilemma	153
Putting the New Bush Doctrine Together	154
Implementation of the Bush Doctrine	162
Why Iraq?	163
A Surrogate War in Iraq	166
U.S. Diplomacy and Multilateralism	169
Immediate Benefits of Invading Iraq	173
Democratization of the Arab-Muslim World	175
The Afghan Experience	176
The Iraqi Experience	178
Conclusion About the Bush Doctrine	181

Chapter Five
The Iraq War—Where Nothing Met Expectations 185

Phase 1: Off to an Apparently Good Start	187
The Easy Part	188
Failures to Adjust to New Realities	192
Phase 2: The Occupation	195
Failure to Plan	195
The Abu Ghraib Prison Disaster	202
Loss of Momentum and Confidence	206
Phase 3: An Interim Government	210
Inability to Bring Factions Together	211
Fallujah—Round II	212
Election Preparations	214
Phase 4: Painful Political Lessons	
and an Intensified Insurgency	219
Sharp Rise in Iraq Insurgency	220
The Process of Democratization	221
Phase 5: An Unexpected Move Toward Civil War	225
Sectarian Violence	226
The Political Implications of Sectarian Violence	227

Conclusions about the War ... 230

Chapter Six
The War on Terror: Recapitulation, Prognosis, and an Unfinished Agenda ... 234

The Explosive Mixture of Politics and Religion ... 234
Current Status of the War on Terror ... 236
   Al Qaeda on the Defensive ... 237
   America on the Offense ... 241
   Muslim Support for Terror Wanes ... 248
   American Support for Iraq War Wanes ... 252
Cementing Victory ... 254
   Back to Multilateralism ... 255
   Lessons Learned about Military Options ... 258
   The Carrot of Freedom and Democracy ... 262
Seeds of Hope—Roots of Change ... 265
   Reform of Islam Needed ... 265
   A Generation of Peace ... 267
   Light Some Candles ... 270

Appendix A: Chronology of Key Events ... 271

Appendix B: Glossary of Arabic Terms ... 281

Appendix C: About the Authors ... 288

Bibliography ... 290

Index ... 304

Authors' Preface

This book provides an update to our 2005 publication, "Winning the War on Terror: A Triumph of American Values" (now out of print), and was written to explain the nature and origins of militant Islamist terrorism and the American strategy that was set in motion to recast the political landscape of the Middle East. Since 9/11, the world has learned that radical, militant Islamism is a deadly disease that must be stamped out because it is a perilous threat to the West and endangers Muslim societies of all types around the world. Militant Islamist leaders are not open to negotiation or reason as many would hope, and their ideology goes far beyond classical Islam's concept of "just jihad," or righteous struggle. To most Muslims, Islam stands for peace, justice, equality, human dignity, rule of law—qualities demonstrated throughout Islam's history, and especially during its "Golden Age." However, Osama bin Laden's theology of hate, death, and destruction, and the type of Islamic law that he and other Islamists contemptuously envision for the world, would be catastrophic. Osama bin Laden, al Qaeda's leader, declared in 1998:

> The ruling to kill the Americans and their allies—civilians and military—is an individual duty for every Muslim who

can do it in any country in which it is possible to do it, in order to liberate the al-Aqsa Mosque and the holy mosque [Mecca] from their grip, and in order for their armies to move out of all the lands of Islam, defeated and unable to threaten any Muslim.

People of all persuasions ultimately will not support such a theology of darkness and hate, and this is why the authors believe that bin Laden and his armies of terror are destined for failure and destruction, nullified by the antidote of freedom.

The first three chapters discuss the causes of radical, militant Islamism and why it erupted in barbarous violence in the name of God in the late 20th century. Also discussed is the enormous impact that vast Saudi oil wealth has had in spreading its country's Wahhabi-Salafist ideology around the world for the last 25 years. Subsequent chapters address how success in the global war on terror will bring the broader Middle East into the world's family of nations politically, economically, and socially. The book does not place blame but rather focuses on how to collectively succeed in the war against the radical, militant Islamists, a war that is vital to the future of Islam, Western civilization, the greater Middle East, and the future of the world.

The real strength of the West resides in its fundamental values of freedom and democracy. Liberal and open societies permit hate-filled, militant ideologues to speak out under constitutional safeguards, even as militants advocate destruction of the West and its ideals, but nothing can justify suicide bombings and beheadings in the name of God, or suicide airline attacks such as those against the World Trade Center and the Pentagon on September 11, 2001. The world's wakeup call to the threat of global terrorism came on 9/11 and subsequent bombings around the world, and it is now clear that tolerance of Islamist extremism—"Bin Ladenism"—will ultimately lead to collective suicide for both the West and the world of moderate Islam.

We also discuss oil and global reserves, because growing dependence on foreign oil has become a severe threat to American and Western security by providing billions in Western monetary support for regimes that have sponsored terrorism—and it also promotes trade imbalance in the process. As journalist Tom Friedman has said, we are funding both sides in the war on terror with our massive oil imports. During the Cold War and up to 9/11, the United States and the West remained hesitant in addressing energy insecurity issues and tolerated Middle Eastern autocrats and despots because of dependence on potentially unreliable sources of imported oil. Saudi Arabia and its neighbors along the Persian Gulf possess nearly two-thirds of the earth's known oil reserves and Saudi Arabia is the world's largest supplier of crude oil and the supplier of last resort in times of global oil shortages. As the leader of the free world and engine of the global economy, the United States has a moral obligation to ensure that Persian Gulf oil remains secure and does not fall under hostile forces that seek to destroy the West, its institutions, and the world's economy.

As the Bush Doctrine developed following 9/11, the United States recognized that it could no longer remain passive toward the Arab Middle East and that it desperately needed to formulate and implement a new foreign policy for its global war on terror. Strategically, the Bush administration determined that the United States had to aggressively pursue al Qaeda and that the best defense against further terrorist attacks on the United States was to remain on the offensive.

The first offensive effort, less than one month after 9/11, was the popular invasion of Afghanistan which resulted in chasing Osama bin Laden into a remote area of Pakistan, toppling the reactionary Islamist Taliban government, and putting Afghanistan on the road to its first democratically elected government in its long history. Over the next year, the United States made substantial progress through tough, behind the scenes negotiations with most countries that possessed nuclear capabilities to secure their nuclear weapons stockpiles and technology from terrorist hands.

In an equally tough set of negotiations with Saudi Arabia, the United States attempted to learn more about Saudi relationships with al Qaeda and to deter the Saudis from providing further financial assistance to bin Laden's terrorist network, an ideological offspring of Saudi Arabia's Wahhabi-Salafist state religion. The authors contend that a sound rationale for the American invasion of Iraq was to modify recalcitrant Saudi behavior. For the first time since President Roosevelt's meeting with King Abdul Aziz Ibn Saud in 1945, the Americans actually out-gulled the Saudis, causing the Saudis to release sensitive information about al Qaeda and take deliberate steps to discontinue funding from both public and private Saudi sources.

The war in Iraq unfortunately was not America's finest hour from a military, intelligence, or ethical perspective, and these shortcomings are outlined in the last two chapters. Much was learned from the Iraq experience, however, and the free elections on January 30, 2005 and again in October and December 2005 literally saved the day for the United States and demonstrated the power of the Bush Doctrine's antidote of freedom and democracy and America's commitment to that ideal. Indeed, the title for the book, "The Triumph of Democracy over Militant Islamism," came from America's Iraq experience where victory was reclaimed by America's reassertion of its democratic ideal, after earlier failures to maintain America's high moral standards.

In the final chapter, our thesis on the war's origins is briefly summarized and the struggle in the war on terror is described. We recommend certain changes to the Bush foreign policy for the remainder of the President's term in office as well as some longer term changes that are required on issues separating the West and Islam.

We conclude that the United States is winning the war against the militant Islamists by holding true to American values of freedom and democracy. The book ends with hope for the future and confidence that mainstream Muslims will find a resounding voice in countering Islamist extremism through the dignity of Islam, reason, educational reform, and democratic practices that will nullify the ideologies of hate and ensure that Bin Ladenism does not spread and take root.

For us personally, it has been a most enjoyable experience that has been accomplished through the wonders of email and the internet. Working separately, we conferred through the internet and we hope our readers will find the book equally fulfilling and informative.

We wish to thank our friends and supporters who have helped make this book possible and will provide regular updates via our web page at http://www.bushwaronterror.com/ as events unfold.

May 15, 2006

B. Wayne Quist   David F. Drake

NOTE: References are listed in the Bibliography. Citations to books or articles are made through the use of brackets around the author's name and, where available, the page number or year of publication following the author's name in the text.

CHAPTER ONE

The Saudi Kingdom and Its Unwholesome Alliance

On September 11, 2001 extremist Muslim killers savagely attacked the American homeland. The attack was the culmination of a series of assaults against American interests by al Qaeda, which until 9/11 was a relatively obscure militant Islamist organization led by a wealthy Saudi Arabian named Osama bin Laden and his fanatical "Afghan Arabs" with ties to the Saudi royal family and wealthy Saudis. Moreover, fifteen of the nineteen jihadist hijackers that attacked the United States on September 11th were from Saudi Arabia, mostly from the conservative, Wahhabi-dominated Asir region in the southwestern province of the oil-rich desert kingdom.

We begin this chapter by discussing the Wahhabi sect of Sunni Islam and how its religious ideology was twisted to suit a political vision for the Arabian Peninsula. We trace the origins of al Qaeda from the early decision of the al Saud royal family to utilize a reactionary Islamist sect in consolidating the Bedouin tribes of the Arabian Peninsula into the modern Kingdom of Saudi Arabia that was founded in 1932. Soon thereafter, in 1938, oil was discovered and oil wealth would eventually finance a worldwide proselytizing effort for this radical sect that bred al Qaeda. But we're getting ahead of the story, which includes a description of Wahhabism, how it was utilized by the al Sauds for realizing their political objectives, a description of the modern state of Saudi Arabia, the role oil has played in its development, and how the Saudis continue to utilize oil and religion for their political objectives.

ISLAM AND ITS RADICAL ELEMENT

The origins of Islam go back to the early 7th century when an Arabian businessman named Mohammed began receiving divine revelations that became the text of the Holy Koran, the sacred book of Islam. In Arabic the word "Islam" means submission and obedience to the will of God. The Arabic language of the Holy Koran has great poetic beauty and splendor, especially when read aloud, and its forceful linguistic power has moved and inspired millions of listeners for centuries. Memorization of the entire Holy Koran is a frequent assignment in fundamentalist Islamist schools and Wahhabi religion classes in Saudi Arabia. Lying under the clear desert firmament at night, as giant stars dot the black sky like marshmallows, the rhythms of ancient Arabic poetry, and the vastness of space itself, are as mesmerizing today as they were centuries ago in the time of the Prophet. Mohammed's divine revelations started in 610 and by 629 he was able to raise an army of loyal believers in his newly proclaimed faith and take control of Mecca and Medina, the holiest cities in the world of Islam. Mohammed died in 632 at the age 63, when having produced four surviving daughters from his eleven wives, the Arabian Peninsula was united for the first time in recorded history.

In the decades following Mohammed's death, Islam spread rapidly east and west by means of violent jihad, or "holy war," throughout the Middle East, Iran, North Africa, Spain and into southern France in the 700s; and then from Southwest and Central Asia through India into

Malaysia, the southern Philippines, and eventually the Indonesian archipelago. Today Islam is the world's fastest growing religion and accounts for nearly a quarter of the world population with almost 1.5 billion believers. After its rapid expansion into Europe and Asia, Islam advanced for nearly a thousand years as the Christian West retreated, and then the Arab-Muslim world fought off invading European Crusaders for nearly two centuries from 1099 to 1244.

The victorious Muslim forces under Saladin, a Kurdish general from present-day Iraq, defeated the Crusaders and were able to retake the holy city of Jerusalem in 1187 from rampaging French Crusaders—the "Franks"—who had earlier captured Jerusalem and massacred thousands of Muslims, an event vividly remembered in the Arab world today. In 1258 invading Mongols from Asia destroyed Baghdad, and in 1453 the Ottoman Turks took Constantinople, renamed the old city Istanbul, and established the Ottoman Empire that extended throughout the entire Arab-speaking world from the Persian Gulf across Africa and into Europe.

During Europe's Middle Ages, and under successive Muslim leaders, cities such as Damascus and Baghdad were well ahead of their European counterparts and renowned during the "Golden Age" of Islam for advanced universities and learning centers, fine libraries, countless book dealers, the first hospitals, opulent public baths, and generous support for the arts and sciences. Ancient Greek and Roman texts were translated into Arabic, saving priceless manuscripts for future generations. Successive Islamic governments admired and supported inquiry into philosophy, higher mathematics, and science, while the medieval Arab-Muslim world made significant contributions to civilization in the fields of astronomy, chemistry, geology, metallurgy, botany, and poetry.

The Ottoman Empire lasted until shortly after the end of the First World War when representatives of the victorious British and French drew present-day Middle East geographical boundaries while sitting around Winston Churchill's dinner table. The Ottomans sided with Germany in World War I and most Arab nations again supported the losing German Nazis and its racial theories of hateful anti-Semitism during the Second World War. The Ottoman Empire was multi-ethnic, pluralistic and generally tolerant of other religions and ethnic groups, but in the aftermath of the First World War and the demise of the Muslim Caliphate in 1924, the newly created Arab-Muslim states were impoverished and impotent, paving the way for corrupt and oppressive governments and radical Islamist terrorism. In a recent interview, Dore Gold [2003], Israel's former ambassador to the UN stated:

> It is important to remember for perspective that Islam, while relegating no Muslims to a second class status, nonetheless showed a remarkable degree of tolerance at times, especially to the Jewish people: the Ottoman Empire opened its doors to Jewish refugees from the Spanish Inquisition in the 15th century and provided land grants for Jewish resettlement in the Land of Israel, well before the British. The Ottoman Sultans were the caliphs of all Sunni Islam, yet this background of limited inter-religious tolerance has been wiped out entirely by the new Islamic militancy, that has been fed by the Wahhabis of Saudi Arabia and the Egyptian Muslim Brotherhood.

Some observers have called the Middle East countries created after the First World War "tribes with flags," because they lacked the typical nationalistic cohesion associated with the development of other countries around the world. However, what bound them together was Islam, and for centuries the Muslim Caliph had been the guardian of Islamic law and the Sunni Islamic state. The loss of the Caliphate and a cohesive Islamic religious leader following the First World War was devastating to the world's Sunni Muslims, especially in the newly created Arab states. Today the restoration of the Sunni Islamic Caliphate is one of Osama bin Laden's major goals and is an emotional issue that resonates loudly and widely throughout the entire Muslim world as an issue all Sunni Arabs can support.

The history of Islam includes a long line of Muslim extremists and ideologues that deeply influenced today's radical Islamist militants, such as the 7th century Kharijites, followed by the 11th century "Assassins," who paved the way as violent Islamist terrorists with tactics and ideology reminiscent of today's militant Islamists. After the death of Mohammed, the Kharijites emerged as ultra-strict, radical fundamentalists with revolutionary zeal and their example has inspired extreme Islamist groups like al Qaeda. The 11th—13th century Assassins, from whom the English word "assassin" is derived, murdered their enemies as a religious duty and used hashish to promote visions of paradise before attacking their victims.

Another radical Islamist ideologist was Ibn Taymiyah (1263-1328), a fierce theologian and religious leader who became the model for the Saudi Wahhabis, Muslim Brotherhood, and Osama bin Laden. A new mosque in Los Angeles, funded by the Saudi government, is named in honor of Ibn Taymiyah but few American Muslims know what the name really implies. Hassan al-Banna (1906-1949), was the influential Egyptian teacher and neo-fundamentalist who established the radical, Islamist Egyptian Muslim Brotherhood, and Sayyid Mawdudi (1903-1979) was a renowned Muslim journalist, reformer and neo-fundamentalist who founded the radical Islamist party Jamaat-i-Islami in Pakistan.

The long succession of Islamist extremists who preceded Osama bin Laden for centuries shared a core belief common to most Muslims today: that Islam is a total, all-encompassing way of life and the Holy Koran is God's revelation and foundation of Muslim life, including Islamic law, which conflicts with man-made law in democratic countries. The radical extremists insist that religion, the state, and society are a single, integrated entity and that separation of church and state is not possible. They insist that Islamic law (Sharia) provides the sole, ideal legal foundation for modern Muslim society and that departure from Islam and reliance on the West are the causes for the decline of the Muslim world since the "Golden Age of Islam."

Ibn Abdul Wahhab (1703-1791), the religious fanatic and zealot who founded Saudi Arabia's Wahhabi or Salafist movement in the 18th century, emphasized a puritanical and militant form of Sunni Islam as a reactionary "reformation" of the religion to bring it back to is earliest days. Preaching an ideology of hatred and a radically intolerant and violent digression from mainstream Islam, Wahhabism came into being under the leadership of Sheik Ibn Abdul Wahhab, partly as a reaction to oppression from the Ottoman Empire and European imperialism, but more from personal loathing of venerated shrines and ancestor worship ("polytheism") practiced by contemporary Muslims. Wahhab was the son of a Muslim religious judge and when he was persecuted for calling Muslims to return to the original form of "pure" Islam, he found refuge in the central Nejd region of Saudi Arabia where a Bedouin tribal leader named Muhammad bin Saud ruled.

In 1744 the religious leader Wahhab concluded an agreement with the tribal leader, Muhammad bin Saud, an ancestor of the first Saudi king, to bring "wayward Arabs" of the Arabian Peninsula back to puritanical monotheism and the "true Muslim faith." The two leaders confirmed their arrangement with an oath and intermarriage pacts between the al Sheik (Wahhab) clan and the al Saud clan that continue to the present day. Through the descendants of the al Sheik and al Saud clans, the lasting partnership between these two large desert families led to the establishment of the Kingdom of Saudi Arabia in the 20th century.

As a demonstration of their religious zealotry and pious iconoclasm, Wahhab's followers destroyed sacred tombs, graveyards, images, and even mosques in Mecca, Medina and Iraq, much as the Taliban destroyed ancient Buddhist monuments and venerated religious icons in Afghanistan in the 1990s. The goal was to return Islam to the "purity" and simplicity of the 7th century, but Wahhabism came to be seen as a deviant and violent Muslim cult, and several mainstream Islamic religious decrees (fatwas) condemned Wahhabism's narrow ultra-orthodoxy. These harsh criticisms caused followers of ibn Abdul Wahhab to call themselves "Salafists," or "Companions of the Prophet" and not "Wahhabis," a practice followed to this day.

Saudi Arabian Wahhabi-Salafists, members of al Qaeda, and the insurgents in Iraq are Sunni Muslims. The fault line between the divisions of Islam lies between the dominant Sunnis in the greater

Middle East and South Asia, and the minority Shiites that are largely located in Iran, southern Iraq, Pakistan, and along the shores of the Persian Gulf, including Saudi Arabia's Eastern Province. Starting shortly after the death of the Prophet Mohammed, mutual hatred and distrust still run deep between the two major Muslim factions based on historical disagreement over leadership succession after Muhammad's death. Another fault line in the Muslim world lies between the 300 million people in the Arab world that represent nearly 20 percent of the world's Muslims and the billion or more non-Arab people who make up the remaining 80 percent around the world.

Wahhabi-Salafists were ruthless with their enemies, especially the Shiites, and their puritanical zeal resulted in the destruction of sacred Islamic tombs, graveyards, paintings, and mosque adornments wherever their Ikhwan army rampaged. Ideologically, bin Laden has ignored some tenets of Wahhabi-Salafism when it suited pragmatic political objectives but the underlying judgment of apostate status for all Muslims who do not accept Wahhabi-Salafism was reflected in the al Qaeda insurgency in Iraq against the Shiite majority in that country. Wahhabism is the philosophical foundation of Bin Laden's al Qaeda and it traces its violent heritage to the Arabian Peninsula in the late 18th and early 19th centuries, as depicted in the Chronology in Appendix A.

THE FOUNDING OF SAUDI ARABIA

The Founder of the Kingdom

By the early 1800s, the al Saud clan ruled much of the Arabian Peninsula from their stronghold in the isolated Nejd region of central Saudi Arabia. The power of the al Sauds and fanatical Wahhabis alarmed the Ottoman Empire and an Ottoman army was dispatched to the interior of the Arabian Desert to contain the influence of the al Saud clan. By 1824 the al Sauds had regained political control over central Arabia and ruled from Riyadh, but were forced into exile in

1891, living along the Rub al-Khali, the "Empty Quarter," before seeking refuge in Kuwait.

In 1902, a young tribal chieftain and colorful desert warrior named Abdul Aziz ibn Saud (1880-1953), known in the West as "Ibn Saud" and affectionately in the desert kingdom as the "Falcon of the Peninsula" [Khaled bin Sultan], captured Riyadh, the capital of present-day Saudi Arabia, and embarked upon a 30-year campaign to unify the Arabian Peninsula under the rule of the House of al Saud, completing for his family a century-old ambition. This event marked the beginning of the modern state of Saudi Arabia.

Following the turmoil of the First World War and the demise of the Ottoman Empire, Ibn Saud established a theocratic monarchy with the support of the Wahhabi partnership created by the earlier marriage alliance between the al Saud and Wahhab (al Sheik) clans. In 1912 Ibn Saud organized his loyal Bedouin tribesmen into a fierce Wahhabi Ikhwan army, a precursor of al Qaeda and today's Saudi Arabian National Guard (SANG), and through severe discipline molded it into a loyal fighting force.

Between 1924 and 1927, in the political vacuum that followed the collapse of the Ottoman Empire, Ibn Saud's Ikhwan army recaptured Mecca and Medina, the holiest cities in the Muslim faith. To break traditional tribal allegiances and avoid family feuds, the shrewd and charismatic Saudi leader settled members of the Ikhwan army and their families in colonies located around desert oases to promote agriculture, forcing the tribes to abandon their traditional nomadic way of life. Members of the Ikhwan army were provided arms and ammunition as well as living quarters, mosques, schools, agricultural equipment, training, and strict Wahhabi-Salafist religious education. The Bedouin tribesmen that formed the Ikhwan army were instructed in fundamentalist Wahhabi-Salafist precepts and their obedience, zealotry, and traditional xenophobia created a disciplined army of dedicated and fierce arch-traditionalists willing to die for their extreme beliefs. The Wahhabi-Salafists and Ibn Saud exhibited exceptional hatred of Islamic minorities such as Shiites and Sufis (mystical, spiritual Islam) and by 1927 had captured Islam's holy cities in western Saudi Arabia.

However, by the late 1920s the army had become difficult for Ibn Saud to control because of fanatical Ikhwan efforts to conquer traditional enemies such as Muslim Shiites and spread their Wahhabi-Salafist faith by the sword in the same way Islam converted infidels in the 7th and 8th centuries. Reactionary Wahhabi clerics even accused Ibn Saud of losing faith—backsliding—because of his support for western innovations such as telephones, telegraph, and automobiles, and for sending one of his several sons to school in Egypt, a country whose people the Ikhwan condemned as "nonbelievers." To reassert authority, Ibn Saud ruthlessly suppressed the Ikhwan army and beheaded many of the leaders, a memory that today's radical Wahhabi clerics do not forget, for merciless suppression of the Ikhwan solidified Ibn Saud's authority and neutralized dissent. On September 23, 1932, Ibn Saud proclaimed the Kingdom of Saudi Arabia as an Islamic state, named himself first king, declared Arabic the national language, and the Holy Koran the Constitution.

Ibn Saud founded a theocratic monarchy and the modern nation state of Saudi Arabia through an alliance of fanatical Wahhabi clerics and devout Bedouin tribesmen of the Arabian Desert. Through the compelling force of his personality, threats of violence and years of war, Ibn Saud established strategic alliances with the various Bedouin tribes by taking 17 wives and fathering 36 or more sons, including subsequent rulers of the Kingdom of Saudi Arabia. When his forces captured the holy Muslim cities of Mecca and Medina, they displayed extraordinary hatred of nonbelievers and other Muslims, especially Shiite and Sufi Muslims.

As a descendant of Mohammed bin Saud and a recognized Wahhabi leader with the title "Imam" (religious leader), Ibn Saud successfully molded Wahhabi-Salafism into the framework of the new Kingdom of Saudi Arabia by integrating the Bedouin tribes of the Arabian Peninsula into a modern state first recognized by Great Britain in 1927. And by marrying into the many Bedouin tribes, Ibn Saud consolidated his power and the al Saud family proliferated, producing as many as 7,000 first tier royal princes today and tens of thousands of other members of the royal family who are lavishly supported by Saudi Arabia's billions in oil income.

The old desert chieftain and first king was wounded many times in battle and is commemorated in epic Saudi poetry. The following tribute to Ibn Saud is very moving when recited aloud around a desert campfire at night under clear skies and brilliant stars:

Abdul Aziz Ibn Saud and the Retaking of Riyadh

Banished was I from the heart of Arabia,
Riyadh, my home, had been stolen by others;
banished was I, and my father and mother,
brothers and sisters, deprived of our birthright.
Sadness we felt for the years that denied us
the feel of sand of the Nejd in our hands.
Kindness we found in Kuwait beyond measure,
but kindness alone could not cure the pain
of living in exile, a life without pleasure,
for pleasure, not nurtured in honor, will wither.
I knew from the earliest years of my living
that I must return to the place of my birth.
They told me that only my death would await me,
(but fear is a far harsher master than death);
they warned of the dangers of crossing the desert
but it was the desert had given me breath.
They asked how a lad could recapture a city,
when put to the sword what my pride would be worth;
I asked how the seed, lying dry in the sand,
at the first taste of rain can emerge from the earth.
"Who will ride at my side on this perilous venture?
Who will risk life and limb to expel Al Rashid?"
Sixty answered my call, young and brave, one and all.
"With all of our strength, we will give what you need;
we will stand by your side when the battle is joined
until each of us falls—or Riyadh is freed."
It was not for the glory we rode from Kuwait;
we held faith as our shield and justice our sword.

THE TRIUMPH OF DEMOCRACY OVER MILITANT ISLAMISM

I sought to regain the land of my fathers
but in all I deferred to the will of the Lord.
We rode towards Riyadh with banners unfurled,
putting trust in the God who created the world.
Ramadan fasting was over, I summoned my kinsmen;
without hesitation they answered my call.
Like shadows that slip over sand dunes at sunset
we gathered in silence beneath Riyadh's wall.
On that night long ago, when the time came to act,
I knew in my heart what it was to be free;
the greatest good fortune in life for a man is
to know he has reached for the best he can be.
Whatever might follow that cold, moonless night
we would know we had fought for a cause that was right.
I chose from my band a mere handful of men;
each one read the risks from the look in my eyes.
We scaled the walls under cover of darkness;
we watched for the sun to put light in the skies.
Outnumbered, we knew that our hope of success
must depend in the end on our use of surprise.
In a fight it is true if you strike off the head of
a man or an army, the battle is won.
The fate of the Emir of Riyadh was sealed,
he must die for the wounds of Al Saud to be healed.
We struck as the lion descends on its prey,
forced open the fortress, brothers then joined the fray.
The garrison knew that resistance was futile;
Al Saud had returned to its home on that day.
Looking back through the decades,
the taking of Riyadh was but one step on a path,
building a nation, devout, proud and strong,
with justice its sword, faith as its shield,
in the land where the message of God was revealed

[Saudi Ministry of Culture and Information].

When Ibn Saud proclaimed his monarchy in 1932, he linked the legitimacy of the Saudi royal family to the tenets of Wahhabi-Salafism and Islamic law. Today Wahhabi Islam is still the basis of the Saudi royal family's legitimacy as a ruling family and its international standing in the Muslim world is derived from its role as the defender and protector of Mecca and Medina, the birthplace of Islam and its holiest cities. By forming a pact to share power with the powerful Wahhabis, the Saudi government gave ultra-conservative Wahhabi clerics control over the entire religious, judicial, and educational system, with reactionary Wahhabi leaders and clerics heading cabinet-level ministries even to this day. And in 1986, to make amends for ostentatious royal living and in deference to criticism by powerful Wahhabi clerics and members of the al Sheik clan who hold senior government posts, King Fahd changed his title from "King" to "Custodian of the Two Holy Mosques," a convention still used by Fahd's half brother Abdullah, the currently reigning monarch.

The Desert Kingdom

Saudi Arabia is a large and arid desert kingdom, over 1,000 miles north to south and 800 miles east to west, nearly the size of the United States east of the Mississippi. The people of Saudi Arabia have tribal roots going back to their ancient nomadic Bedouin origins and are well known for their fierce fighting capabilities, abundant desert hospitality, genuine warmth, grandiose poetic expression, and noble graciousness. Saudi Arabia in the 21st century is really just entering the modern world even though its significant oil wealth and financial strength have recently provided the external trappings of modern society. The problem the West faces with Saudi Arabia is that beneath a thin veneer of modern shopping centers, advanced Western technology, and a costly social welfare system for its exploding population, is an all-pervading, severe, and absolute fundamentalist religious establishment that dominates every element of Saudi society in ways that appear medieval to Western observers.

If it was not for oil, and now radical Islamist terrorism, the West would not pay much attention to Saudi Arabia, but the fact remains that the United States is by far the world's largest consumer of oil, importing 60 percent of all its oil from foreign sources. Saudi Arabia is the world's largest oil producer and exporter, with 25 percent of the earth's proven reserves in its Eastern Province along the Persian Gulf. Moreover, Europe and Asia are even more dependent on Persian Gulf oil, making the world's interconnected global economy hostage to Persian Gulf oil where nearly two-thirds of the earth's known oil reserves are located. And today, China's gigantic thirst for oil accounts for well over half of the oil transported daily through the narrow and vulnerable Straits of Hormuz from the Persian Gulf.

Most importantly, Saudi Arabia is the birthplace of Islam and home to its holiest cities near the Red Sea. Mecca is the birthplace of the Prophet Mohammed where he received his first revelation from Allah, and Medina is the burial site of the Prophet. Mecca is also the destination for the annual Hajj pilgrimage that brings more than two million Muslims from around the world to the Great Mosque, the site of the Kaaba—"the cube" or holy black stone—supposedly given by God to the Prophet Abraham. In the first years of the monarchy the principal revenues supporting the kingdom were fees collected from the annual flow of Muslim pilgrims to the holy cities. Cash generated from the pilgrims was stored in a strongbox carried by the king's financial advisor and was considered Ibn Saud's private purse.

To understand Saudi Arabia is to appreciate the profound influence of the harsh Arabian Desert on the Saudi people and the culture of Islam as an all-encompassing way of life, totally integrated into government and personal affairs alike. Saudis, like many Arabs, believe that conservative Islamic values are far superior to Western secular values and this belief is buttressed by the importance of the tribal nature or extended family structure of Saudi society, wherein old and trusted family loyalty and self-assurance exceed allegiance to the state, which is a relatively new concept. Another feature of Saudi society is its culture of consultation and consensus wherein, "the king is both chief consensus maker and chief executive" [Long]. A form of Bedouin tribal democracy goes back centuries in the harsh desert environment and calls for consensus among tribal leaders as well as the opportunity for tribal members to discuss grievances with their leaders.

Many Westerners have attempted to understand Saudi behavior based on years living and working in the kingdom, but the Saudi mindset can be an enigma. A character trait that often appears to Westerners as paranoia may derive from Bedouin tribal culture and centuries of polygamy that predate Islam. Under Islamic law, men are permitted up to four wives at a time, although members of the royal family appear to have taken many more than four over the course of their lives. "Gulling," or deception and duplicity, seems to be a Saudi character trait that may be tied to the problems and jealousies that arise from juggling family responsibilities between multiple competing wives and many children from each.

Saudis have also exhibited an exceptional sense of insecurity due to historical Bedouin perceptions of being surrounded by enemies and the need to defend their unusually harsh form of Islam. Saudi beliefs are based on an ultra-conservative Wahhabi interpretation of the Holy Koran that serves as the Constitution of the country and a formal set of rules that guide every aspect of living. Under Saudi Arabia's harsh Islamic law, the state and religion are inseparable and no churches, synagogues, temples, or shrines of any religion other than Wahhabi-Salafism are permitted. Proselytizing by other faiths is prohibited by law and even nonbelieving Muslims are persecuted, their books banned, and sensitive government jobs denied to the approximately two million Muslim Shiites who live in the oil-rich Eastern Province.

Discovery of Oil

Oil and tar has been used over the centuries in the Middle East and documented evidence of the presence of oil has been available since the 19th century. In 1871 a German group visited Iraq and reported abundant supplies of oil. In 1907 another German mission reported that Iraq was a "lake of petroleum" and the following year oil was found in Iran. Iraq began exporting oil in 1934, shortly after the major Iraqi oil field was discovered at Kirkuk in 1927. In 1932, the British discovered oil in Kuwait and Bahrain off the east coast of Saudi Arabia and in 1938 the Eastern Province of the Saudi kingdom gushed forth with "black gold." The beginning of Saudi oil wealth actually started in 1933 when Ibn Saud granted exclusive rights in a concession to Standard Oil of California (SOCAL) to explore, extract, and sell oil for 60 years. SOCAL was the first American company to enter into competition with the British for Middle East petroleum. A few years later, American oil companies known today as Exxon, Chevron, Texaco, and Mobil formed the Arab American Oil Company (ARAMCO) in a unique partnership with the Saudi government. Oil was initially transported by barge to Bahrain, then by oil freighters, and in 1950 a pipeline was completed through the desert to Lebanon and the Mediterranean Sea. ARAMCO continued to explore for oil in the Arabian Peninsula, finding even larger fields in the 1950s, and liquefied petroleum gas processing started in Saudi Arabia a decade later.

Even before the SOCAL oil concession was granted, the old Saudi king had been exposed to several prominent American doctors and missionaries in the Eastern Province of Saudi Arabia. He perceived Americans as non-threatening and manageable, particularly when compared with "untrustworthy" Europeans. Most importantly, Ibn Saud was fearful of European colonial ambitions, especially the British, and he was very adept at playing power politics as he had demonstrated with the Ottomans, British, and French during the First World War. Americans were seen as being gullible, easy to work with and manipulate—easy infidels to "gull"—because they were naïve in their willingness to do good and because they came from far away and had no special axe to grind regarding local or regional politics.

Earlier, Kuwait had granted an oil concession to the British-Iranian Oil Company, known today as the British Petroleum Corporation (BP), and the old king's trusted British advisor, Harry St. John Philby (1885-1960), was instrumental in assuring that Saudi Arabia's oil did not go to the British as in Kuwait. Philby was a dedicated Arabist and British civil servant who grew dissatisfied with British policy toward the Arabs following the First World War. In 1930 Philby left the British Foreign Service in Transjordan (today's Jordan) after being accused of spying, joined the Saudi monarch in Riyadh, and converted to Islam with the name "Hajj Abdullah." During World War II, Philby's son, Kim, became an even more infamous British spy and it is ironic that an American company received the 60-year concession to the vast Saudi oil fields at the urging of a British advisor to the shrewd Saudi king.

Through the troubles of the Great Depression and global war in the 1930s and 1940s, Saudi Arabia stood apart from the rest of the world, guided by its wise and charming desert warrior-king. Saudi oil had become important enough during the Second World War for President Roosevelt to hold a meeting in February 1945 with Ibn Saud aboard the presidential yacht shortly after his Yalta meeting with Stalin and Churchill. During the war, the United States desired to secure its access to Middle East petroleum supplies and acquire a base in the Middle East that could link aerial routes from the Mediterranean to Asia. Roosevelt's historical meeting aboard the "USS Quincy" in Egypt's Great Bitter Lake in the Suez Canal resulted in an agreement between the two countries that eventually established a major United States Air Force base at Dhahran in the Eastern Province and the U.S. Military Training Mission to Saudi Arabia (USMTM). The historic meeting between the first Saudi king and President Roosevelt to protect the Saudi oil fields was important to both sides and although the agreement was not formalized until the Eisenhower administration, it remains in effect today.

The old king died in Taif, Saudi Arabia on November 8, 1953, and was buried in an unmarked grave in Riyadh according to Wahhabi ritual and custom. As a devoted Arabist, Harry St. John Philby remained in Saudi Arabia after the death of his friend the old king, and died there himself in 1960. Today, Saudi Arabia's immense crude oil reserves are critical to the security and stability of the global economy but serve as an Achilles' heel for the industrialized world.

THE KINGDOM OF OIL AND ALLAH

Unprecedented oil wealth made it possible for the Saudi religious establishment to spread its radicalized form of Wahhabi Islam around the world over the last 25 years. Saudi Arabia is the world's largest and cheapest oil producer and exporter, controlling a quarter of the earth's proven oil reserves and there may be even far more oil and gas reserves in the vast "Empty Quarter," or Rub al-Khali, of the Arabian Desert, which has never been fully explored.

Saudi Arabia did not become a wealthy nation overnight but proceeds from its "black gold" soon made profound changes in the poor and arid desert kingdom. Oil generated only about $2 million in royalty payments in 1938 but by 1948 Ibn Saud received nearly $50 million in annual royalties. In 1973, Ibn Saud's son King Faisal, who was raised in a Wahhabi household and whose sons currently serve as ambassador to the United States and Saudi foreign minister, initiated the Arab oil embargo that resulted in the quadrupling of oil prices by the late 1970s.

By 1978 Saudi oil wealth had mushroomed to $50 billion and exceeded $100 hundred billion two years later. Global oil prices fell in the 1990s but Saudi oil revenues still averaged $70 billion from 1999 to 2003, reaching nearly $110 billion in 2004 and more than $160 billion in 2005 when oil prices peaked at $70 per barrel following Hurricane Katrina and then declined to the mid $60s, only to peak again at $75 on April 21, 2006 due to continued high global demand and geopolitical risk caused by instability in the Middle East, Nigeria and Venezuela.

Today Saudi Arabia has the largest known petroleum reserves in the world, ranks as the world's largest producer and exporter of petroleum, and is a leading member of the Organization of Petroleum Exporting Countries (OPEC). It has also served as the only oil producer willing and able to pick up slack in global oil production when demand peaks or supply problems develop elsewhere in the world's oil network. Saudi Arabia's "swing capacity" of nearly two million barrels per day has made it a key American ally in maintaining price stability for global oil markets, independent of OPEC, but the Saudi "swing capacity" is diminishing. Saudi Arabia has an oil-based economy with the central government controlling its oil reserves as well as the country's major economic activities. Petroleum accounts for about 75 percent of Saudi Arabia's budget revenues, 45 percent of its gross domestic product (GDP), and 90 percent of exports [CIA].

Whether we like it or not, oil—imported oil—is the lifeblood of Europe, Asia, the United States, and the entire global economy. Without imported oil, the world's economic engines would slow to an idle. The source of the world's oil is predominantly from Muslim countries where Islam is struggling for its ideological heart and soul in what might someday be called the Muslim Reformation. The Persian Gulf, or the Arabian Gulf as the Saudis prefer to call it, is a 600-mile-long body of water between Iran and the Arabian Peninsula. It is one of the world's strategic waterways because of oil, and at its narrowest in the Straits of Hormuz, the Gulf is only a few miles wide with limited navigation, a choke point that could easily bottle up the world's oil supply. Saudi Arabia leads the world in crude oil reserves by a long margin and in its ability to pump nearly 12 million barrels of oil per day and provide a surge capability during global shortages and crises. Table 1.1 contains estimates of the world's crude oil reserves summarized by the top 15 countries with the highest reserves. Five of the first six countries are Persian Gulf states. Muslim states are indicated with a double asterisk.

Table 1.1
2004 Crude Oil Reserves by Country*

Rank	Country	Proven Reserves (billion barrels)
1	Saudi Arabia**	263
2	Canada	178
3	Iran**	130
4	Iraq**	115
5	United Arab Emirates (UAE)**	98
6	Kuwait**	97
7	Venezuela	78
8	Russia	69
9	Libya**	36
10	Nigeria**	34
11	United States	29
12	China	24
13	Mexico	16
14	Algeria**	11
15	Norway	10

*Multiple Sources: U.S. Energy Information Administration, *International Energy Annual Report*, March 4, 2005 http://www.cia.doe.gov/emeu/international/reserves.html; *World Oil*, Vol. 224, No. 8, Aug. 2003.
** Muslim countries

Until 9/11, America's relationship with Saudi Arabia was nearly all about oil and little else, other than the offsetting effect of lucrative contracts for American companies to build the Saudi infrastructure and sell expensive weapons and other American products not on the Saudi blacklist. Saudi Arabia still tracks foreign companies that do business with Israel, based on an Arab League boycott that dates to 1951 shortly after the establishment of Israel. For years, the Saudis had boycotted companies like Ford and Coca-Cola for doing business with Israel but they were subsequently taken off the official blacklist as the Saudis amassed greater oil wealth.

After 9/11, the Saudi-American equation became more complex and expanded from simply maintaining freely flowing Persian Gulf oil at moderate prices for the global economy to including cooperation with the United States in the global war on terrorism. But even the importance of the war on terrorism did not override oil as the central factor in the relationship between the two countries because Western dependence on Persian Gulf oil has steadily increased. American crude oil production peaked in 1970 and has declined steadily since, to the point where the United States now imports over 60 percent of its oil.

The world consumes over 82 million barrels of oil each day, with the United States accounting for about 25 percent of the world's total consumption, and the numbers are growing so rapidly that by 2030 global consumption will reach 120 million barrels per day, with 60 percent of the increase coming from Asian countries such as China, Japan, Korea and India, who today import about 50 percent of their oil directly from the Persian Gulf.

To make matters worse, each day Americans burn about 45 percent of all gasoline that is refined in the world, so better mileage efficiency for automobiles and other conservation efforts can result in significant savings in the total amount of oil the United States imports. However, the Paris-based International Energy Agency (IEA) [2006] reports that there is no immediate fear that the world will run out of oil anytime soon, based on estimates of energy demand up to 2030. The report states in part, "The earth contains more than enough energy resources to meet demand for many decades to come." Today's problem is caused by rising global demand for oil that grew more rapidly than projected in the past decade, especially from Asia, where dependence on imports is even higher than in the United States. More and more, the issue is now becoming the reliability of the oil supplying countries.

As China's top oil supplier, the growing oil-for-arms relationship between China and Saudi Arabia is alarming, suggesting a significant post-9/11 realignment of Saudi Arabian security relationships away from the United States. In early 2006 King Abdullah traveled to China for the first ever state visit by a Saudi monarch to China. Saudi Arabia has had long range Chinese missiles for several years and recently negotiated a stake in a Chinese refinery. China's SINOPEC also received a Saudi contract to develop natural gas in the vast and barren Rub al Khali, Saudi Arabia's unexplored "Empty Quarter." Because of its severe energy shortage and recent dependence on Persian Gulf oil, China also signed a $70 billion oil and natural gas agreement with Iran in the fall of 2004 to supply China with 150,000 barrels of oil per day for 25 years.

Japan and Korea are even more dependent on foreign oil, importing almost 100 percent of their oil, and nearly one-third of that from the Persian Gulf. This is why a large Japanese consortium consisting of major Japanese companies such as Mitsubishi, Mitsui, Marabena, Itochu, Tomen, Chiyoda, JGC, and Toyo recently negotiated an agreement with Iraq for strategic claims to Iraqi's vast oil fields.

European imports have also grown to a point where today Europe imports 80 percent of its oil, over one-third of it from the Persian Gulf. Second only to Saudi Arabia, Russia is also a major oil supplier to the world with great potential from its abundant oil reserves that rank sixth in the world, and Canada has vast reserves of retrievable oil sands. Emerging suppliers in Central Asia on both sides of the Caspian Sea as well as Iran are also significant players in the global oil calculus, and one of the world's largest undeveloped sources of crude oil lies underwater off the west coast of Nigeria. Finally, Iraq has significant oil reserves and its oil production has the potential of rivaling Saudi Arabia as additional fields are explored and neglected infrastructure is developed and improved.

While there is little danger of the world running out of oil in this century, the crux of the issue for the United States and the West is the reliability of the sources of imported oil. The fact remains that most of the major oil-producing regions of the world are controlled by Muslim countries where suspicion of America's motives and disenchantment with American Middle East policies have increased since 9/11 due to the war on terror and American military action to liberate Afghanistan and Iraq.

As American domestic oil reserves peaked and started a steady decline in the early 1970s, global oil prices quadrupled later in that decade as a result of the Arab oil embargo following the October 1973 Arab-Israeli Yom Kippur War and the formation of OPEC. That is when Saudi oil wealth began to mushroom and Western firms began implementing contracts worth billions of dollars in infrastructure development and weapons purchases in the kingdom.

To counter the threat of further oil shortages in the 1970s and make a political statement, President Jimmy Carter put in place America's first conservation initiatives since the Second World War, mandating a 55 MPH speed limit on freeways and increased mileage standards for automobiles. In time, these initiatives took hold and the pace of American demand for oil lessened, eventually driving down global prices a decade later. President Carter laid the groundwork for another American initiative shortly after revolutionary Shiite Muslims overthrew the Shah of Iran in 1979 by announcing what became known as the "Carter Doctrine" in his State of the Union speech in January 1980, stressing that security of Persian Gulf oil was considered an American "vital interest" to be defended "by any means necessary, including military force."

President Reagan confirmed this policy in the 1980s during the Iran-Iraq war (1980-89) and President George H. W. Bush invoked the Carter Doctrine when Saddam Hussein invaded Kuwait in 1990 and threatened Saudi Arabia and its Persian Gulf oil facilities. The first President Bush formed a massive global coalition that drove Iraq from Kuwait and neutralized the Iraqi threat to the Persian Gulf oil fields. The Carter Doctrine remains in effect today and the United States can be expected to invoke its terms again if Persian Gulf oil is once more threatened.

American oil companies and their global partners have operated in the Persian Gulf for nearly 70 years. They know the region and its problems well, but have done little to help the United States lessen its dependence on imported oil. American energy security objectives have been based on the premise that oil demand is tied to the long-term health of the world economy, but successive American administrations since Carter have failed to meet their stated energy security goals:

U.S. ENERGY SECURITY GOALS

- Promote diversity of energy sources to avoid dependence on oil and lower American dependence on foreign suppliers
- Avoid dependence on a single supplier nation and reduce price volatility
- Protect national and economic security by promoting a diverse supply and delivery of reliable, affordable, and environmentally sound energy
- Protect national and economic security by providing world-class scientific research capacity and advancing scientific knowledge
- Protect the environment by resolving the environmental legacy of the Cold War and by providing for the permanent disposal of high-level radioactive waste [U.S. Department of Energy]

In fact, American energy independence has been a dismal failure on almost all counts, especially diversity of suppliers and flexibility, because OPEC possesses the only real flexibility. In the fall of 2004 oil peaked at more than $55 a barrel and in late August 2005 following Hurricane Katrina oil topped $70 per barrel and then reached $75 per barrel in April 2006, an all-time high, while American imports of foreign oil rose to 60 percent of total domestic consumption, another all-time high. The United States and the West have little flexibility in the global oil market because Muslim OPEC nations control most of the world's oil reserves and spare production capacity. For the next several years, almost all of the world's additional production lies along the Persian Gulf and most of that is in Saudi Arabia. When oil prices peaked in late 2004, 2005 and again in 2006, OPEC spare capacity was only one million barrels per day and almost all of that was from Saudi Arabia, making the United States and the West hostage to the very country most responsible for fomenting radical, Islamist fundamentalism—hardly a successful energy security policy for the world's largest economy [Bremer and Hawes].

MODERN SAUDI ARABIA

In less than three generations, Saudi Arabia literally vaulted from its 7th century Bedouin origins to approach a modern 21st century society, skipping intermediate phases of development that typically require centuries. What the West faces in Saudi Arabia today is the gigantic task of successfully moving a country with ultra-conservative medieval values into the 21st century. The United States created many of Saudi Arabia's governmental institutions to the point that modern Saudi Arabia today is largely an American creation, and one that came back like Frankenstein to haunt its creator on 9/11. The formation of the Saudi bureaucracy and establishment of modern governmental institutions started in earnest in the 1960s during the reign of King Faisal and accelerated with the advent of oil wealth and fallout from the 1979 Iranian Shiite revolution. Physically, organizationally, and economically, most Saudi Arabian bureaucratic institutions resemble agencies of the U.S. government—all funded by massive Saudi oil wealth from the 1980s. In a 2003 interview, Thomas Lippman described the humanitarian origin of United States-Saudi relationships that were initiated and cemented with the first king of Saudi Arabia, Ibn Saud, by American medical missionaries in the 1930s:

The relationship began not with the signing of the first oil contract but with the work of medical missionaries from the missionary hospital in Bahrain that was established at the beginning of the twentieth century by the Reformed Church in America. The first Americans that King Abdul Aziz [Ibn Saud] met were doctors from the Bahrain missionary hospital, who requested to come into the kingdom, where medical conditions were terrible. People suffered from tuberculosis, malaria and all kinds of chronic diseases. [Lippman, 11/2003].

American Imprint
Beginning with President Roosevelt's commitments to the old king in 1945 and the gift of a DC-3 civilian airliner, President Truman's "Point Four Program" followed in the 1950s, and American support for Saudi Arabia continued under each successive American administration. The first American institution established in Saudi Arabia was the Arabian American Oil Company (ARAMCO) in 1933. Before being nationalized by the Saudi government in 1982, ARAMCO had grown into a gigantic American presence in the Eastern Province and thousands of American expatriates and their families lived in secluded American housing compounds that resemble suburban America of the 1950s and 1960s.

During the Roosevelt-Ibn Saud meeting after the Yalta Conference with Allied leaders in 1945, the United States agreed to help protect the Saudi oil fields in return for an American air base in the Eastern Province. The emerging Cold War against atheistic communism following the Second World War caused the Saudis to side with America in the post-war environment and to place great value on the ARAMCO relationship that produced such unbelievable wealth for the royal family.

Except for oil and ARAMCO, American involvement in Saudi Arabia evolved without fanfare and publicity until the 1973 Arab-Israeli war and the Saudi-led Arab oil embargo. That same year, the Saudi government acquired 25 percent ownership in ARAMCO and the British announced their intention to depart the Persian Gulf where they had been the dominant military force for decades. In 1974, President Nixon established the U.S.-Saudi Joint Economic Commission and American involvement in Saudi Arabia increased dramatically following the overthrow of the Shah of Iran in 1979 by Ayatollah Khomeini's Shiite Islamist fundamentalist revolutionaries. Nixon's "Twin Pillar" Persian Gulf policy had called for dual support of both Iran and Saudi Arabia, but that policy collapsed when the Shah and his family fled for their lives, greatly alarming the Saudi royal family amidst serious concern regarding the loyalty of the Saudi Shiite minority living in the Eastern Province and proselytizing Iranian fundamentalists across the Persian Gulf.

With massive, new oil wealth and renewed concern for security against a radical Iranian Shiite threat, the Saudis contracted with American businesses and the U.S. government to create and transform governmental offices and develop a modern Saudi bureaucracy, creating agencies and departments that closely resemble their American counterparts.

The Bedouin/Islamic Influence

The Arabian Peninsula was never colonized during the 18th, 19th and 20th centuries like most Arab countries in the region, and for countless centuries, nomadic Bedouin tribes wandered the open Arabian Peninsula, well known for their insular, traditional, and xenophobic Bedouin culture and rigid "code of the desert" required for survival. The barren heartland in the center of Saudi Arabia around the capital, Riyadh, formed a natural barrier to the Ottoman Turks, Portuguese, British, and other European colonial powers. Since its inception in 1932, Saudi Arabia has been an absolute monarchy—a true authoritarian oligarchy—without elected representative institutions or political parties until partial municipal elections in February 2005.

Legitimacy of the monarchy comes from its relationship with the Wahhabi religious leaders. Wahhabism is the most fundamentalist Sunni Muslim sect and the Wahhabi clerics prefer to call themselves "Salafists" for advocating an ultra-conservative version of Islam that demands Islamist states, Islamic law, and a return to the "pure" days of 7th century Islam. Saudi Arabia is a uniquely Islamic country where church and state are a single entity with no separation possible because it would be contrary to the Wahhabi interpretation of Islam. To Wahhabi believers, separation of church and state cannot be tolerated because it would undermine Islam's doctrine of church and state as an integrated entity. According to Wahhabi-Salafist thinking, secular states are governed by man-made laws and Islamic states like Saudi Arabia are governed by what they believe to be God's laws as revealed in the Holy Koran and writings of the Prophet Mohammed. Disfavored Muslims such as Shiites and Sufis and all other religions are banned in Saudi Arabia, and Saudi Wahhabis have been especially virulent in their persecution and discrimination against the Shiite minority in the Eastern Province near the oil fields that makes up 10-15 percent of the Saudi population.

The Wahhabi-controlled Commission for Promotion of Virtue and Prevention of Vice under Prince Nayef's Ministry of the Interior has cabinet rank in the government, and strict Wahhabi Islamist norms are enforced by the Commission's Muttawa religious police who operate much like the severe Taliban Islamist fundamentalist regime in Afghanistan that was overthrown by the United States in November 2001. Saudi Arabia is governed by Islamic law (Sharia) derived from the teachings of the Holy Koran, which is believed to be the Word of God, and from the Sunnah, the words and deeds of the prophet Muhammad as recorded in the Hadith. The term "Sharia" in Arabic literally means "the path to the watering hole" and as Islamic religious law, it serves as a religious code for living, much more rigid than the moral system of the Bible for Christians. Moreover, Saudi Arabia has the strictest and most lethal interpretation of Sharia anywhere in the world.

The judicial system in Saudi Arabia is closed to the public and the government does not permit demonstrations or criticism, although there has been some loosening because the advent of the internet and satellite television has changed the ability of the Saudi government to control its people. Moreover, the Iraqi national elections in January,

October and December of 2005 served as a driving force for reform throughout the Middle East, including Saudi Arabia. Yet, if people demonstrate or criticize the royal family or the Saudi government, they risk detention or torture. Until recently, defendants have not had the right to representation by a lawyer, are poorly informed of the status of legal proceedings against them, and trials are generally held behind closed doors. When individuals are brought to trial before an Islamic court, the proceedings do not meet accepted international standards for fairness and punishments are medieval and brutal.

The consumption of alcohol is punished by whipping, theft by the amputation of limbs, and under full implementation of Islamic law, 100 lashes and death by stoning are mandated for married women convicted of adultery or fornication. Beheading and stoning for "sorcery" and nonbelief are routine under Saudi law, ranking Saudi Arabia first in the world for beheadings and second only to China for the number of deaths by capital punishment. "Executions by the law of God" (Iaqmet al-Had in Arabic) is the weekly public beheading spectacle held after noon prayers each Friday, either in the court of the main mosque or in a square in front of the regional governor's palace. Crucifixion for 24 hours is adjudged for crimes like robbery accompanied by premeditated murder, followed by swift public beheading using a long, curved scimitar. Saudi Arabian security forces and religious police have been guilty of serious human rights abuses, conduct closed trials, provide no legal counsel for defendants, and implement barbarous punishment such as beheading, amputation and stoning for "sorcery," nonbelief and blasphemy [U.S. State Department Report, February 2004].

Sayyid Qutb, intellectual theoretician of the Egyptian Muslim Brotherhood, admired the Saudi legal system and commended it as the basis for other Islamist states and a solution to the world's ills. Saudi Arabia is governed day-to-day by the king as head of state and a Council of Ministers established in 1953. The Council of Ministers consists of 29 cabinet-level members and is responsible for all affairs of state. The Council meets weekly and is presided over by the king or his deputy, the crown prince. Various ministries and government agencies serve under the Council of Ministers and most are located in the capital, Riyadh. Regional governors, who are senior members of the royal family with cabinet-level rank, head 13 regional provinces. The governors are responsible to the Minister of Interior for regional governance matters, hold power over the local tribal leaders, and are authorized to carry out capital punishment.

Saudi legislation called the "Basic Law" was implemented in 1993. The Saudi Basic Law essentially established ground rules for the structure and organization of the Saudi government and a "Bill of Rights for Saudi Citizens." The Basic Law was an attempt for the first time to formalize a written constitution and it further defined the government's rights and responsibilities to Saudi citizens and established a Consultative Council called the "Majlis Al Shura," a Bedouin form of tribal participation. Initially 60 members and now 120, all appointed by the king, the Majlis al Shura was established to bring together distinguished Saudi representatives from a mixture of clans, religious and business leaders and professionals to serve four-year terms and advise the king on matters effecting the country. The concept of a tribal council is well established in Bedouin culture and the Saudi Majlis al Shura resembles its earlier Bedouin models. Members are appointed by the king and not elected, and the king is the final arbiter on all issues. The Majlis al Shura is unique in that any member of the clan or tribe may appeal to the local sheik or leader to express the nature of a problem and seek redress for a perceived wrong, regardless how small or trivial. The Saudis implemented the Majlis al Shura as their version of representative government, declaring that it was not a step toward Western-style democracy but rather an extension of Saudi tradition that goes back to the days of the Prophet Mohammed and even before.

The Al Saud-Wahhab Partnership Continues

Senior Wahhabi religious leaders form the Ulama, which has a long and significant history that started in 1744 with the political and religious alliance between the al Saud family and Mohammed bin Abdul Wahhab [Saudi Ministry of Culture and Information]. The

Saudi Ulama enforces rigid standards of Wahhabism, controls the Ministry of Religious Affairs, Ministry of Education, and Ministry of Justice in the Saudi government. In this capacity, the Ulama implements Islamic law and jurisprudence (Sharia), judges all legal cases in the courts according to Islamic law, administers public education at all levels, supervises 100,000 imams and mosques including what is preached both at home and abroad, and controls international funding and support for mosques and schools in foreign countries. As strict Wahhabi religious leaders, the Ulama has played a key role in the country from its inception and continues to influence and control elements of the Saudi government that have even a remote relationship to religion, including the preaching of Islam abroad.

Treatment of women is especially harsh in the Saudi kingdom. Women's rights as known in the West are virtually nonexistent in Saudi Arabia because of the Ulama's ultra-strict and literal interpretation of Islamic law. Stoning, amputation, and public beheading for capital crime are common and Saudi cultural taboos create immense problems for Saudi women in their efforts to enter the 21st century. Other Muslim countries differ significantly from Saudi Arabia in their interpretation of the Holy Koran, which shows that it is not Islam, as a whole, but rather the strict Saudi interpretation of the Holy Koran and sayings of the Prophet that has failed to adapt to the modern world.

The plight of women under strict Islamic law in Saudi Arabia is medieval and barbaric by Western standards, both in interpretation and practice. As laid out in the Holy Koran in the 7th century, Islamic law in Saudi Arabia governs women's activities and all aspects of behavior outside the home. The list of female restrictions and prohibitions is lengthy, starting with rigid segregation of the sexes, even to the point that Saudi women have separate entrances to their homes. Outside the home, women must be fully covered in black, including a black facial veil that must be worn even in oppressive desert heat, and when they leave their homes, a male family member who typically wears cooler white robes, must escort them.

Social customs and tribal taboos are so formidable in some remote and especially conservative parts of Saudi Arabia such as the Al Kharj region south of Riyadh that not even a woman's husband or children are permitted to see her face until she dies [Qusti, 9/3/03]. The 5,000-man Muttawa religious police strictly enforce Islamic law, calling the faithful to prayer five times a day and arresting violators of rigid Wahhabi rules for fraternization between the sexes and violation of the rigid female dress code. In 2004 the Muttawa was strengthened to pacify senior Wahhabi clerics in the government in the wake of the government crackdown on extremists following successive al Qaeda attacks within the kingdom.

Different standards prevail for women in Saudi Arabia, as in almost everything, and capital punishment is even more extreme for women. Under Islamic law, a woman may be stoned to death if she has been raped or convicted of extramarital sex, but capital punishment for women is normally by firing squad, while men are beheaded with a sword slightly longer than one meter. Under the law, women are treated as chattel with limited rights and are the personal property of the husband or father, while men may practice polygamy and are permitted to have up to four wives simultaneously. Women are prohibited from driving cars and are frequently forced into arranged marriages as early teenagers. Inheritance rights favor men over women—two shares for men and one for women—and divorce and child custody are strictly male prerogatives, legally ordered upon peremptory demand by the husband with no objection permitted by the wife. Under Islamic law the right of revenge belongs to the heir of the victim, and in cases of murder or other wrongful death, the heir can exchange this right for cash compensation called the "blood-price." In the death of a woman, however, the heir receives only half the blood-price of a man. The same discount formula applies to the death of a Jew or Christian.

Female obesity is a problem in much of the Arab world because men consider heavyset, overweight Arab women attractive. Young girls are frequently force-fed to make them gain weight at an early age and increase their marketability for marriage, a practice that often leads to early health problems. Evidence in court from a woman is only valid if a male member of her family accompanies the woman and even then, evidence from a female counts as only half of a man's testimony. Women also have limited career opportunities and are generally restricted to teaching and medicine, although some women have recently been attracted to businesses they can operate within the limitations of Islamic law. To travel outside the country requires permission from a male family member, and the many restrictions on women caused by rigorous interpretation of Islamic law and Saudi cultural taboos are pervasive.

So, many questions remain: Is modern Saudi Arabia prepared to join the rest of the world in the 21st century or will it remain mired in reactionary clerical hatred and continue to propagate the world with Islamist terrorists bent on returning to a violent and primitive past? Where do the people of Saudi Arabia begin their efforts to initiate reform, and how do people and institutions change their basic outlook when religious ideology seems so opposed to everything modern and the rapid pace of change?

SAUDI RELATIONS WITH THE WORLD

Saudi Arabia's relationships with other nations have been greatly influenced by American oil companies and the American government, but the kingdom's underlying motives for the conduct of its government and its relations with other nations still reflect the decisions of its founder, King Abdul Aziz Ibn Saud. By most counts, the first king had over 50 children from his many wives and his sons have successively ruled the country since his death in 1953. And over the years, the Saudi monarchy has been run like a family business, not for the benefit of Saudi citizens, but for the benefit of the family, and keeping control of the family business has been the first responsibility of Ibn Saud's successors.

Ibn Saud's Successors

Ibn Saud's oldest son, Saud, became king in 1953 when his father died but he was deposed by members of the royal family 10 years later, who were repulsed by his profligacy and failure to become an effective leader. During Saud's ten-year reign, Saudi Arabia had little impact on the world except to form the Organization of Petroleum Exporting Countries (OPEC) in 1960 to serve as a cartel to fix oil prices by establishing production quotas for member nations. Saudi Arabia assumed the role of the swing nation that changed its oil production to meet global oil demand and regulate world oil prices, which was largely ineffective from a cartel standpoint because of OPEC's inability to accurately predict changes in world demand. During Saud's reign, Arab nationalism was seen as a threat to the Saudi monarchy and Wahhabi extremists were encouraged to go to Egypt to join and assist the Muslim Brotherhood in its efforts to topple Abdel Gamal Nasser from leadership in Egypt and among the Arab League members. Those efforts subsequently succeeded in the assassination in 1981 of Nasser's successor, Anwar Sadat, who had signed the Saudi-hated peace treaty with the Israelis in 1979.

Saud's successor, King Faisal, was clever like his father and actively supported Arab efforts to destroy Israel in the last of three wars the Israelis easily repelled. However, in 1973 when the Arabs, led by the forces of Egypt, Jordan, and Syria, surprised the Israelis on Yom Kippur with its fourth attack, the United States had to come to Israel's rescue with a last-minute delivery of vital military aid that turned the tide against the Arab aggressors. Incensed, King Faisal imposed the 1973 Oil Embargo on Western oil purchasers and oil prices quadrupled later in the decade. The world witnessed the greatest transfer of wealth, this time to OPEC, since Spain removed tons of gold from the New World in the 16th century. Many Saudis became overnight billionaires and the excesses of the Saudi royal family became legendary. Faisal was subsequently assassinated in 1975 by a deranged, Wahhabi-influenced nephew seeking revenge for his brother who had been killed in a clash with Saudi security forces in 1966. He died without fully understanding how his oil embargo would profoundly change Saudi Arabia and the world over the next thirty years.

THE TRIUMPH OF DEMOCRACY OVER MILITANT ISLAMISM

King Khaled followed Faisal and was "amiable but ineffectual," [and] "troubled by a weak heart and paid little attention of governing" [Lippman, 2005]. The country was really run by Crown Prince Fahd who eventually succeeded King Khaled when he died in 1982 from heart failure. But in 1979, Fahd presided as Crown Prince over the most tempestuous year in Saudi Arabian history since the Ikhwan army's revolt against Ibn Saud in the late 1920s. Beginning with the fall of the Shah of Iran to rioting Shiites who quickly installed the fundamentalist Grand Ayatollah Khomeini, the year 1979 ended with the Soviet invasion of Muslim Afghanistan and a Wahhabi revolt in the holy city of Mecca, an event highly reminiscent of the earlier Ikhwan rebellion against Abdul Aziz Ibn Saud.

On November 20, 1979, the beginning of the fifteenth Muslim century and a few days after a Shiite revolt in Eastern Saudi Arabia that had closed the oil fields, a group of Wahhabi and Muslim Brotherhood extremists captured and claimed the Grand Mosque in Mecca while their leader proclaimed himself the mahdi—literally, "the guided one"—who according to both Sunni and Shiite traditions is a messianic figure who appears at the end of time to restore righteousness" [Gold]. Because the leaders had valid Wahhabi credentials (from a family of an Ikhwan soldier who had been killed by Ibn Saud in 1929), the royal family was now confronted with a legitimate dispute over its religious credentials. King Khaled had no choice but to seek permission from the Ulama to deal with the dissidents. Crown Prince Fahd, the King's representative whose profligate living style during his youth limited his negotiating power with the Ulama, was at a distinct disadvantage. The highest religious authority in the kingdom took a full four days of deliberation before it granted the monarchy permission to invade the Grand Mosque and remove the protestors with force, but not before extracting a very heavy price on the monarchy for its previous ostentatious behavior—a commitment from the royal family to spend a large portion of the kingdom's oil wealth on international assistance programs to help poor Muslims and to proselytize worldwide for Wahhab-Salafism. In addition, the Ulama's authority in supervising the kingdom's "Wahhabi character" was expanded.

COLONEL B. WAYNE QUIST AND DR. DAVID F. DRAKE

The royal family had sustained a substantial diminution in its governing authority. Consequently, in 1981 when Egypt and Syria exiled members of the Muslim Brotherhood after Sadat's assassination, the royal family welcomed these Islamist radicals to Saudi Arabia and provided many of the exiles positions in Saudi schools of higher education. Even earlier, as a result of Nasser's rising Arab nationalism, exiled members of the Muslim Brotherhood from Egypt and Syria had infected Saudi universities with their brand of militant and violent Islamist radicalism, and Saudi Arabia's radical Wahhabi clerics reinstated the medieval concept of jihad, or "holy war," against nonbelievers and any type of progressive thinking. With an ideological motivation similar to the old king's Ikhwan army, the stepchild of Saudi Wahhabi-Salafist ideology—"Bin Ladenism"—was born, seeking to convert infidels or, failing that, advocating the murder of innocent people, including women and children, with guarantees of martyrdom and heavenly rewards in the afterlife for the fanatical perpetrators.

As Crown Prince and later as King, Fahd had an increasingly difficult problem with his governance partner, the Wahhabi clerics. He had an excess number of devoted, even radical, Wahhabi-Salafist followers in the kingdom who were becoming increasingly critical of the royal family and he had to find a way to divert their religious energy away from the royal family. The Saudis quickly joined the Americans in a cause that suited both nations' objectives—thwarting the Soviet Union's 1979 invasion of Afghanistan. The United States under President Reagan sought to not just contain communism but to defeat the Soviet Union as part of its Cold War strategy and the Saudis wanted to be seen as defenders of Islam in coming to the aid of a fellow Muslim nation against atheistic communism. The Saudi royal family readily agreed to a joint program of assistance to the Islamist forces in Afghanistan. The Saudis defused their Wahhabi-Salafist extremists by using funds promised to the Ulama for proselytizing Wahhabism, worked to strengthen their longstanding relationship with Pakistan, and encouraged Wahhabi-Salafist extremists to launch a jihad against the Soviet communists, which spirited many of the radicals out of the country, at least for the short-term. King Fahd also enhanced the royal family's image by employing funds generated from the oil price bonanza into "an unprecedented construction, and reconstruction, movement in the kingdom. Virtually every community was transformed. Within the life of a single generation the Saudi urban habitat changed beyond recognition" [Taheri, 8/2/2005]. These extravagant spending programs were consistent with Fahd's long-held belief that money could solve all problems.

But Fahd faced one more crisis—this time an outside threat by Saddam Hussein's reckless 1990 invasion of Kuwait and thousands of Iraqi troops positioned ominously on the Saudi border. By the time of the Iraqi invasion, Saudi jihadists in Afghanistan had triumphantly returned from their victory over the Soviet Union. Speaking for his "Afghan Arabs," Osama bin Laden offered to wage war against the invading Iraqis, who were to bin Laden's thinking "as easy as pie" compared with the Soviet Union, one of the world's two superpowers. Not only did Fahd fear what the future consequences might be for the royal family if bin Laden's boast proved correct, but he had a better offer from the first President Bush for United States military forces to drive Saddam out of Kuwait. After assuring himself that the Americans would not topple Hussein in their military action against Iraq, Fahd invited the Americans to honor their longstanding commitment to protect its oil fields by stationing 550,000 American and nearly 450,000 other troops in Saudi Arabia to protect the Saudis and serve as a launching pad for taking Kuwait back from the Iraqis. Not only was bin Laden crest-fallen by Fahd's dismissal of his offer, but he was enraged when he learned that the king had invited nearly a million infidels to the holy land of Islam. This was blasphemy according to his strict interpretation of Wahhabism and bin Laden declared war on the Saudi monarchy and the United States, the next "great Satan." Plans for a great jihad, the global war on terror, began formulation in 1990.

King Fahd spent his remaining years on the throne quietly cementing better relations with the United States. But it was Fahd who had directed millions and ultimately billions into international Islamic charities that funded radical militant Islamist groups around the world and established Wahhabi-Salafist schools and mosques with hate-filled messages against nonbelievers. Fahd authorized the use of Saudi oil wealth to ultimately spread Saudi Arabia's fanatical and frightening form of ultra-conservative Islam across North Africa and Central Asia, and into Indonesia, the Philippines, Europe, and even the United States.

Between 1975 and 2002 it has been estimated that the Saudi government directed as much as $70 to $90 billion in Islamic aid projects around the world, far more than the Soviet Union spent on propaganda during the entire Cold War. This vast sum does not even include the very substantial amount of additional funding from private Saudi sources, providing aid to the families of suicide bombers and motivating young Muslims around the world to kill infidels and commit unspeakable acts of violence in the name of God. More than 60 percent of the suicide bombers in Iraq following the overthrow of Saddam Hussein were identified as young Saudis [Pas], many just teenagers who were exposed to a steady diet of Wahhabi-Salafist propaganda during their impressionable and rigidly dogmatic school years. With drastic consequences for the world, the genie of Wahhabi-Salafist fundamentalism was unleashed by radicalized Saudi clerics using billions of petrodollars from the two trillion in oil revenue generated by the Saudi oil fields since the 1970s.

The Board of Directors

Born in 1921, King Fahd was incapacitated following a series of strokes in 1995 and 1996 and finally died in 2005. His half brother, Abdullah, born in 1923 or 1924, served as crown prince and de facto ruler for nine years (like Fahd under Khaled), and was ordained by the royal family as King Abdullah on August 1, 2005. Significantly, King Abdullah is not one of the so-called "Sudairi Seven," full brothers and sons of the old king's favorite wife, Hassa bint Ahmad Sudairi. King Fahd was a Sudairi and two other aging Sudairis, Prince Sultan and Prince Nayef, remain in waiting for their turn at the throne, as do younger generations of princes from the Sudairi line. The remaining Sudairi brothers, listed below, are now in their late 70s and early 80s and confront the health problems of aging, but continue to control powerful government institutions.

The Sudairi Seven

Fahd bin Abdul Aziz ibn Saud	Deceased King and Prime Minister
Sultan bin Abdul Aziz ibn Saud	Crown Prince and Minister of Defense & Aviation
Abdul-Rahman bin Abdul Aziz ibn Saud	Vice Minister of Defense & Aviation
Nayef bin Abdul Aziz ibn Saud	Minister of Interior
Salman bin Abdul Aziz ibn Saud	Governor of Riyadh
Ahmad bin Abdul Aziz ibn Saud	Vice Minister of Interior
Turki (II) bin Abdul Aziz ibn Saud	Chairman, Arabian Cement Company, Ltd.

Through decades of extravagance and royal vice, the Western press and Wahhabi clerics have criticized members of the Saudi royal family for their unrestrained self-indulgence. It is widely known that King Fahd used alcohol excessively, smoked heavily and lived extravagantly, especially at his villa in Marbella, Spain where Roman-style decadence abounded. Like many members of the royal family, Fahd lived a life of ostentatious wealth and consistently demonstrated a belief that money could solve all problems, such as the ransom he paid the Ulama after the seizure of the Great Mosque in Mecca in 1979 by Wahhabi extremists.

King Abdullah, however, has a far different reputation. He grew up in the desert among the remote northern tribes before the discovery of oil and raced horses and camels with his loyal Bedouin followers. By 1962 Abdullah was selected to command the Saudi Arabian National Guard (SANG), now consisting of well over 50,000 loyal and highly-trained Bedouin tribesmen responsible for internal security. Today Abdullah's strengths rest with his reputation for integrity and hard work and the fact that the National Guard he has commanded for over 40 years is loyal to him personally. Abdullah's sons are also in senior positions in the National Guard where they maintain strong Wahhabi and Bedouin tribal connections. The modern Saudi Arabian National Guard is a direct descendant of the Wahhabi Ikhwan militia and was formed for internal security purposes as a counterweight to the more traditional military forces under Prince Sultan, one of the Sudairi Seven and a full brother of King Fahd.

Abdullah and his family have close family ties to the Saudi Arabian Shamar confederation, a large and powerful Wahhabi Bedouin tribe that reaches from northern Saudi Arabia into western Iraq, eastern Syria, and eastern Jordan. Iraqi Wahhabis have been among the fiercest insurgents fighting American forces in the Sunni Triangle northwest of Baghdad and most are from the Shamar confederation. Abdullah's family also controls the tribal council that rules the holy cities of Mecca and Medina and he maintains strong relationships with the Ulama, the powerful Wahhabi religious hierarchy that controls the influential Ministry of Religious Affairs, Ministry of Justice, and Ministry of Education. Abdullah has spent little time outside Saudi Arabia and has been very critical of America and the West in the past, but he has recently taken steps to appear more moderate, as in a 2002 interview with New York Times reporter, Tom Friedman, when he offered a Saudi solution to the Arab-Israeli stalemate. Nevertheless, as late as the spring of 2004, Abdullah was quoted as saying:

> It became clear for us and I say, not 100 percent but 95 percent, that Zionists hands are behind what is going on now. Unfortunately, they deceived some of our sons. The Devil made them daring and they are supporters of the Devil and colonialism.

THE TRIUMPH OF DEMOCRACY OVER MILITANT ISLAMISM

Abdullah's rivals are his Sudairi half brothers, Crown Prince Sultan, born in 1924, and Prince Nayef, born in 1934. Sultan's official title is "His Royal Highness Crown Prince Sultan Ibn Abdul Aziz, Deputy Prime Minister, Minister of Defense and Aviation and Inspector General." As Minister of Defense, Sultan controls the entire Saudi military establishment except for Abdullah's countervailing National Guard. Sultan and his Sudairi brother, Abdul-Rahman, and Sultan's son Khaled control the traditional Army, Navy and Air Force. Another of Sultan's sons, Bandar, was the influential and popular Saudi ambassador to the United States in Washington, DC from 1983 until 2005. Until 9/11, Bandar was a highly effective Washington power broker with close personal connections to high-ranking Republicans and Democrats alike. Since 9/11, however, Bandar appeared less frequently in public and Abdullah eventually replaced him in the summer of 2005 with Prince Turki al Faisal (son of King Faisal) to have his own representative in Washington. Bandar is among the next generation in the line of succession for the monarchy and returned home in 2005 as Secretary-General of the newly created National Security Council, reporting directly to the new king. Sultan and Bandar tend to tilt toward the West, but Sultan is a loyal family member and supporter of the existing Wahhabi power structure while having grown extremely wealthy from years of alleged corruption and huge commissions on military contracts that he controls through the Ministry of Defense and Aviation (MODA).

Prince Nayef is Minister of Interior where he and his full Sudairi brother, Ahmad, are in charge of internal security and control the secret police and Mattawa religious police. Saudi Arabia is a tightly controlled oligarchy and Prince Nayef is a strong Wahhabi supporter with close ties to prominent Wahhabi clerics in the ministries that report to him. Prince Nayef has headed the interior ministry and its secret and religious police since the early 1970s. His ministry is responsible for enforcing Islamic law and it is well documented that torture is commonly used to obtain confessions. Executions are sanctioned for capital crimes and offenses other than murder such as witchcraft, adultery, sodomy, robbery, sabotage, apostasy (renunciation of Islam), and a catchall charge of "corruption on earth." In early December 2002, Prince Nayef told a Kuwaiti magazine, "Who committed the events of September 11?...I think they [the Zionists] are behind these events," even as questions abound regarding corruption at high levels and royal family support of al Qaeda [Bergen 12/18/2002].

Crisis in the Kingdom

Competition has always existed among the royal princes, but today outward signs point to a growing struggle between Abdullah, Sultan and Nayef and powerful reactionary Wahhabi clerics. Few Western observers understand the inner workings of the royal family that rules the inscrutable desert kingdom, but many experienced observers believe that the serious problems caused by al Qaeda attacks in the kingdom, hard pressure from the United States for reform, and the strength of the Wahhabis within the government, have placed the royal family in the most serious crisis of its existence and with a diminishing chance of compromise. The outlook for the survival of the royal family as an institution is less than promising because of its lethargy at a time when it needs to forcefully adapt itself into a constitutional monarchy with a broadly representative government capable of controlling the reactionary Wahhabi clerics.

With nearly 7,000 first tier princes and tens of thousands of other members of the Saudi royal family dependent on overly generous oil stipends and expensive tastes, there is a strong potential for a bloody struggle within the Saudi royal family over the future role of Wahhabism in the kingdom. Many younger members of the royal family, like Prince Bandar and influential Saudi businessmen, have been educated in the West and understand the problems faced by the ruling family and the need for reform. Many of these people desire reform, but in the final analysis, the tale of the Saudi royal family is an ancient story of royal excess replete in the annals of history, symptomatic of failing absolute monarchies and reminiscent of the final years of the Shah of Iran and other absolute rulers. As the royal family prepares to hand power to the third generation of al Sauds, the aging sons of the old desert warrior who founded the kingdom have no doubt pondered the comments of Ibn Khaldun (1332-1406), the wise 14th century Arab historian, who said the following about Arab dynasties:

> "The first generation takes power, the second consolidates it, the third uses it to live in luxury and licentiousness, and the fourth generation squanders it all as new and hungry forces sweep in from the desert."

In 2004, Osama bin Laden warned that the Saudi royal family is destined to meet the same fate as the Shah of Iran due to corruption, ostentatious living, and wayward policies. The first and primary goal of al Qaeda is the overthrow of the Saudi monarchy, followed by restoration of the Sunni Caliphate, and installation of a Taliban-like regime with a rigid Wahhabi legal system in Saudi Arabia and around the world. But to the Saudi monarchy, any suggestion of reform looks like weakness, inviting even more al Qaeda-inspired violence.

If the Saudi royal family falls to radical, militant forces, world markets will tremble, the price of oil would soar to $300 per barrel or higher, and the world economy would sink into severe global recession. The alternative for the West at that time would be to unite behind U.S.-led NATO forces to secure the Saudi oil fields in the Eastern Province and help mainstream, moderate Muslims internationalize the holy cities of Islam in Mecca and Medina, possibly under traditional Hashemite rule. The Saudi rulers are faced with daunting challenges of uncertain royal family succession as well as the monumental task of bringing the desert kingdom, its people, and its ultra-conservative religious clerics and culture into the 21st century while facing rapid and enormous global change.

The royal family has had a long history of peacefully accommodating and then violently smashing the Wahhabi religious clerics when they defy authority, and that is what might happen again if the royal family is pushed further into a corner. When the Wahhabi Ikhwan rose up against Abdul Aziz Ibn Saud in 1928-30, he publicly beheaded the leaders, and when Wahhabi extremists seized the Great Mosque in

Mecca during a 1979 religious rampage, the Saudi regime executed over 60 of the extremists, with public beheadings throughout the country as an example [Lippman, 2004]. Today's Wahhabi clerics understand full well the inherent risks in pushing too hard against the monarchy, and so does the royal family.

Besides the problems of its religious clerics, the Saudis also face dramatic population growth, fluctuating oil revenues, deficit spending (until recently), plus the difficulty of accommodating incessant forces of globalization and modernization. The future portends many problems relating to social dislocation caused by rapid modernization and runaway population growth that will double the Saudi population in 20 years. High wages and an uncompetitive economy in the global market are the result of a poor Saudi work ethic, high salary expectations and a failed public school system that does not provide needed job skills or training. Unless the royal family is successful in quickly implementing critically needed reforms, these conditions could result in the overthrow of the monarchy by a radical Islamist government dominated by the military and with little hope of a Western-style democracy.

Other developments are also disturbing. The Saudis are wedded to huge levels of defense spending and rampant corruption, with about 13 percent of Saudi GDP devoted to defense versus 4.3 percent for China and 3.2 percent for the United States by way of comparison. Moreover, the Saudis acquired 50 ballistic missiles from China some years ago with a range of 2,000 miles and recently negotiated an arms-for-oil exchange to upgrade the missiles with the latest Chinese technology as well as other potentially destabilizing security arrangements with China and Pakistan. China is motivated to secure its sources of oil because it imports nearly two-thirds of what it consumes and has recently negotiated large deals with both the Saudis and Iran. Meanwhile, it has been widely reported in open sources that the Saudis funded $7 billion for nuclear weapons programs in Iraq under Saddam Hussein and in Pakistan. It is further alleged that the Saudis have an agreement with Pakistan to receive nuclear warheads for upgraded Chinese missiles to be used as a deterrent to Israeli and potential Iranian nuclear capability across the Persian Gulf.

All in all, trouble lies ahead for the absolute monarchy that has been dubbed the kingdom of "intolerance swaddled in faith" [Cohen]. The reality after 9/11 is that the United States can no longer take Saudi Arabia for granted as it has in the past, and as many desert warriors have observed, "the desert winds are blowing"—change is in the wind—but it is well to remember, "nothing is easy in the desert."

With this in mind, the next chapter looks at al Qaeda and its ideological origins to further identify the influence of Saudi Arabian Wahhabi-Salafism and its impact on the world today, as today's "Bin Ladenism" has taken Saudi Arabian Wahhabism to a new level of violence, and xenophobic intolerance.

CHAPTER TWO

Al Qaeda's Origins, Plans, Next of Kin, and Arab-Muslim Problems

Al Qaeda was formed in the late 1980s and early 1990s after bin Laden's "Afghan Arabs" helped defeat the Soviet Union in Afghanistan. It is a descendent of a long line of radical Islamist movements that have been offshoots of militant Islamist thought over the centuries. This chapter begins by reviewing the history of al Qaeda's founding, outlines the radical offshoots and their relationship to al Qaeda, and concludes by discussing problems in the modern Arab-Muslim world.

Today's radical, militant Islamists are generally well educated, use modern technology effectively, and argue that science and technology must be harnessed to pursue the will of God. They also argue that personal and violent jihad are necessary and justified by the Holy Koran to solve problems in the Arab world by Islamizing society and eventually the entire world. Long legal arguments have been developed by Muslim scholars making the case for violent jihad and justifying the use of nuclear weapons against the West because of perceived damages that go back to the Crusades. Ultimately, the arguments of today's radical Islamist militants call for death to nonbelievers or conversion to an extremist form of Islam with no compromise or tolerance for other beliefs. A rallying goal of Osama bin Laden and other extremists is to restore the Islamic Caliphate, a goal that has broad support throughout the Muslim world. The origins of al Qaeda and militant Islamism—"Bin Ladenism"—started before the creation of modern Saudi Arabia and its marriage to Wahhabism, an ultraconservative and puritanical sect of Sunni Islam born in the Arabian desert over 200 years ago.

Saudi citizens are al Qaeda's largest single nationality and according to reliable news reports, nearly one-quarter of the prisoners held by American forces at Guantanamo Bay, Cuba were Saudis, mostly young men who had traveled to Afghanistan to participate in relief work for their Muslim brothers. In 2004, the United States and Saudi Arabia reached agreement whereby some of the younger Saudis held in Cuba were repatriated to Saudi custody for trial back home, but many of these young, hard-line terrorists may have been freed to seek martyrdom in Iraq. Even yet today the legacies of Ibn Saud are evident and at work throughout the vast oil empire that the old king crafted in the early 20th century.

The source of today's militant Islamist terrorism is the Wahhabi-Salafist religious creed practiced in Saudi Arabia reinforced with the discipline of the radicalized Muslim Brotherhood movement. The 9/11 terrorists were indoctrinated in militant Wahhabism and were predominantly from Saudi Arabia. Osama bin Laden and fifteen of the nineteen hijackers were born and raised in Saudi Arabia and were profoundly influenced by militant Wahhabi-Salafism that is still taught today in the Saudi Arabian school system and in Saudi-funded Wahhabi schools in Europe, the United States and around the world.

BIN LADENISM

Osama bin Laden is a hard core Islamist who hates America and all that it stands for with fierce determination and deadly passion. For bin Laden and his followers, there is no compromise. America and its allies are bin Laden's primary enemy but he also names the corrupt Saudi royal family as even more deserving of eternal punishment for many real and perceived sins against the Muslim people. America, in bin Laden's mind, represents all that is wrong in the 21st century because the world's greatest democracy implements laws that are made by people as opposed to laws delivered from God. He also hates America because it conspires with Islam's enemies to drive a globalization process that showers massive and unwanted technological and social change upon the poor and teeming Muslim masses. Bin Laden, like all Islamists, believes that Islam is an all-encompassing religio-political system with its own legal, economic and social structures as well as its moral and religious base. Bin Laden believes democracy must be destroyed because it is corrupted by immoral, depraved, and godless people and follows man-made laws that result in anarchy and oppression of Muslims.

Bin Laden's view of the world would only permit God's laws as revealed in the Koran and as interpreted and codified over the centuries in rigid Islamic law known as Sharia. Bin Laden is at war with the West and rationalizes the use of nuclear weapons and other types of mass destruction because the American people—not just their misguided leaders—are guilty of sins and crimes against the Muslim world since the American people freely elect their leaders and create their own laws in defiance of God's law. Drawing from multiple sources, each with distinct ties to his native Wahhabi-Salafism, Bin Laden has adopted and molded an ideology of hate that justifies terrorism because his fierce and determined but scattered forces are incapable of direct assault against well-trained conventional armies such as the American military, his primary enemy. He believes terrorism against non-believers thus suits his cause, even if it results in the death of innocent people—Christians, Jews, and Muslims alike. We ask ourselves, "How and where did this type of thinking originate?" Yet, such hatred of the West is not new to Islam and has been around for several hundred years, surfacing and resurfacing over the centuries with Muslim ideologists that date to even before the Crusades.

THE TRIUMPH OF DEMOCRACY OVER MILITANT ISLAMISM

Osama Bin Laden's Story

Osama bin Mohammed bin Laden is Saudi Arabian by birth and grew up as the youngest son in a large and wealthy though somewhat untraditional Saudi family. He was born around 1957 (the family is uncertain of his exact birthday) in the capital city Riyadh and came of age during the tumultuous 1970s and 1980s when radical members of the Muslim Brotherhood had taken control of leading Saudi universities. A radical Islamist regime had overthrown a neighboring monarch across the Persian Gulf in 1979 and oil wealth began to indelibly transform the provincial desert kingdom. Bin Laden's father, Mohammed bin Laden, came to Saudi Arabia from Yemen in the early part of the 20th century as a poor migrant worker and before long established a close relationship with the first king, Ibn Saud. Bin Laden's father became a trusted member of the king's inner circle and, as the king's preferred building contractor, he was awarded lucrative construction jobs for many of the most important and sensitive projects in the kingdom, including military facilities and the Grand Mosque in Mecca. Bin Laden's father had several wives and like the old king fathered over 50 children. Osama bin Laden's mother was his father's only Saudi wife, which affected how he was raised, especially in his early years and when compared with his brothers whose mothers were more emancipated Egyptian, Lebanese, Syrian, and Jordanian women. The family moved from Riyadh to Jeddah in the western province in the 1960s and later to Medina, Islam second holiest city. Like many immigrant parents, bin Laden's father emphasized the value of education, but the elder bin Laden was killed in a plane crash in 1968 when his youngest son was only eleven.

As global oil prices quadrupled following the Saudi-led Arab oil embargo in 1973, ballooning Saudi oil wealth started to transform the kingdom and cranes dotted the desert landscape. Building construction boomed and, under the leadership of his older brothers, the bin Laden family business prospered while Osama bin Laden attended high school in Jeddah, the relatively liberal Saudi port city on the Red Sea where young people were routinely exposed to Western influence as well as radical, militant Islamist propaganda originating from the radical Muslim Brotherhood in Egypt. In preparation for a career in the family business, bin Laden went from high school to study business, management, and economics at King Abdul Aziz University in Jeddah, considered at the time one of the best schools in the country. Although exposed to Western influence from an early age, bin Laden gradually grew more religious and inward-looking and began to show increased interest in Islam as a teenager [Bodansky, 3]. His father's intentions had been to move him into one of the several family businesses that had grown rapidly as the new oil wealth transformed the previously impoverished desert kingdom, but his unexpected death in 1968 and the tempestuous events of the 1970s changed the family's plans. The disastrous Arab-Israeli Yom Kippur War in October 1973 and the ensuing peace treaty between Egypt and Israel, the assassination of King Faisal in 1975, and in 1979 the overthrow of the Shah of Iran by Shiite Islamists, followed by the takeover of the Grand Mosque in Mecca by radical Wahhabi militants, and the invasion of Afghanistan by the atheistic Soviet Union all in the same year were tumultuous events with shocking implications for the Saudi royal family and for young people in the kingdom like Osama bin Laden. Meanwhile, influential radical, militant Islamists from the Muslim Brotherhood exiled Egyptians, Syrians and Palestinians had risen to prominent and influential positions in Saudi universities in Mecca, Medina and Jeddah, including one of the most prominent and charismatic of the radical Islamist militants, Dr. Abdullah Azzam (1941-1989), distinguished and charismatic professor of Islamic Studies at bin Laden's university in Jeddah.

Bin Laden's Mentors and Colleagues

Just what direct contact Osama bin Laden may have had with Abdullah Azzam when he was a student at Abdul Aziz University is unclear, but he probably attended Azzam's popular lectures and was profoundly influenced by Azzam. Bin Laden and Azzam were among the first Arabs to go to Afghanistan shortly after the Soviet invasion in late December 1979 and it was there that he again came in contact with the distinguished professor and lecturer, probably some time in early 1980. Azzam has been called the "Godfather of Jihad" because he was a scholar and Islamist ideologue of great importance and served as bin Laden's spiritual mentor in the formative years of al Qaeda [Bergen]. Steve Emerson [2001], writer and producer of a PBS documentary on Jihad in America, stated, "Azzam is more responsible than any Arab figure in modern history for galvanizing the Muslim masses to wage an international holy war against all infidels and non-believers until the enemies of Islam were defeated."

Abdullah Azzam was Palestinian by birth, born in the province of Jenin in the West Bank, and became a member of the Muslim Brotherhood at an early age. Azzam received his early education in Jordan, studying agriculture at a local college, and received a B.A. degree in Islamic law (Sharia) from the Sharia College of Damascus University 1966. Following the disastrous Arab loss to Israel in the 1967 Six Day War, Azzam joined Yasser Arafat in terrorist activity against Israel but soon broke with the Palestinian leader as he became disillusioned with the Palestinian struggle and realized that Arafat was insufficiently Islamist in his outlook and was driven more by nationalist and Marxist ideology and disturbing agreements with the communist and atheistic Soviet Union. Azzam believed that Islamism was a far higher cause than provincial Arab nationalism or Palestinian independence and that the struggle of all Muslim people should be taken onto the global stage against Islam's "far enemies," atheistic communism and the hated democratic West. These ideas later coalesced with the emerging ideas of Dr. Ayman al Zawahiri, bin Laden's Egyptian deputy, and the writings of the spiritual Islamist leader of Sudan, Dr. Hassan al Turabi. Azzam soon found that his true calling was not fighting on the battlefield as a militant Palestinian terrorist but rather as an ideological leader and educator with a determined worldview of Islam, profound knowledge of Sharia, and mesmerizing oratorical skills. According to Emerson [2001], "Those who met Azzam were dazzled by his spellbinding oratorical skills, his capabilities as a military strategist, and his interminable energy." Even today, the Hamas military wing of the Palestinian Liberation Organization (PLO) is called the "Abdullah Azzam Brigade" and

Azzam and his writings are revered throughout the world of radical, militant Islamism.

After breaking with Arafat, Azzam traveled to Egypt where he earned a Master's degree in Sharia and Islamic Studies at Cairo's renowned and influential Al-Azhar University, infiltrated as early as the 1950s with Saudi money. The Saudi royal family and their Wahhabi clerics had been highly successful since the old king's first initiatives in the 1950s in planting seeds of Wahhabi-Salafism at Al Azhar through lucrative stipends to Islamic scholars and professors and by radicalizing the faculty in support of intolerant Wahhabi-Salafist goals. After receiving his Master's degree, Azzam returned to Jordan to teach in Amman but was expelled in 1970 as a radical militant. Azzam received another scholarship to continue work toward his Ph.D. in Sharia which he received from Al-Azhar University in 1973. It was during this critical period in Cairo that Azzam came to know such ideological and future terrorist leaders as Sheik Omar Abdul Rahman, who was responsible for the first World Trade Center bombing; Dr. Ayman al Zawahiri, who is bin Laden's deputy and chief ideologue; and other followers of Sayyid Qutb, the ferocious ideologue of the Muslim Brotherhood.

Qutb's ideology and belief in the inevitability of a "clash of civilizations" between the world of Islam and the world of nonbelievers drove Azzam's view of violent revolution as the only alternative to secular government and the critical need to re-establish the Sunni Muslim Caliphate under an Islamic state strictly ruled by Sharia. After receiving his Ph.D. from Al-Azhar, Azzam returned to Jordan to again teach at Amman University but was expelled a second time because of his radical views and took refuge in Saudi Arabia where other exiled and well-educated Muslim Brotherhood ideologues, including Qutb's brother Mohammed, had found refuge as teachers. It was here at King Abdul Aziz University in Jeddah where Azzam took a position as lecturer in Sharia and Osama bin Laden most likely heard the charismatic Dr. Abdullah Yusuf Azzam lecture for the first time in the late 1970s.

In the early 1980s, Osama bin Laden brought family money and youthful passion to Azzam's revolutionary ideas that included hatred of Christians and Jews. Operating from western Pakistan, Azzam and bin

Laden established what became known as the "Services Bureau," a forerunner of al Qaeda, which bin Laden expanded into an international network designed to attract Islamists with all types of special knowledge, from medicine to engineering and drug smuggling [Bodansky, 12]. Bin Laden returned home in the early 1980s to raise money for his Arab army in Pakistan and Afghanistan and recruit youthful Saudi volunteers. It was during this time that bin Laden allegedly secured financial support and commitments from senior members of the Saudi royal family, including King Fahd's brother, Prince Salman bin Abdul Aziz, and the chief of intelligence, Prince Turki bin Faisal, the current Saudi ambassador to the United States. Bin Laden also met with the late King Fahd and Crown Prince Abdullah, the current king, and secured support for his Afghan cause with impassioned pleas to the royal family. By the early 1980s, over 3,000 Arabs were in Afghanistan and the numbers continued to climb to nearly 20,000 by the mid 1980s when Afghanistan had become a magnet for militant Islamists from all over the world. Egyptian Islamists with military background, fugitives from Sadat's crackdown on radical militants, soon arrived and provided military knowledge and discipline for bin Laden's growing cadre of Arab fighters that emerged victorious over the Soviet Union's disastrous venture into Afghanistan.

By the late 1980s bin Laden had established recruitment centers in fifty countries and later set up training centers in western Pakistan and Afghanistan to provide special training and physical conditioning for the newly recruited militants arriving to do battle with the "Great Satan," the occupying Soviet Union. The Berlin Wall fell in 1989 and the "evil empire" finally collapsed in 1991. On November 24, 1989 Abdullah Azzam and two of his sons were killed in western Pakistan when unknown assassins land-mined his car. Osama bin Laden was the likely suspect due to an alleged fallout with Azzam over the next jihad target following the withdrawal of the Soviet Union from Afghanistan. Azzam was prepared to carry the struggle back to his native Palestine but by this time bin Laden had become further radicalized and was convinced that the next enemy was the West. With the death of Abdullah Azzam in late 1989, Osama bin Laden was the undisputed leader of the victorious

Afghan Arabs and was a hero of Robin Hood proportions both in his own country and among radical Islamists worldwide.

In the early 1980s another of bin Laden's mentors, Dr. Ayman al Zawahiri, had opened a jihad bureau in Cairo and through his dedication and personal charisma became the undisputed leader of the Egyptian Islamic Jihad movement. Shortly after the assassination of Anwar Sadat in 1981 by radical militant Islamists, Zawahiri was forced to leave Egypt following President Mubarek's crackdown. Having since merged his organization with al Qaeda, Zawahiri became bin Laden's top lieutenant and chief ideologue for what bin Laden calls "The World Islamic Front for Jihad Against Jews and Crusaders." This is al Qaeda.

Zawahiri's rise to Islamist leadership crossed paths with many people, including Abdullah Azzam and Hassan al Turabi, each subsequently influencing bin Laden's emerging ideology in profound ways. Zawahiri first met Abdullah Azzam in Cairo when Azzam was a student at the revolutionary font of Islamist ideology, Al-Azhar University. But it was Zawahiri's relationship with Hassan al Turabi, who has been called the "Pope of Terrorism" [Joscelyn], that is in many ways more significant. Turabi hosted bin Laden's exile in Sudan after his expulsion from Saudi Arabia following the Gulf War and bin Laden's criticism of the Saudi royal family. Turabi was born in Sudan in 1932, studied law in Khartoum, London and Paris, rose to prominence in several Sudanese governments, and became the chief mentor of Ayman al Zawahiri. All have had profound influence on Osama Bin Laden. The FBI lists Dr. Ayman al Zawahiri as one of its most wanted terrorists and offers a $25 million reward leading to his apprehension. [FBI "Most Wanted," 2005]

Ayman al Zawahiri was born in suburban Cairo in 1951 to a comfortable middle class family and was radicalized by the 1967 Six Day War with Israel, becoming a member of the Muslim Brotherhood and follower of Sayyid Qutb while still a teenager. Zawahiri's father was a pharmacologist and it was natural for the bright, young Zawahiri to study pharmacology, psychology, and human behavior. Zawahiri received a degree in medicine from Cairo University in the late 1970s and by 1979 had become even more radicalized. Along with dozens of fellow Islamists, Zawahiri was arrested following the assassination of Egyptian President Anwar Sadat in 1981, but the government had insufficient evidence to convict him of the murder, jailing him only for illegal possession of firearms. When released from prison in the mid 1980s, Zawahiri met Osama bin Laden in Afghanistan through Abdullah Azzam. Following the Afghan war he returned briefly to Egypt and then traveled extensively throughout the 1990s, even to the United States, using multiple passports, assumed names, and nationalities. With bin Laden's assistance, Zawahiri organized the "Brotherhood Group," more than 100 extremely wealthy Arabs in Saudi Arabia and the Persian Gulf region [Bodansky, 43]. Bodansky goes on to say:

> The objective of this financial system is to conceal the money trail so that it will be impossible for Western security authorities to connect the terrorists with the sponsoring-states. The key members of the Brotherhood Group have a well-known and established presence in the West—sixty-five of them have major companies and businesses in the United States....Some eighty members have comparable services in Western Europe.

Zawahiri is one of the most highly lethal and perniciously effective terrorist organizers in the world and has been sentenced to death in absentia by the Egyptian government for his involvement in the 1997 massacre of approximately 60 foreign tourists in Luxor, Egypt. Along with bin Laden, he is likely cornered in a remote area of western Pakistan with limited communications and drastically decreased effectiveness, amidst persistent rumors of his death. Zawahiri's mentor, on the other hand, was recently freed from house arrest in Sudan and though he is now in his early 70s, Hassan al Turabi has shown no signs of easing or moderating his radical Islamist views that continue to provide fuel to the flames of radical, militant Islamism in Sudan and with al Qaeda exponents around the world.

Hassan al Turabi's influence on Ayman al Zawahiri and Osama bin

Laden has been substantial. He was once the speaker of the Sudanese parliament, has been in and out of high office and a political prisoner in his own country, and is considered the ideological power and spiritual leader behind the Islamist government that has fueled genocide in Sudan's Darfur province. By the early 1950s, the Muslim Brotherhood had taken root in the University of Khartoum and Turabi joined the radical movement while studying law there. After obtaining a degree in law in 1955, Turabi received a Master's degree in law from the University of London and completed his Ph.D. at the Sorbonne in Paris in 1964. He is a multilingual and charismatic Islamist like Azzam and advocates pure Islamist solutions to the problems in Sudan and the broader Muslim world. By the mid sixties Turabi was back in Sudan and rose to lead the radical Muslim Brotherhood in Sudan at about the same time Sayyid Qutb was imprisoned in Egypt. He published numerous political and religious works at the time and gained fame in Islamist intellectual circles, including the influential Al-Azhar University in Cairo where Abdullah Azzam and Ayman al Zawahiri were students and gaining increased prominence. Turabi's political theology was based on a fundamentalist interpretation of the Koran that formulated a strategy for the Muslim faithful to take on the evil and hated West, especially the United States, to establish Islamist societies as a cure for the problems and ills facing the Muslim world. This was a vision that appealed to Azzam and Zawahiri, and when Osama bin Laden took refuge in Sudan in the 1990s, Turabi further impressed his thought and philosophy upon the successful leader of the Afghan Arabs. According to Bodansky [33], "Turabi has been instrumental in translating this [his] doctrine into action. Since…[the early 1990s]…there has been a fundamental, if not historic, evolution in Islamist terrorism, subversion and violence."

Together, Abdullah Azzam, Ayman al Zawahiri, and Hassan al Turabi have played profound roles in guiding, shaping, preparing and molding al Qaeda and Osama bin Laden's thinking. Turabi was freed from imprisonment in Sudan in the summer of 2005 and Zawahiri remains active in the field today as al Qaeda's spiritual leader, ready and willing to die for radical, militant Islamism.

Al Qaeda's Goals and Objectives

Osama bin Laden has clearly stated his goals and objectives to the world several times between 1996 and 2004:

1. Replace the Saudi royal family with an Islamist state as Khomeini did with the Shah's regime in Iran.
2. Drive the U.S. from the Middle East, reinstate the Muslim Caliphate as leader of the Sunni Muslim polity.
3. Utilize Saudi oil proceeds to establish Islamist regimes throughout the Middle East, gain control over the Muslim world, and launch a final attack on the West.
4. Drive the United States into bankruptcy in the process.

These goals were largely formulated as a result of bin Laden's experience in Afghanistan and his cool reception from King Fahd after his return to Saudi Arabia in 1989. Bin Laden was euphoric about his victory over the Soviet Union and even took personal credit for its almost immediate collapse in 1991. He thought, "If we can overturn the mighty U.S.S.R., why can't we defeat the remaining superpower in the world, the United States?" Bin Laden took credit for bankrupting the Soviet Union and believed he could do the same with the United States. Similarly, while the Saudis had supported the Taliban Islamic state in Afghanistan, why not establish a similar Islamic state in Saudi Arabia and the rest of the Muslim world? The only goal that did not flow directly out of bin Laden's Afghanistan experience was the nostalgic dream of restoring the Muslim Caliphate, but this time it was his distinct desire that the Caliphate would be of Wahhabi-Salafist persuasion, not just any type of Sunni Islam.

In addition to bin Laden's four goals, Fouad Hessein, a Jordanian journalist, has written a biography (available only in Arabic) of Abu Musab al Zarqawi, a fierce Takfir wal Hijra, who is bin Laden's chief of operations in Iraq, that purports to contain a 20-year plan for al Qaeda's domination of the world:

Phase 1: The "awakening" in the consciousness of Muslims around the world following the 9/11 attacks, aimed at provoking the U.S. into declaring war on the Islamic world and mobilizing Islamic radicals.

Phase 2: "Opening eyes," the current period, where the "Western conspiracy" would become aware of the "Islamic community" as al Qaeda continues to form secret battalions.

Phase 3: "Arising and standing up," which should last until 2010 and bring increasingly frequent attacks against secular Turkey and archenemy Israel.

Phase 4: "Anti-Arabic government," from 2010 and 2013. This phase will see the fall of hated Arab regimes, including Saudi Arabia and Jordan, and will be accompanied by attacks against oil suppliers and the U.S. economy, using cyber terrorism.

Phase 5: "Declaration of Islamic states and/or establishment of a Caliphate," from 2013 to 2016. Western influence in the Islamic world will be reduced, Israel will be weakened, resistance will not be feared and the Islamic state will bring about a new world order.

Phase 6: "Total confrontation," 2016 until 2018, the Islamic army will begin the "fight between believers and non-believers" predicted by Osama bin Laden.

Phase 7: "Definitive victory," by 2020, the Caliphate will prove victorious, the world will be beaten by an army of "one and a half billion Muslims."

Although we cannot authenticate Hussein's formulation of al Qaeda's plan as truly a product of bin Laden, it is internally consistent with bin Laden's goals and the first two phases of the plan are also consistent with what al Qaeda has done since September 11, 2001. It's not exactly a *Mein Kampf*, but it does owe a striking debt to the kind of megalomania that produced Hitler's master plan and wreaked havoc on the world in the 20th century.

Al Qaeda is extremely dangerous, more so because these religious zealots really believe they can accomplish their goals as God's work. As we evaluate the American response to al Qaeda later in the book, the early phases of this 20-year plan serve as a useful metric for measuring the success of American efforts to thwart the grand plans of Osama bin Laden and save the world from the mad dreams of Islamist religious zealotry.

AL QAEDA'S ANTECEDENTS AND ALLIES

Several Islamist organizations have contributed to the development of bin Laden's poisonous ideas and al Qaeda's world terrorist network. Bin Laden, today a man without a country and a with large bounty on his head, has nevertheless demonstrated striking political skill in bringing together a variety of Islamist organizations to serve his goal of terrorizing the West to create a worldwide Islamist state.

The Muslim Brotherhood
As we have seen, al Qaeda is the product of the merger of two Egyptian Islamist fundamentalist factions, the Islamic Group and Egyptian Islamic Jihad. Al Qaeda's top philosopher and theoretician, Dr. Ayman Al Zawahiri, founded the Egyptian Islamic Jihad and has long-standing ties to Takfir wal Hijra, probably the most aggressive Islamist terror organization in the world today. Bin Laden's al Qaeda terrorist organization is a dynamic, transnational movement that gained strength as the result of a marriage between Zawahiri's Egyptian killers and bin Laden's fanatical "Afghan Arabs" who, after the Afghanistan war against the Soviet Union, had become professional jihadists no longer welcome in ultra-conservative, theocratic Saudi Arabia. The Saudi-Egyptian marriage joined bin Laden's "Afghan Arabs" and their radicalized Saudi Wahhabi-Salafist ideology with Zawahiri's Egyptian terrorists and their long-standing radical, militant

ideological background. Their common ground was Saudi Arabian Wahhabi-Salafism influenced by the writings of radical members of the Muslim Brotherhood.

Al Qaeda's Egyptian factions had evolved from Egypt's Wahhabi-influenced, Islamist movement, the Muslim Brotherhood, called "al-Ikhwan al-Muslimun" in Arabic, and were guided by the principle Islamist philosopher and theoretician, Sayyid Qutb (pronounced "Kuh-tahb"). Osama bin Laden was profoundly influenced by the writings of Qutb (1907-1966) and the strict Wahhabi-Salafist interpretation of Islam that he absorbed during his impressionable and formative years in the Saudi Arabian educational system.

The Muslim Brotherhood was founded in Egypt in the late 1920s by Hassan al-Banna (1905-1949) and has distinct Wahhabi-Salafist ideological roots that emanate from an influential Egyptian intellectual writer early in the 20th century who was on the payroll of the first Saudi king, Ibn Saud [Gold, 54-5]. This early Saudi effort to buy intellectual influence marked the beginning of a consistent Saudi effort over the years to "gull" its friends and "manage" its problems by silencing critics with money and buying endorsements from international scholars and politicians. Saudi lobbying behavior continues to this day, especially in American and European capitals and prestigious universities like Harvard, Georgetown, and Oxford that have received large Saudi endowments for their departments of Middle East Studies in Faustian bargains that limit academic independence and objectivity.

Having extended itself far beyond Egypt, the Muslim Brotherhood today is a secretive, militant society, active in more than 70 countries and well-documented links to terrorism [Mintz and Farah, 2004]. The Muslim Brotherhood has devoted followers around the world, including the United States, but especially in Europe where it is the dominant movement among large European Muslim communities. The Muslim Brotherhood extends throughout the Muslim world today and has gained legitimacy because of continued strong financial support from the government of Saudi Arabia and its billions in oil revenue. The message of the Muslim Brotherhood resonates loudly as the guiding principle for today's Islamist terrorists and suicide bombers:

> God is our objective; the Holy Koran is our constitution; the Prophet is our leader; struggle is our way; and death for the sake of God is the highest of our aspirations.

Sayyid Qutb's sharp intellect and prolific penmanship helped him rise quickly as the leading writer and intellectual spokesperson for the Muslim Brotherhood. Qutb advocated classical Wahhabi tenets such as strict Islamic law (Sharia) and a return to the so-called purity of the early days of Islam as a counter to what he believed were the devastating effects of America and the modern world. When Gamal Abdel Nasser overthrew Egypt's King Farouk in 1952 and formed the Egyptian Republic, Qutb initially collaborated with Nasser's pan-Arab socialist movement and appealed for Islamic law as the only basis for a new Egyptian Islamic state. But Qutb's outspoken initiatives were rejected by the new Egyptian government, and after the Muslim Brotherhood attempted to assassinate Nasser, Qutb was imprisoned and subsequently executed in 1966 for his uncompromising rigidity and militant, Islamist beliefs. Even while enduring torture in prison Sayyid Qutb wrote voluminously, focusing on the plight of the Arab-Muslim world in the 20th century. He posed fundamentalist Islamist solutions to the many problems he envisioned when he studied in Colorado in 1948-1949 and articulated sharp theological criticism of modern Western life that in his view demanded violent jihad against imperialistic Western interests and corrupt Muslim regimes. Qutb wrote that the human condition had become unbearable not only in America, but around the world, because humanity had lost its soul and touch with God.

Many of the problems Qutb envisioned in modern Western society are similar to those deplored by conservative Christians in America today: godlessness, permissive attitudes toward sex, unfettered female freedom, declining moral standards, pornography, homosexuality, adultery, divorce, corruption, corporate larceny, violence, obscenity, profanity, gluttony, sloth, obesity, unchecked gambling, and people saying, "Since there is no God or Hell, let's enjoy ourselves here on earth, indulge our appetites, without fear of punishment after death."

Most conservative Christians in the United States would agree with Qutb that the spread of wealth in the West had weakened the religious and ethical base of societies that had originated in fear and poverty. They would also agree that sin had grown as wealth increased, that so-called "modern" people had come to resent old-fashioned ethics because modern life was to be enjoyed, that the sources of immorality—wealth, falling moral standards, political strife, war—had left people unanchored in a global sea of violence. They would agree that when society declared the Ten Commandments to be man-made and not divine, the moral code lost its effectiveness, taboos disappeared, expediency and pleasure reigned supreme. Guilt and fear of sin diminished, conscience was free to take the easy path, people no longer yearned to be good, for the ends would justify the means, and immorality became another form of individualism.

This is what Qutb saw when he lived in the United States following the Second World War. He observed that man's inspiration, intelligence, and morality had degenerated, especially in the infidel West, and that sexual relations between men and women had deteriorated "to a level lower than beasts." He further stated that humanity had become anxious and skeptical, causing spiritually unhappy people to turn to drugs, crime, alcohol, and away from religion. The solution according to Qutb was a rigidly fundamentalist version of Islam that rejected modernism and the secular West's separation of church and state.

The Brotherhood Spreads to Saudi Arabia

Followers of Qutb, like Osama bin Laden, believe that Islam has been under attack from the globalizing, imperialistic, capitalist West for centuries and that the mission of true Muslim believers today is to preserve Islam from extinction by the West's rampant forces of globalization through any tactic necessary, including terrorist bombings, beheadings, murder and the destruction of sinful societies in North America, Western Europe, and Asia. Bin Laden's followers are not concerned about dying in their effort to change the world, for death and immortality are seen as the culmination of righteous struggle or "jihad" in the name of Islam, and this type of struggle means ultimate martyrdom for their cause and a special place in Heaven.

After the execution of Sayyid Qutb by Nasser in 1966 and the disastrous Six-Day Arab-Israeli war that followed in 1967, Sayyid Qutb's brother Mohammed and many other members of the Muslim Brotherhood were expelled from Egypt and Syria and found highly sympathetic refuge among ultra-orthodox Wahhabi clerics in Saudi Arabian universities in Jeddah and the two holy cities. As early as 1961 the Saudi royal family had permitted the Muslim Brotherhood to start the Islamic University in Medina, and following the 1967 Six-Day War with Israel, the Muslim Brotherhood splintered into a radical movement that further penetrated the Saudi educational system. Mohammed Qutb became a distinguished professor of fundamentalist Wahhabi Islamist studies at King Abdul Aziz University in Jedda and was later one of Osama bin Laden's influential teachers. It was during this turbulent time in Egypt following the 1967 Arab-Israeli war that Saudi Arabia and its Wahhabi clerics became a magnet for Egyptian and Syrian Islamist fundamentalists and theoreticians who ultimately became leading professors at Wahhabi fundamentalist universities in Mecca and Medina. In his statement to the 9/11 Commission, Mamoun Fandy [2003], senior fellow at the United States Institute of Peace, outlined the role of the Muslim Brotherhood in Saudi Arabia:

> The Muslim Brotherhood movement was born in the Egyptian coastal city of Ismaeliya in 1928. After they were thrown out of Egypt during the Arab cold war between Nasser and King Faisal of Saudi Arabia, the Muslim Brothers went to Saudi Arabia. There they worked in the field of education. They were responsible for radicalizing Saudi students who were raised in the strict but quietist Wahhabi tradition... When the Saudis welcomed the members of the Muslim brotherhood they did so naively— not thinking that they were giving them a chance to influence young Saudis. It is the "brothers" who were responsible for development of certain radical teachings in

the Saudi education system and for the spread of the radical *madrasas* (religious schools) throughout the Middle East and South Asia. And, while some Saudis influenced by the teachings of the Muslim brothers remained faithful to that organization, others developed even more radical versions of its doctrines, creating the new organizations that gave us Osama bin Laden and al Qaeda. This was in part because many Saudis felt that this originally Egyptian organization was trying to steal the mantle of Islam from Saudi Arabia. Saudis felt that to compete with a global organization such as the brotherhood, they too would have to establish similarly wide-reaching networks of influence. This is what led to the rise of the Muslim league and the Muslim youth organization and many other charities that we know now have been directly or indirectly linked to terrorism.

The Arab world faced another disastrous defeat by Israel in the October 1973 Yom Kippur War, and as oil prices quadrupled in the 1970s, Saudi Arabia's Wahhabi religious leaders now had access to hundreds of millions in oil money and began exporting the writings of Sayyid Qutb and their version of radical Wahhabi-Salafist Islam around the world. The Saudis had formed the Muslim World League in 1962 as well as several international Islamic charities and began endowing professorships and funding entire departments at prominent universities such as Al-Azhar University in Cairo, the oldest and most distinguished university in the Muslim world. Forty years later, nearly all Al-Azhar professors had received Saudi stipends and the Saudis soon followed a similar process in Europe and the United States, establishing Middle East Studies departments at distinguished universities and buying off academicians and the rigor of academic independence with large cash grants and endowments. Al Qaeda received much of its strength and legitimacy throughout the Arab world from pernicious Saudi funding and the influence and inspiration of Sayyid Qutb, making the organization popular and well funded today, with powerful ideas, global capabilities, and a level of sophistication and resiliency that has surprised and confounded its enemies.

Al Qaeda's Next of Kin—Takfir Wal Hijra

Al Qaeda has many links to other extremist Islamist terrorist operations around the world. Significant among these is the Takfir wal Hijra, the most brutally violent Islamist terrorist operation in the world today and an extreme extension of Wahhabi-Salafist doctrine. It expresses unrestrained hatred of Shiite Muslims and, like Osama bin Laden, calls for restoring the Sunni Caliph, the Islamic political and religious leader of prior Muslim empires. Abu Musab al Zarqawi is an exceptionally fierce Takfiri fighter who gained notoriety in 2004 by leading Sunni terrorists in a holy war of true believers against infidel American and coalition forces in Iraq. Zarqawi is a Jordanian-born Palestinian and in late 2004 Osama bin Laden announced that Zarqawi had officially aligned his terrorist forces in Iraq with al Qaeda. Prior to the American invasion of Iraq in 2003, Zarqawi had operated without notice in Iraq but with Saddam Hussein's knowledge and support, and he even established a terrorist training camp in Afghanistan with bin Laden's assistance. Today Zarqawi's organization consists of some of the most violent and dedicated jihadists in the world, most notorious for their gruesome violence against Shiites and videotaped beheadings in Iraq.

The principle al Qaeda theoretician, Dr. Ayman Al Zawahiri, is the most prominent Takfiri. His leading role and influence within al Qaeda helped spread Takfir's radical and violent ultra-orthodoxy in the belief that all non-Muslim leaders in the world must be overthrown by any means possible, including assassination and violence. In Zawahiri's view, all infidels as well as all Muslims who do not fit the Takfir ideal are subject to sanctions including death. The ideology of Takfir—accusing other Muslims of apostasy—has also been identified as the incubator of extremism in the Saudi school system that created thousands of young, radical Saudi followers of bin Laden and teenage suicide bombers in Iraq. Takfir wal Hijra is active in Europe and the United States, and its origins, like so many terrorist groups, trace back to Egypt with Saudi Wahhabi-Salafist ideological underpinnings. In fact, it is safe to say that wherever a Salafist movement exists in the world, the fingerprints of Saudi funding and Wahhabi ideology are evident. This type of radical Islamist ideology has spread rapidly to thousands of young

European Muslims through internet sites and online chat rooms, resulting in grotesque throat-slitting murders in the United States and Europe by Takfiri Islamists.

Takfir wal Hijra is exceptionally capable in its ability to infiltrate Western societies and uses clever subterfuge by permitting members to disregard the normally strict injunctions of Islamic law against alcohol and illicit sex to help them blend into infidel societies and advance their specific terrorist mission. Mohammed Atta, the leader of the 9/11 airline hijackers, was a Takfiri. Atta and his 9/11 accomplices dressed as Westerners and rationalized going to bars and discos, using alcohol and calling prostitutes to their hotel rooms because they believed such activities supported their mission against the enemy, infidel America. In 2002, the U.S. Justice Department charged four Takfiri men in Michigan for planning shoe bombings, airline attacks, and conspiring to attack Disneyland, a Las Vegas casino, and the American Embassy in Jordan. Takfiri groups are guided by influential radicals like al Qaeda's Dr. Ayman Al Zawahiri and Sheik Omar Abdel Rahman, the exiled Egyptian cleric now imprisoned in the United States for the first World Trade Center bombing in 1993, and who issued the following fatwa in 1998:

> Cut all links with the [United States]. Destroy them thoroughly and erase them from the face of the earth. Ruin their economies, set their companies on fire, turn their conspiracies to powder and dust. Sink their ships, bring their planes down. Slay them in the air, on land, on water. And [with the Command of Allah] kill them wherever you find them. Catch them and put them in prison. Lie in wait for them and kill these infidels. They will surely get great oppression from you. God will make you the means of wreaking a terrible revenge upon them, of degrading them. He will support you against them. He will cure the afflicted hearts of the faithful and take all anger out of their hearts.

Even bin Laden was not pure enough and became a Takfir target during a 1996 assassination attempt in Sudan but in the final analysis, al Qaeda and its Bin Ladenism ideology serve as an umbrella organization for many Islamist terrorist operations around the world with varying degrees of ferociousness. What they all share in common is a hate-filled ideological framework that predates all of their organizations and is directly influenced by violence-inspiring Saudi Wahhabi-Salafism and its interconnected relationship with the Muslim Brotherhood and Sayyid Qutb's philosophy of violent jihad.

The Concept of Islamist Jihad

Jihad has had many interpretations throughout the history of Islam and confusion continues today with various interpretations of the meaning of jihad by Muslim and Western apologists for Islamist terrorism. Radical militant Muslims, many mainstream Muslims, and some Western apologists do not consider bin Laden and Islamist warriors as terrorists but see them as mujahadeen—"warriors of jihad"—fighting for the Muslim faith and defending against attack. In Islam, the world is uncompromisingly divided into the House of Islam (the faithful) and the House of War (infidels who have not yet surrendered to Islam) and there are two types of jihad. "Greater jihad" is defined as personal and of a spiritual nature, while "lesser jihad" is justified for violent and militant actions to expand the faith and defend Islam when the religion is threatened. When Saudi Wahhabis started exporting their version of Islam they reintroduced the concept of violent jihad to the Muslim world. The basic concept of jihad is found in the Holy Koran's seemingly reasonable command for believers to "struggle" in the path of God, striving to lead a good life and create a just society in the name of God. But in practice jihad goes far beyond a personal struggle to lead a good life. The mission of jihad has been defined as expanding Islam through personal "struggle" as well as by creating conditions where Muslims rule and Islam ultimately prevails. It calls for believers to spread the message of Islam through struggle in support of oppressed people, defending the faith, and violently overthrowing governments that threaten Islam, calling for death to nonbelievers to preserve the pure faith.

Jihad has been present throughout Islam's history and the goal of jihad is to spread the Muslim faith, either by conversion or by submission. Islamic history and jurisprudence have traditionally established only three choices for non-Muslims facing jihad: conversion to Islam, death, or submission under Islamic rule and second-class citizen status. In the 7th century, jihad was ordered against Christians in Egypt and Syria and the practice of violent jihad continued throughout the spread of Islam, culminating in 1683 at the gates of Vienna when Islam's march into Europe was halted and violent jihad became less common, reappearing once again with Wahhabism in Saudi Arabia and its recent offshoot, "Bin Ladenism." One of the problems today is that many mainstream Muslims are silent and do not take a stand against violent jihad due to fear and because the concept of jihad has such deep roots in Islam's history and is easily exploited by Islamist terrorists. Bernard Lewis [2003] describes the Muslim duty of jihad: "…the presumption is that the duty of jihad will continue, interrupted only by truces, until all the world either adopts the Muslim faith or submits to Muslim rule."

Modern Wahhabi-Salafism or "Bin Ladenism"

Saudi Arabia's Wahhabis are a virulent minority sect of Islam intricately entrenched into the autocratic monarchy and theocratic government that rule Saudi Arabia. Before becoming infected with the teachings of Sayyid Qutb and the Egyptian Muslim Brotherhood in the early 1960s, Saudi Wahhabis were a cloistered and seemingly harmless fundamentalist fringe movement within Sunni Islam and few in the West took them seriously. However, with their relatively recent oil riches, Saudi Arabian Wahhabis and their worldwide missionary movement have sponsored international terrorist organizations such as al Qaeda and Hamas and spread deep hatred for the basic values of Western civilization such as freedom, democracy, religious tolerance, separation of religion from government, universal suffrage, women's rights, free press, free trade, free unions, and free political parties. Wahhabi-Bin Ladenism also displays unusually venomous attacks against perceived American and Western imperialism and justifies violence and stirs hatred by blaming others for persistent Arab failures.

THE TRIUMPH OF DEMOCRACY OVER MILITANT ISLAMISM

Wahhabism as practiced by ultraconservative clerics in Saudi Arabia is a distortion of the mainstream teachings of Islam and is manifested in conflicting Saudi government policies of rigid religious intolerance on the one hand and the promotion of modernization and Westernization on the other.

Well-educated Saudis and members of the Saudi royal family frequently blame others, especially the United States and Israel, for endemic and systematic problems in the Arab-Muslim world. This mindset refuses to admit the nature of systemic problems and is quick to advance the Wahhabi state religion of Saudi Arabia as the solution. Saudi Arabian leaders are also well known for "double-dealing" and "gulling" the West, trading oil for security as King Abdul Aziz Ibn Saud did in the early days and as the Saudis are doing now, buying support from prestigious international universities, while permitting its state religion to spread hatred for the West and death threats to nonbelievers.

As a result, there is growing agreement in the West that Saudi Arabia cannot be trusted and is no longer a reliable ally and may in fact have become an unpredictable antagonist in the global war on terror. However, since the May 12, 2003 terrorist attacks in the Saudi capital Riyadh and several subsequent attacks in 2004 and early 2005, then Crown Prince Abdullah and the Saudi royal family have taken some steps against homegrown terrorists that have attempted to destroy the increasingly dysfunctional and corrupt Saudi government. Abdullah has also indicated some willingness to provide a more open government, but not all observers agree that reform is possible.

The Saudi government has been a key backer of the international Islamist terror network and has been active at multiple levels of international terrorism for well over 20 years. Senior members of the royal family, like Interior Minister Prince Nayef, have stated that 9/11 was a Zionist plot involving the CIA and many remain wedded to the reactionary belief that Wahhabi-Salafism must continue to be promoted around the world as the solution for the world's problems. As a result, the events of 9/11 and a significant lack of subsequent Saudi cooperation forced the Bush administration to reassess Saudi Arabia's reliability as a credible regional ally and to develop a new grand strategy for American policy and strategic relationships in the region. That strategy became codified in the post-9/11 Bush Doctrine and is now unfolding in the Middle East, as chapter 4 describes.

The answer to how the Saudis could have opened Pandora's Box and released the genie of radical, militant Wahhabism into the world lies in the tangled history of Saudi Arabia's development as a theocracy. Wahhabism started in the Arabian Peninsula 250 years ago while American revolutionary leaders were developing principles of freedom and democracy so antithetical to Wahhabi-Salafism. From the beginning of its origins as a desert nation of nomadic Bedouin tribes, Wahhabism has been the state religion of Saudi Arabia. Wahhabis control the Ministry of Education, Ministry of Religious Affairs, and Ministry of Justice where harsh Islamic Law is implemented with exacting cruelty. Saudi Arabia's Islamic law, Sharia, is based on the Holy Koran, and is the same Islamic legal system that the world witnessed in Afghanistan under the Taliban with routine public executions and rigid oppression of women. Before 9/11, the West either ignored Saudi Arabia's Wahhabis or viewed the sect as a lunatic fringe of Sunni Islam, even though Saudi Arabia's vast oil wealth had permitted the export of Wahhabi-Salafism and promoted death to infidels and nonbelievers for many years. But even then, few in the West took note or were able to penetrate the complexities of the Byzantine desert kingdom.

PROBLEMS IN THE MODERN MUSLIM WORLD

Radicalism Is Only Part of the Problem

The Muslim world is wide and diverse and it is important to remember that the "bad guys"—the militant Islamists—are a distinct though growing minority that represent a small fraction of the world's nearly 1.5 billion Muslims. There are several classifications of the various representations of Islam in addition to the major Sunni and

THE TRIUMPH OF DEMOCRACY OVER MILITANT ISLAMISM

Shiite divisions and it is clear that the "bad guys," the enemy, are the radical, militant Islamists like the Taliban, al Qaeda, Hamas, and Palestinian Islamic Jihad who resort to violence in an attempt to create totalitarian Islamist states. It has been said that in recent years, "Not all Muslims are terrorists, but all terrorists are Muslims." A corollary reads, "Not all Salafists are terrorists, but all terrorists are Salafists." These are the "bad guys"—the radical, militant Bin Ladenists. There are also traditional fundamentalists in the Muslim world, like perhaps 70 percent or more of the population of Saudi Arabia and its ultra-orthodox Wahhabi religious establishment that support bin Laden's goals and provide funding for al Qaeda and other radical militant Islamists. Another group consists of traditional Muslims such as moderate-conservative Shiite mullahs in Iran who wish to preserve orthodox Shiite norms and old-fashioned behavior, while more liberal Shiite reformists such as Grand Ayatollah al-Sistani in Iraq have traditional goals, but are more flexible and innovative in compromising with modernity. Though their governments are not democratic by any means, Sunni leaders of Egypt, Jordan, and Libya could be called modernists in the sense that they accept the fact that Islam can be compatible with the modern world, while secularists such as Ataturkists in Turkey go even further and clearly separate religion from the public sector by law.

Turkey is unique in that it is Muslim but not Arab, straddles both Asia and Europe, and sits astride the Arab-Muslim world with its historical Ottoman legacy. Turkey and its 70 million people provide a natural partner for helping stabilize the region because Turkey is a long-standing member of the North Atlantic Treaty Organization (NATO) and the only Muslim member. Moreover, Turkey could become the first Muslim member nation of the European Union (EU) as early as 2015 and has vested interests in accommodating and nurturing Western values. With the fall of Saddam Hussein in Iraq, the world's only remaining fascist-oriented Baathist Party is in Syria, where along with a sprinkling of reactionary Socialists and Communists, religion is generally discarded and used to its own advantage, as Saddam Hussein did in Iraq.

Al Qaeda's late prolific propagandist, Yusuf al Ayyiri, asserted visceral hated of the United States and the West, stating that the United States and Israel must be destroyed because they are leaders of a global anti-Islamist movement. The goal of what Ayyiri called "Zio-Crusaderism" is to destroy "true Islam" and achieve dominion over the Middle East and its valuable oil resources. The enemies are Jews, Christians, Shiites, lax Sunnis, and secularists, but to the al Qaeda extremists, America's most fearful weapon is the export of Western concepts of freedom and democracy. Democracy and popular sovereignty separate church and state, which in turn disembowel "true Islam." Because religion and the state are one and the same, only God's laws can be implemented and not the man-made laws of secular democratic states. The logical result of democracy and unbridled freedom in al Qaeda's way of thinking is anarchy and destruction of Muslim society and its moral standards. Al Ayyiri condemned cable television and the internet for unleashing torrents of filth and idolatry. He detested the United States because of its support for Israel and pervasive Jewish influence on the American government and because the West inspires godlessness, permissive attitudes toward sex and female freedom, and permits moral standards to decline. In Ayyiri's view, the result is fatal erosion of pure Arab-Muslim culture from within and therefore all enemies, including women and children, must be destroyed through violent jihad and by any means possible.

Other Contemporary Arab-Muslim Problems

The area of the Arab-Muslim world extends from the Persian Gulf across the Middle East to North Africa, and encompasses 22 Arab nations and over 300 million people, with Arabic a common language in varying accents. Although Muslim, Turkey and Iran with populations of about 70 million each are not ethnically Arab and are not included among the 22 Arab League countries in the greater Middle East and North Africa. For many years, Cairo has been the traditional seat of Arab knowledge and a venerated center of Arab culture. But since the end of the First World War and the demise of the ruling Ottoman Empire and the Muslim Caliphate, the Middle East has been a hotbed of Islamist militancy and radicalism with declining economic influence and corrupt, oppressive governments.

There are many complex reasons for the political and economic decline of the Arab-Muslim world and the subsequent rise of Islamist militancy. They include remaining vestiges of European imperialism, the creation of artificial Arab states following World War I, the establishment of Israel at the end of World War II, and a yearning by modern day Islamist fundamentalists to return to the glory days of Islam when Saladin defeated the Christian Crusaders and recaptured Jerusalem in 1187, or to the "pure" days of Mohammed. But the unfortunate fact remains that today the 22 Arab nations have a collective gross domestic product (GDP) that is less than Spain's, even with vast Arab oil riches and if oil income is subtracted, combined Arab GDP is less than the market capitalization value of a public company such as Nokia, the Finnish public telecommunications company [United Nations, 2005].

The victorious French and British arbitrarily established present-day Middle Eastern boundaries after defeating and dismantling the Ottoman Empire that had sided with the Germans during the First World War. In the 1930s and 1940s, Arab nations supported Fascism and Nazism that produced harsh and vitriolic anti-American and anti-Semitic propaganda still present in many Arab schoolbooks today and now augmented with Wahhabi-Salafist ideology exported by the Saudis in free textbooks printed in Arabic that include instructions on how to cut off the heads of infidels and statements such as the following:

> …everywhere you meet Jews, kill them…it is forbidden to have mercy on a Jew…beware of Jews, they are treacherous and disloyal…Muslims are commanded to kill non-Muslims…anyone supporting Western methods of government deserves excommunication from God's mercy, from Islam.

Most Arab nations of the Middle East sided with the Germans during the Second World War and once again witnessed humiliating defeat. Hajj Amin al-Husseini, the Grand Mufti of Jerusalem and leader of the Palestinians during the war years, was an advisor to Hitler and the Nazis, visited Auschwitz with Heinrich Himmler, and made plans to open a Palestinian death camp for Jews following German victory over the Allies. But that did not happen and after the war, as Soviet Communism rose over the ashes of Eastern Europe, a new Cold War emerged that pitted the Soviet Union's Warsaw Pact against the West's North Atlantic Treaty Organization (NATO). The result was even more rabid anti-American and anti-Semitic propaganda spread throughout the Middle East by the Soviet Union, as the Communist monolith attempted to gather allies in the oil-rich Arab world. Years of Western neglect and post-World War II concern for oil, stability, and a rigid anti-Soviet status quo, created a vacuum of freedom in the Middle East and a sense of hopelessness among people facing oppression and corruption from their governments.

For the last sixty years or more, political, economic and social stagnation, oppressive governments, tyranny, autocracy, and terrorism have been the norm in the Arab-Muslim world. Even the quadrupling of oil prices in the 1970s and 1980s had little impact in pulling the region out of its misery, as was hoped at the time. Unfortunately, the Arab-Muslim world—the "axis of oil"—did not enjoy a liberating political evolution that energized other parts of the world over the last 50 years, especially after the collapse of the Soviet Union in 1991. Ironically, as oil wealth created billionaires it also imprisoned and impoverished millions of people in an autocratic status quo. The result was even greater stagnation and dependence that pulled the region down further when compared with the rest of the world. State-controlled economies, often on the Soviet model, failed to attract foreign investment due to corruption, bureaucratic meddling, and high investor risk, and even wealthy Arabs preferred to invest in Europe and the United States for higher returns and far less risk. During this time, the only political alternatives in the region, with the exception of Turkey and Israel, were limited to:

(1) Autocratic absolute monarchy model like Saudi Arabia and some other Arab countries;
(2) Baathist model like Syria or Saddam's Iraq with fascist ideology;
(3) Socialist model with a rubber-stamp parliament and military dictator as in Egypt; or
(4) Theocratic model such as the Iranian Shiite Ayatollahs and harsh, uncompromising Islamic law.

The Arab nations have a long way to go to catch up with the rest of the world because of inherent problems caused by repressive, autocratic regimes whose primary goal has been and remains political survival for the rulers. From 1980–2000 Arab nations had combined earnings of about $2.5 trillion, 90 percent from oil, but they employed fewer than one million of their 300 million people in the oil, refining, or petro-chemical sectors. Since 1980, Arab oil revenues and foreign aid made up virtually all income and it went either to the state or directly to corrupt rulers who doled out government subsidies to the people through bloated, corrupt, and nonproductive bureaucracies [Rivilin and Even].

To bolster power and prestige, repressive Arab regimes have focused on security and the result has been massive and excessive expenditures on weapons. Together, the 22 Arab states of the Arab League spent nearly $50 billion on armaments in 2002, in addition to billions of dollars in military aid provided by the United States to Jordan and Egypt. Arab armed forces also tend to operate in centralized, authoritarian political systems and as a result use outmoded, bureaucratic, and top-heavy military organizational models and doctrine inherited from the Soviet Union. This caused them to become overly cumbersome and rigid on the battlefield, made worse with poor training, especially for unmotivated enlisted men with limited education. Nearly 70 percent of Arab military expenditures were by Persian Gulf states that have questionable needs for such massive weapons programs and much of what they acquired has not been operated or maintained effectively, resulting in enormous waste and corruption. Even with the billions Saudi Arabia spent on its weapons systems, the Saudi army was no match for Saddam Hussein's forces during the First Gulf War and needed massive international assistance to oust the invading Iraqi forces. The most significant Saudi military investments were for air defense systems, communications, and military infrastructure that proved effective in hosting thousands of coalition forces in 1990-1991.

In 2001 six Arab states spent more on arms than they did on health or education, and even with such massive expenditure on weapons, Arab states performed dismally in battle with their expensive arms. Egypt is an important example. With a population that has doubled in the last 30 years to more than 75 million today, Egypt is the largest country in the Arab world and is a very important and influential Arab country for historical, political, cultural, and social reasons. Egypt is highly Westernized and urbane, desires to be recognized as a major factor in regional development, and wishes to strengthen its relationship with the United States. But even in a country as relatively open and modern as Egypt, there is no real democracy and important decisions are made centrally by a rubber-stamp parliament and not through the open discussion of a democratic decision-making process. Large bureaucracies and oversized armed forces, as in Egypt, ensure political survivability for rulers who often threaten force against their own populations. A glimmer of hope emerged in 2005 when President Mubarak allowed multiple candidates in the 2005 presidential election, but most Arab regimes provide little accountability to the people and few checks and balances to challenge government actions.

Throughout the Arab world, the government or a single political party frequently control newspapers, television, and radio, and open participation in the political process is limited to party leaders or other insiders, resulting in enormous benefits from ingrained corruption throughout the system. The consequence is that a viable Arab middle class has failed to develop due to a minimal role for the private sector and a lack of public debate in the political process. This in turn has caused economic stagnation and few political alternatives except for Islamist fundamentalism that has been ruthlessly put down in countries like Egypt and Algeria, but latent Islamism smolders menacingly throughout the entire Arab world due to lack of hope among the people and the overriding tenets of Islam that mandate struggle—jihad—against unjust rulers and nonbelievers. A cycle of hope and repression has repeated itself nearly every generation during the last century and Arab states have remained desperately trapped in a closed system designed to provide political survival for autocratic Arab rulers, despite a high number of political assassinations, but without basic economic, political, and social reform for the people.

Moreover, the legal system in most Arab countries is a disaster, causing high risk for invested capital and little incentive to attract foreign investment from Europe, Asia, or the United States. Decrepit, command economies are vestiges of socialism that failed and even the wealthiest Saudis, until recently, have invested much of their capital outside the Arab world, mainly in the United States and Europe, instead of in Arab economies because of high risks and poor returns. Anti-Semitic and anti-American propaganda dating to the Nazi and Soviet eras are endemic throughout the Middle East and have been so effective that wildly concocted Arab propaganda continually distorts reality, causing totally uncorroborated stories to be accepted as truth, such as the claim that the 9/11 attackers were Jews and CIA agents. Arabs are well known as the world's greatest conspiracy theorists and they tend to be overly suspicious, even of each other, often out of fear from living under oppressive governments and within violent environments. State-controlled Arab media frequently blame Israel and the American CIA as conspirators intent on the destruction of Islam and as reasons and excuses for long-festering social and economic problems. To this day, many Arab people do not believe that 9/11 was an Arab-led act of terrorism but rather an Israeli-CIA conspiracy designed to place blame on Arabs and Islam.

Unfortunately, the voices of moderation in the Arab-Muslim world are few and muted due to intimidation and fear, most frequently because of the blare of Saudi-funded propaganda aired on mass media such as Al Jazeera and Al Arabiya, funded and controlled by the Saudi royal family and fed with odious Wahhabi-Salafist propaganda. This does not mean to say that there are no moderate Arabs, for there are many, and they have the same aspirations for a better life as other people around the world. But high birth rates in the Arab-Muslim world have resulted in rapidly growing, youthful, and restive populations, creating a large base of young people who are deeply angry and frustrated with their dispossessed state of affairs and poor prospect for opportunity in the future. And the young people have been further hampered by a failed educational system that recycles Nazi, Soviet, and Wahhabi-Salafist propaganda in hate-filled textbooks. The result, at best, has been poorly trained young people and a brain drain of the brightest young Arab people to the United States and Europe for those fortunate enough and with the means to escape the cycle of poverty, oppression, and violence.

Powerful demographic forces are also operating, especially in the Middle East. Today there are over six billion people in the world, up from three billion only 30 years ago, and demographers forecast that world population will peak at about 9 billion between 2050 and 2070 and then begin a period of global decline due to falling birth rates. Of the more than six billion people currently in the world, there are approximately two billion Christians (33%); nearly 1.5 billion Muslims (23%); and 1.2 billion Hindus and Buddhists (22%). In sharp contrast, there are only 14 million Jews in the world, with 36 percent of the world's Jews living in the United States and only 35 percent in Israel, all with low birth rates. Islam, which is about 90 percent Sunni, is the fastest growing religion in the world, with impoverished people and corrupt, repressive governments especially among the Arab nations. Estimates of Muslim populations vary widely due to lack of reliable census information and in some cases deliberately inflated statistics. In Lebanon, for example, there has been no official count since the 1932 census was conducted under the French League of Nations mandate and in Saudi Arabia the official census has always been kept a state secret. Population estimates below were developed from the CIA [2006] and other independent sources.

In addition to overpopulation, the Muslim world also suffers from unemployment, authoritarianism, suicidal terrorism, and opposition to new ideas by conservative religious clerics, all of which have combined to stifle progress for decades. The Muslim world has the highest unemployment rates in the world today and the highest rate of population growth in the world during the last half century. One-third of the Arab population is under the age of 15 and these teenagers will soon enter a bleak job market during their childbearing years.

Saudi Arabia has always closely guarded its population statistics because of the embarrassingly small numbers of Saudis in contrast with its large number of foreign workers. With an annual 3 to 4 percent growth rate, the Saudi population has exploded from about 3 million in 1970 to 17-20 million Saudi citizens today, not counting the 6-7 million expatriate foreign workers in Saudi Arabia. At this growth rate, one of the highest in the world, the population of Saudi Arabia is expected to double in 20 years to about 40 million people.

Saudi Arabia's failed higher educational system produces more degrees in religion than any other discipline, with two thirds of all Ph.D.s awarded in Islamic studies. Few if any useful practical skills are taught in Saudi schools controlled by ultraconservative Wahhabi clerics and the Wahhabi-controlled Ministry of Education, resulting in high unemployment for young people with limited skill sets. Even though Saudi Arabia is the world's largest oil producer and still possesses vast oil wealth, the country has, until recently, run a large budget deficit for more than a decade. The Saudis, like most Arabs, have a fixation on security and the cost of massive Saudi arms purchases has outpaced the country's ability to pay. Moreover, the Saudi royal family routinely skims billions from the flow of petrodollars, and these illegal proceeds often wind up in private international bank accounts of family members. Evidence of widespread corruption and excessive government spending has been well documented over the years, and it does not stop, even with new and stricter rules of the game. To sweeten their deals, members of the Saudi royal family prefer to deal directly with private companies on arms purchases to facilitate payment of illegal commissions through complex subcontract arrangements as opposed to using the United States or British government as intermediaries to manage large arms sales. Some

Table 2.1
World & Muslim Population (2004) – Millions

Continent	Total Population	Muslim Population	Muslim %
Asia	3,830.1	1,010.7	26.4
Africa	861.2	414.3	48.1
Europe	727.4	51.2	7.0
North America	323.1	6.6	2.0
South America	539.8	1.6	.03
Oceania	32.3	.4	1.2
Total	6,313.9	1,484.8	23.5

Source: Central Intelligence Agency, *The World Fact Book*, Washington, DC: Government Printing Office, 2004.

Table 2.2
Population Summary
League of Arab States (Arab League) *

Country	Population (Millions)	Growth Rate (Percent)
Algeria	32.0	1.3
Bahrain	0.7	1.5
Comoros	0.7	3.0
Djibouti	0.5	2.1
Egypt	76.0	1.8
Iraq	25.0	2.7
Jordan	5.6	2.7
Kuwait	2.2	3.4
Lebanon	3.8	1.3
Libya	5.7	2.4
Mauritania	3.0	2.9
Morocco	32.0	1.6
Oman	2.9	3.4
Palestine	3.6	3.5
Qatar	0.8	2.7
Saudi Arabia**	26.0	3.5
Somalia	8.0	3.4
Sudan	39.0	2.6
Syria	18.0	2.4
Tunisia	10.0	1.0
United Arab Emirates (UAE)	2.5	1.6
Yemen	20.0	3.5
Total	318.0	

* Source: Central Intelligence Agency (CIA), *World Factbook 2004*, Washington, DC, Government Printing Office: 2004
** Includes approximately 6.5 million foreign guest workers

countries, like France, Russia, China and others have no problem paying illegal commissions but the United States' Foreign Corrupt Practices Act strictly prohibits such illegal payments.

Expatriate workers in Saudi Arabia make up about two-thirds of the total Saudi workforce and 95 percent of the labor force in the private sector, but half of the expatriate jobs are drivers and maids to support a large and growing female population that is prevented from driving or working in most jobs. Nearly 70 percent of the Saudi population is under the age of 25, creating a pool of millions of potentially radicalized and restive young Saudis, trained only in Saudi-funded Wahhabi schools, and many willing to die in battle against the perceived "Great Satan," the United States of America, with the blessings of Allah and their parents. In typical Bedouin fashion, King Abdullah, while Crown Prince, said that Saudi Arabia must continue to increase its population and does not have an excessive birthrate, even though the Saudi population is projected to double in 20 years. The current generation of Saudi leaders in the royal family has been exceptionally sensitive about Saudi Arabia's true population and in the past has even inflated its census statistics, but the fact remains that the Saudi population has mushroomed in the last 30 years, creating a serious unemployment problem for its large number of restive, young people. The Saudi government must seriously address how the economy can support so many young people and how the Saudi culture can accommodate the impending changes that result from such rapid and tumultuous growth. Unfortunately, the Saudi leadership seems to believe that its ideology can one day rule the world, and to do that, it must have as many home grown true believers as possible.

On the other hand, fertility rates are declining globally and except for Saudi Arabia are falling faster in the Middle East than anywhere else on earth, changing the demographic dynamics over the next generation. This is a global phenomenon and even populous China will face huge problems due to its "4-2-1" problem (four living grandparents and two living parents for each worker), and by 2050, Mexico will be an older society, on average, than the United States. As a result, global demographic trends hold promise for some optimism.

The task, then, is to establish a generation of peace through ideas, jobs, and hope for the young people of the Middle East because the war on terrorism is essentially a generational battle of ideology. The United States and the West must aggressively work to create a generation of peace and opportunity for the angry, young Arab population that is growing far faster than the population in Europe or the United States. Wahhabi-Salafist propaganda, fueled by Saudi oil wealth, has made Saudi Arabia a major destabilizing force in the world, with an ideology of intolerance that underlies a ruthless, hate-filled religious faith championed by reactionary clerics. The West must overcome this propaganda assault with its own ideas of freedom and democracy to shine light into the darkness of Wahhabi-Bin Ladenism and its deadly creed.

Since the late 1970s, oil wealth has created a huge pool of Saudi capital, with hundreds of thousands of Saudi citizens investing billions of dollars in the American economy through investments in public and private companies, although several millions in Saudi investments have been repatriated from the United States since 9/11. With offices in Bahrain, New York, London, and Atlanta, Investcorp and Arcapita (formerly Crescent Capital) invested billions in Saudi royal family funds through the First Islamic Bank of Bahrain and acquired dozens of well-known brands ranging from Gucci in Italy, Saks Fifth Avenue and Tiffany's in New York, to Caribou Coffee and Jostens in Minnesota. These prestigious investment firms made many other strategic acquisitions throughout the United States and Europe, following strict Islamic prohibitions regarding payment of interest or ownership in non-Islamic businesses that sell alcohol or promote gambling, but many other investments by private Saudi citizens have been far more liberal and less Islamic. Robert Kaiser [2002] observed:

> After nearly three decades of accumulating this wealth, the group referred to by bankers as "high net-worth Saudi individuals" holds $500 billion to $1 trillion abroad, most of it in European and American investments. Raymond Seitz, vice chairman of Lehman Brothers in London and a

former U.S. ambassador to Britain, said Saudis typically put about three-quarters of their money into the United States, the rest in Europe and Asia. That would mean Saudi nationals have invested perhaps $500 billion to $700 billion in the American economy. That is a huge sea of fungible assets supporting the American economy and belonging to a relatively small group of people. Managing these hundreds of billions can be a lucrative business for brokers and bankers in London, Geneva and New York. Which financial institutions get the business? .... Robert Hormats, a vice chairman of Goldman Sachs in New York, ... paused for a moment, then answered: 'Every major financial institution in the world has some links with Saudi money.'

The problem Western civilization faces today has its antecedents within Islam itself but more specifically in Saudi Arabia. The Saudi kingdom is a vast, barren, oil-rich, desert oligarchy that was isolated for centuries and is ruled by an aging theocratic monarchy with a medieval legal system based on the Holy Koran and dominated by ultra-conservative Wahhabi religious leaders. It is in Saudi Arabia that some answers to vexing questions can be found regarding the nature of militant Islam's 21st century warriors and their fanatical, totalitarian ideology.

The next chapter discusses the global threat of Saudi Arabian Wahhabi-Salafism. With billions in oil wealth, the Saudi government and wealthy Saudi citizens have pumped unprecedented amounts of money into Islamic charities that funded mosques, schools and Wahhabi-Salafist religious materials, while most Americans and Europeans had no idea they were contributing to a Wahhabi-Salafist mosque and Wahhabi-Salafist propaganda each time they bought gasoline. The chapter also discusses U.S.-Saudi relations and how changing that relationship became vital to winning the war on terror that al Qaeda declared on America on September 11, 2001.

CHAPTER THREE

The Worldwide Threat of Saudi Arabian Wahhabism and America's Response

Of the nearly 1.5 billion Muslims living in 57 countries around the world, several million are sufficiently radicalized to actively support militancy based on an ideology derived from Wahhabi-Salafism that is deeply antithetical to Western values of freedom and democracy. The radicals are generally well educated and young, especially in the Middle East where nearly two-thirds of the population is under the age of 24. A majority of the world's Muslims lives under oppressive governments and the young radical militants have had little hope for the future except for a religious faith that rejects traditional Islam in favor of a deadly and literalist interpretation of the Holy Koran. Their numbers extend from the Persian Gulf across North Africa and into Europe, through Southwest and Southeast Asia, and into North America. The extremists among the young radicals are prepared to die for their beliefs. For many years, thousands of Wahhabi-Salafist missionaries have been funded by Saudi Arabia while promoting hatred of the West. They have identified America as the "Great Satan," and have demanded the overthrow of elected democracies and installation of totalitarian Islamist governments under Islamic law and Saudi Arabian Wahhabi-style Sharia like the Taliban.

The world of Islam is now struggling for its very heart and soul in a deadly tug of war between forces of moderation and radical, militant Islamists who, like the Wahhabi-Bin Ladenists and the Taliban, wish to turn back the clock to the 7th century and the time of the Prophet. However, historians will likely document the early 21st century as the period of the start of the Muslim Reformation, driven by new technology—satellite TV and the internet—much as the Christian Reformation in the 16th century was enabled by the new technology of its age, the printing press, that unleashed the genie of freedom and human expression.

Meanwhile, the message of the radical, militant Wahhabi-Salafists has been exported around the world and into the United States and Europe with Saudi money. In the last 20 years, approximately half of the 1,500 mosques and Muslim schools in the United States were built with Saudi money distributed through Saudi-controlled Islamic charities that control 80 percent of the mosques in the United States and Europe. The fingerprints of Saudi Wahhabi funding of Salafist groups in the United States and Europe with ties to the radical Muslim Brotherhood movement are well documented. American and European mosques have routinely received weekly faxed messages, directly from conservative Wahhabi clerics in Saudi Arabia, containing hate-filled sermons that call for death to Jews, Christians, and other nonbelievers and victory in the jihadist struggle against the Allied forces in Afghanistan and Iraq. The well endowed, Saudi-funded Wahhabi lobby in the United States hires top public relations specialists and routinely exploits American weaknesses through the generally pro-Palestinian orientation that exists among the political left and on campuses of American colleges and universities.

COLONEL B. WAYNE QUIST AND DR. DAVID F. DRAKE

WAHHABISM IN THE WEST

Wahhabism in America

According to a recent survey, two million American Muslims say they are associated with a mosque, while the number of mosques in the United States has increased 25 percent since 1994 to about 1,500 today [Hartford Seminary]. Nearly two-thirds of all American mosques were founded since 1980 and there are about 1,625 Muslims associated with each American mosque, which translates to nearly 2.5 million Muslims in the United States, a reasonable estimate. Of that number, according to the poll, about 30 percent are converts to Islam and nearly 90 percent of American mosques have Asian, African-American, and Arab members. The ethnic origin of regular participants in American mosques and the percentage of the American Muslim population for each group are shown in Table 3.1 below:

Table 3.1
Ethnic Origin of Mosque Participants in the U.S.

Region of Origin	Percent of Total
South Asian (Pakistani, Indian, Bangladeshi, Afghani)	33.0
African-American	30.0
Middle East/Arab	25.0
Sub-Saharan African	3.4
European (Bosnian, Tartar, Kosovar, etc.)	2.1
White American	1.6
Southeast Asian (Malaysian, Indonesian, Filipino)	1.3
Caribbean	1.2
Turkish	1.1
Iranian	0.7
Hispanic/Latino	0.6
Total	100.0

Source: Hartford Seminary "Mosque in America: A National Portrait," *Faith Communities Today*, April 2001.

About 90 percent of American mosques say they strictly follow the Holy Koran and Sunnah (sayings and teachings of Mohammed) and 20 percent of American mosques operate a full-time school associated with the mosque. Radical Islamists coming into the United States often use mosques as a base of operation and to exploit American qualities of openness, fairness, and helpfulness when aiding and assisting immigrants from foreign cultures and religions. When identified in the press as Wahhabis or Wahhabi-inspired and supported Salafists, American Muslim groups often claim to be victims of slander while at the same time slandering their critics and demanding government protection under the freedom of religion clause of the American Constitution. These groups do not typically identify the sources or amounts of their financial support, especially foreign funding.

In early 2005, the Boston Herald reported that a particularly violent East Boston-based street gang called MS-13 with roots in El Salvador consisted of alleged rapists and violent, machete-wielding criminals with links to the al Qaeda terrorist network [McPhee 1/5/2005]. Raed Hijazi, an al Qaeda operative charged with training the suicide bombers in the attack on the USS Cole, lived and worked in East Boston and was allegedly tied to MS-13, "[which has] an estimated 8,000 to 10,000 members in 33 states in the United States…" [Campo-Flores 3/28/2006]. The commercial jet airliners that destroyed the World Trade Center towers in New York City on 9/11 were hijacked from Logan International Airport in Boston, leading investigators to track the possible role of MS-13 in aiding the 9/11 hijackers.

Zacharias Moussaoui, a 9/11 conspirator captured in Minnesota shortly before 9/11 and was an al Qaeda Takfiri inspired by Wahhabi-Salafist teachings. Moussaoui operated from Minnesota because of Wahhabi-funded support that he was able to receive from the large Muslim Somali community in Minnesota and proximity to the porous Minnesota-Canadian border and is serving a life sentence in federal prison in the United States.

Wahhabis have also actively recruited prison convicts in the American federal prison system, especially black and Hispanic prisoners. Chuck Colson [6/24/2002] commented: "Alienated, disenfranchised people are prime targets for radical Islamists who preach a religion of violence, of overcoming oppression by jihad." Al Qaeda training manuals specifically identify American prisoners as candidates for conversion because they may be disenchanted with their country's policies. Wahhabi-affiliated American organizations such as the American Muslim Council (AMC) actively proselytize, but they have a tendency to look down on Black American Muslims as deviants from true Islam. Yet the AMC readily counts Black Americans in their numbers to inflate the size of the American Muslim population for political influence and as a potential resource for future terrorist operations.

Muslims in the American armed forces are even more problematic. Unknowingly, the Pentagon has used Wahhabi-backed organizations in the United States to select and train Muslim imams (prayer leaders) for the U.S. Army chaplain corps. Chaplains are in a unique position to indoctrinate and influence converts about their faith, placing U.S. military officials in a difficult position if Wahhabi clerics were to preach subversive sermons or incite vulnerable, new converts to violence in private talks with Muslim members of the American military. The best estimate is that there are as many as 15,000 Muslims in the American military, but no one knows for sure because Muslims do not commonly declare their religious affiliation and are not required to do so. Some military personnel are Muslim by birth but most are converts, the majority black and some Hispanics.

The American military first addressed the issue of conversion to Islam in Saudi Arabia during the First Gulf War in 1990-1991 and, since then, has had serious problems with the way Muslim military chaplains are selected and trained. In March 2002, a Customs Service task force raided a Muslim chaplain school and network of Islamic nonprofit organizations and businesses in suburban Virginia outside Washington, DC. The raid established evidence that Saudi-funded organizations funneled money to al Qaeda, Palestinian Islamic Jihad and other groups that support radical, militant Islam.

Moreover, in the aftermath of the First Gulf War, ultra-conservative Saudi Wahhabi clerics aggressively tried to recruit U.S. service members stationed in Saudi Arabia, especially American Blacks and Hispanics. Under the guise of lectures on Saudi Arabian culture, American troops were forced by their commanders to sit through many hours of Wahhabi propaganda. An article by John Mintz and Gregory Vistica in *The Washington Post* on November 2, 2003 summarized Saudi Wahhabi missionary efforts:

> Just after the 1991 Persian Gulf War against Iraq, huge tents were erected in Saudi Arabia near the barracks of U.S. military personnel. Inside, day and night, Saudi imams [Wahhabi prayer leaders] sent by their government lectured the GIs about Islam and made aggressive pitches to convert them. Saudi officials had promised that the discussions would touch only on Arab culture. But within months, about 1,000 soldiers, and perhaps as many as 3,000, converted to Islam—the largest surge of Muslims ever into the U.S. armed forces. 'It was quite aggressive,' said David Peterson, then the military's top chaplain in the region. 'In retrospect,' he said, 'there was reason for concern that foreign clerics had gained influence over the troops, but military officials were slow to grasp the implications,' he said. [Mintz and Vistica]

Sitting in the audience with his fellow American soldiers was Timothy McVeigh, the convicted bomber (executed in 2001) of the 1995 Oklahoma City Federal Building, who served in Saudi Arabia during the First Gulf War. It is conceivable but unproved that Wahhabi ideology may have influenced and motivated McVeigh's violence, for he was alienated toward his country and was an ideal ally for radical, nihilistic, Wahhabism and especially al Qaeda-inspired Takfirism. Recent circumstantial evidence has revealed intriguing evidence of a possible Wahhabi connection to McVeigh and his accomplices, Michael J. Fortier (released from federal prison in early 2006) and Terry Nichols. McVeigh first met Nichols and Fortier during their basic training with the Army at Fort Benning, Georgia in 1988.

Directly after the Oklahoma City atrocity, unsubstantiated reports indicated possible involvement of Middle Easterners in Oklahoma City in the days leading up to the bombing. Next was an unusual trip to the

Philippines by McVeigh's co-conspirator Terry Nichols, who may have met with members of the al Qaeda-linked Islamist extremist group Abu Sayaff. Richard A. Clarke [2004, 127], former member of the White House National Security Staff, summarized his suspicions regarding Nichols' trip to the Philippines:

> Another Conspiracy Theory intrigued me because I could never disprove it. The theory seemed unlikely on its face: Ramzi Yousef or Khaled Sheik Muhammad had taught Terry Nichols how to blow up the Oklahoma Federal Building. The problem was that, upon investigation, we established that both Ramzi Yousef and Nichols had been in the city of Cebu on the same days...on an island in the central Philippines. Yousef and Khaled Sheik Muhammad had gone there to help create an al Qaeda spin-off, a Philippine affiliate chapter, named after a hero of the Afghan war against the Soviets, Abu Sayaff. Could the al Qaeda explosives expert have been introduced to the angry American who proclaimed his hatred for the U.S. Government? We do not know, despite some FBI investigation. We do know that Nichols's bombs did not work before his Philippine stay and were deadly when he returned. We also know that Nichols continued to call Cebu long after his wife returned to the United States. The final coincidence is that several al Qaeda operatives had attended a radical Islamic conference a few years earlier in, of all places, Oklahoma City."

Clarke's theory regarding the Oklahoma City bombing and a possible connection to al Qaeda is intriguing and plausible, even more so because of the aggressive Saudi missionary efforts to convert American soldiers such as McVeigh, Nichols and Fortier to Wahhabism. What we know for certain on the Saudi side is that shortly after the Gulf War senior Saudi military and religious leaders were directed to identify and assess potential American military converts to

Islam. We also know that McVeigh was in Saudi Arabia at the time, was exposed to the Wahhabi lectures, and would have made a prime candidate for conversion, meeting the ideal profile of a dissenter desiring to undermine and discredit his country and make war against its policies.

In his memoirs of the Gulf War, Prince Khaled bin Sultan [1995], American General Norman Schwarzkopf's Saudi counterpart during the war, refers to his religious aide, a senior Wahhabi cleric. It is common practice for conservative Wahhabi clerics to be assigned to the staffs of Saudi military commanders to enforce Wahhabi-Salafist doctrine among the troops, similar to the way the KGB operated in the Soviet Union military structure to enforce Communist Party discipline at all levels of command and in the ranks. Wahhabi clerics are assigned and operate at every level of the Saudi military command structure for religious purposes, but one of the primary tasks during the Gulf War was missionary work to proselytize infidel allies, especially Blacks and Hispanics and disaffected American soldiers like McVeigh. Recruitment included expensive gifts as well as the long-standing Saudi practice of providing cash grants for new converts to travel to Mecca for the annual Hajj pilgrimage. Prince Khaled and his Wahhabi religious advisors deliberately gulled their American military partners into permitting these unusual activities during the long and boring redeployment phase of the Gulf War after hostilities had finished. In the American tradition of freedom of religion, American military leaders felt that the Wahhabi lectures would please their Saudi hosts while benefiting the educational and religious needs of American soldiers who were bored while waiting to return home. These unusual Saudi missionary efforts resulted in hundreds of American converts to Wahhabi Islam and additional military converts have come from Wahhabi-funded mosques located in the United States.

Unless Terry Nichols or Michael Fortier shed additional light on the subject, we may never know for certain if Timothy McVeigh was motivated and inspired by Saudi brainwashing to bomb the Federal Building in Oklahoma City. But what we do know is that Muslims in the American military pose a unique problem of trust and risk, as evidenced by Sergeant Hasan Akbar. Prior to joining the U.S. Army as a Muslim soldier, Sergeant Akbar attended the University of California Davis and a nearby radicalized Wahhabi-funded California mosque. Akbar threw hand grenades that exploded in an American command center in Kuwait on March 22, 2003 just as American forces were about to launch their attack into Iraq. After tossing the grenades into the command tents, Akbar shot several soldiers with an automatic weapon as they ran from their tents, killing two officers, an American Air Force major and Army captain, and wounding fourteen others.

Massive Saudi propaganda efforts, extensive missionary work, and nearly inexhaustible Saudi funding for mosques and Islamic schools have created extraordinary problems unimaginable before 9/11 and have served to intimidate much of the mainstream American Muslim community into silence, although encouraging signs finally began to emerge in 2005 when the North American Muslim community started to react to promising developments in the Middle East and to the vulgar beheadings, atrocities and utter horror that were perpetrated by bin Laden's followers in Europe, Saudi Arabia and Iraq.

The European Problem

Another problem that the West faces is the so-called "European Problem" because radical, militant Islamism supported by Saudi Arabian Wahhabi-Salafist theology now resides in the heart of modern Europe, making Europe not only a base of militant Islamist operations but also a prized target. The Arab-Muslim world spans Europe's soft underbelly and Europe's demographic pressures have resulted in Muslims leading the wave of post-World War II immigration into Europe from the more than 300 million Muslims that reside along Europe's Mediterranean southern rim, with a rapidly expanding population. The majority are under age 20 and 40 percent are below the age of 14. At the same time, native European populations are aging and shrinking, making immigration an economic necessity and Europe has failed to integrate its large Muslim population into the broader social fabric.

Europeans have a different perspective than the United States regarding Muslims and terrorism, largely because Europe has such a large Muslim population and is geographically closer to the Arab-Muslim world than North America, and because Europe has such a long history of active involvement in the Arab-Muslim world due to its recent colonial past. Europeans in general, and certainly the French and Germans, believe that Americans do not understand the problems of the Arab-Muslim world because the United States is a relatively young nation and is situated far away from the Muslim world and Europe, where it is literally driving distance from France or Germany to Chechnya and Iraq. Moreover, many Europeans have believed that Americans, as relative newcomers to the Middle East, exaggerate the problem of radical, militant Islam and the threat of global terrorism. While European attitudes began to change in 2005 due to the London bombings and Muslim riots in France, many Europeans still believe that the United States lacks the type of "old world" patience required to manage problems the "Arab" way because Americans are naive on the one hand and rash bullies on the other, and lack experience in the Arab world.

As the dominant colonial power for many decades, the United Kingdom has had long experience in Iraq, Jordan, Egypt, Oman, India, Pakistan, and elsewhere in the world. France feels that it knows and understands the people, culture and history in Syria, Lebanon, Algeria, and Morocco from its colonial past, just as the Netherlands is particularly knowledgeable in the complexities of the world's largest Muslim country, Indonesia. Germany believes that it understands Turkey and Iran better than other nations due to its large Turkish "gast arbeiter" population stemming from well-established relationships with the Ottoman Empire and ventures like the Berlin-to-Baghdad railroad. Because of these historical ties, large Muslim populations range throughout Europe, from Italy in the south to Sweden in the north.

While there are few reliable Muslim population statistics, it is generally accepted that more than 50 million Muslims live in greater Western and Eastern Europe. Approximately 18 million Muslims, as summarized in table 3.2 below, live in the 25 countries of the European Union (EU), several times more than the relatively small Muslim population in the United States.

Table 3.2
Western Europe Muslim Population (Millions)

Country	Total Population	Muslims	% Muslim	# Mosques
Austria	8.2	0.5	6.1	-
Belgium	10.4	0.6	5.8	380
Denmark	5.4	0.2	3.7	-
France	60.4	5.9	9.8	1,500
Germany	82.4	4.2	5.1	2,400
Italy	58.1	1.1	1.9	250
Netherlands	16.3	1.1	6.7	400
Norway	4.6	0.1	2.2	10
Spain	40.3	1.1	2.7	400
Sweden	9.0	0.5	5.6	-
Switzerland	7.5	0.4	5.3	-
United Kingdom	60.3	1.8	3.0	1,600
TOTAL	**362.9**	**17.5**	**4.8**	**5,340**

Source: Central Intelligence Agency, *The World Fact Book*, Washington, DC: Government Printing Office, 2004.

A majority of Europe's Muslims live in the Balkans and southeastern Europe, areas once part of the Ottoman Empire. In Western Europe, the largest numbers of Muslims live in France, Germany, and the United Kingdom, with many immigrants coming from Turkey, Algeria, Morocco, Tunisia, and Pakistan, having remained in their European host countries as "guest workers." Their children are now native-born citizens of the European Union with EU passports and there is also a growing number of European converts to Islam. Today, the obvious presence of Islam is readily seen throughout Western Europe where there are about 2,400 mosques in Germany, 1,500 in France and 1,600 in England, most built recently and funded by Saudi Wahhabi-Salafist sources.

In Great Britain, there are nearly two million Muslims and in 2004, the name "Mohammed" was listed for the first time in the top 20 most commonly chosen names of baby boys, according to the British Office for National Statistics. In England, more Muslims attend mosque each week than Anglicans attend church, and Oxford University has established a lavish new Center for Islamic Studies, funded by the Saudis, with a large prayer hall, traditional Muslim dome, and towering minaret [Ferguson, 4/18/2004].

In Germany there are over four million Muslims but the native German population is projected to decline from 82 million in 2004 to about 67 million in 2050 while its Muslim population explodes. Saudi-funded Muslim institutions have become the spiritual home to Islamist terrorists, as evidenced by the 9/11 investigations into the al Qaeda cells that operated freely in Hamburg, Germany prior to the al Qaeda attacks against the American homeland on September 11, 2001. Similar cells now operate with relative ease throughout Europe, primarily due to open borders resulting from liberal and relatively unrestricted EU travel policies that have eliminated the requirement to show passports at borders. Today Muslim extremists can move freely through Europe and travel largely undetected all the way to Iraq through Turkey.

The King Fahd Academy was recently established in Bonn, Germany, the former capital, as a personal gift from King Fahd. Currently, German-Muslim children are taught the same hate-filled curriculum used in Wahhabi schools in Saudi Arabia. The German public was recently shocked by surreptitiously taped radical Islamist sermons in a German mosque that revealed calls for holy war against Jews and infidels. Testifying before the U.S. Senate Subcommittee on Terrorism, Technology and Homeland Security, Dr. Alex Alexiev, Senior Fellow, Center for Security Policy, stated:

> The typical modus operandi in taking over a mosque or similar institution follows approximately the following pattern: Saudi representatives offer a community to subsidize the building of a new mosque, which usually includes an Islamic school and a community center. After completion of the project an annual maintenance subsidy is offered making the community dependent on Saudi largess in perpetuity. Saudi chosen board members are installed, a Wahhabi imam [prayer leader] and free Wahhabi literature are brought in and the curriculum changed in accordance with Wahhabi precepts. Visiting speakers of extremist views are then regularly invited to

lead Friday night prayers and further radicalize the members. The most promising candidates are selected for further religious education and indoctrination in Saudi Arabia to be sent back as Wahhabi missionaries as the circle is completed" [Alexiev, 2003].

A German television report on June 30, 2004 indicated that Germany has 2,400 mosques compared to 1,500 to 2,000 mosques in the much larger United States, and that the state of North Rhine-Westphalia announced the results of a study of textbooks used in the private Islamic school that the Saudi government established in Bonn. Muslim children were taught that, "…the Muslim people's existence has been threatened by Jews and Christians since the Crusades, and it is the first duty of every Muslim to prepare to fight against these enemies."

In France there are over six million Muslims although the number might be as high as eight million. According to a French undercover police study reported in the French daily Le Monde, there has been a marked increase in the number of Islamist radicals taking over mosques in the greater Paris area, with 32 out of 373 Paris mosques reported to be under the control of extremists:

> According to the police, extremists take over by first criticizing the older generation's interpretation of holy texts and then bringing up political issues such as the ban of Muslim headscarves in French public schools, the Israeli-Palestinian conflict, and discrimination against Arabs. To maintain and increase community support, the radicals open day-care centers and nursery schools associated with the mosques and undertake the teaching of Arabic and the Holy Koran. Some Salafist radicals [Takfirs] are linked to al Qaeda and other terror groups and the increase of radical-controlled mosques is regarded as a threat to security in France and Europe [CNS News, 6/30/2004].

French researchers believe that radicalization of mosques is a result of the growing Salafist movement in Europe inspired by Saudi Wahhabi-Salafism. It appeals to young, second-generation Arabs who feel rejected by Western society and alienated from their immigrant family culture and traditional Islam, which they reject. The increase of this radical form of Islam has also occurred in other urban areas of France, Germany, and Britain. The radicals target young people and gradually take over by isolating older clerics who have practiced moderate Islam in their mosques. Stephen Schwarz [2002] has described the danger of Wahhabi-funded mosques:

> What makes a Wahhabi mosque so dangerous? First, Wahhabi preaching and teaching to such a congregation will be fundamentalist, indoctrinating young and old in hatred, contempt, and distrust of Jews, Christians, and non-Wahhabi Muslims. Second, it will propagandize in favor of violence in places such as Iraq, Israel, and Chechnya. Wahhabi mosques serve as centers for the dissemination of extremist literature, including the "Saudi edition of the Holy Koran," a revised version of the Islamic scripture with insertions and distortions that make it an extremist document. The collection of money and the distribution of videos extolling jihad combatants also take place in these mosques. The step from such activities to direct recruitment of these combatants is small, as evidenced by the enlistment of British subjects to fight in Chechnya and American citizens who become al Qaeda operatives [Schwartz, 2002].

Although there are fewer than 750,000 Jews in France and Germany combined, disturbing and growing trends of malevolent anti-Semitism are now present in Europe, and especially in France, mostly driven by militant Islamists. European anti-Semitism has reemerged because European Muslims share common and unified hatred of Israel and support for Palestinians. They also share a deep distrust of the

United States, fed by daily Al Jazeera television news, because of unswerving American support of democratic Israel and the American-led war in Iraq. According to an officially commissioned European Union study in 2003, almost all neo anti-Semitism in Europe comes from Muslim groups:

> Muslims and Palestinian groups were behind many of the [anti-Semitism] incidents it examined...Physical attacks on Jews and the desecration and destruction of synagogues and cemeteries were acts often committed by young Muslim perpetrators...radical Islamist circles were responsible for placing anti-Semitic propaganda [Benoit, 2003].

What is particularly disturbing is Europe's reluctance to address the problem of European anti-Semitism and its causes, especially Wahhabi-Salafist funding and support provided to anti-Semitic activities by Islamic charities. Saudi funding for Europe's poor and isolated Muslim community has been seen as benign, but there is well-documented proof that Saudi money and radical Wahhabi ideology in Saudi-backed schools, mosques, and foundations have caused increased support for terrorism among Europe's young and disaffected Muslims.

In Spain, Europe's largest mosque is located near Madrid, built by the government of Saudi Arabia with weekly directions for what will be preached at Friday's call to prayer and how funds may be spent. In Greece, the King Fahd Foundation of Saudi Arabia financed an Islamic Center in suburban Athens. The Greek government recently donated the land for a large mosque funded by a Saudi Arabian Wahhabi foundation to accommodate the approximately 200,000 Muslims in the greater metropolitan area of Athens. The Muslim phenomenon in Europe is driven by changing demographics that are rapidly transforming the European landscape:

> Today, the Muslim birth rate in Europe is three times higher than the non-Muslim one. If current trends

continue, the Muslim population of Europe will nearly double by 2015, while the non-Muslim population will shrink by 3.5 percent [Taspinar, 2003].

While population trends mean that European Muslims will soon have proportionally more influence in elections, European Muslims are even more alienated and distrustful following 9/11 and with recent exposure of al Qaeda-Takfir cells in Germany, Italy, France, Belgium, Spain, and the Netherlands. Al Qaeda's March 11, 2004 attack in Spain was a resounding victory for bin Laden, with near simultaneous bombings of four trains that killed nearly 200 people. Moreover, the attack in Spain knocked a major American ally out of the Iraq war. The world reacted in horror to successive 2004 al Qaeda beheadings in Iraq and Saudi Arabia and then later to the savage and violent murder of Theo Van Gogh in Amsterdam on November 2, 2004 by a Muslim militant who had connections to an al Qaeda-Takfir terrorist cell and a radical, Wahhabi-inspired Salafist mosque in Amsterdam. An encouraging development in March 2005 came from Spanish Muslim leaders when they announced a fatwa (religious ruling) against Osama bin Laden on the anniversary of the Madrid train bombings saying that according to the Koran, "the terrorist acts of Osama bin Laden and his organization al Qaeda…are totally banned and must be roundly condemned as part of Islam" [CNN, 3/11/2005]. Renewed European efforts to combat the Islamist terror threat followed the London bombings and French riots in 2005.

An early casualty of these developments is Europe's widely accepted doctrine of multiculturalism, where all cultures have been considered equal, but less so in France where students and teachers were banned from wearing headscarves in state schools in 2004, igniting fierce criticism from Muslim groups that claimed banning Muslim headscarves is a form of discrimination against Islam. Five German states also introduced headscarf bans for teachers in 2004 but restricted only teachers, not students, from wearing Islamic headscarves. Bavaria's culture minister was quoted as saying, "The veil is widely abused by Islamic fundamentalist groups as a political symbol." The

Social Democratic Party (SPD) and Greens, both left-of-center parties that rule in a coalition at the national level in Germany, voted against the ban in the regional parliament and sided with Muslim groups, a trend that has shown the European and American political left aligning with radical Muslim interests in Europe and the United States.

It is possible that France will have a Muslim majority at the national level within 25 years. The problem of militant Islamists in France is becoming acute due to extreme isolation, alienation, and discrimination against Europe's Muslim population and an uncertain future for young Muslims—a trend that is redefining Europe from Sweden and Norway in the north to Italy and Spain in the south. Caroline Wyatt, Paris correspondent for the BBC, recently noted: "Women in black chadors and abayas make Burgundy feel more like Barbary." She went on to say that family members, asylum seekers, and illegal immigrants add to the growing immigrant population who live in bleak French public housing, causing resentments of young Muslims to grow, while their French classmates move on to better positions in society [Wyatt, 12/20/2003].

Germany, with Europe's second largest Muslim population and ultra liberal political asylum policies, has also failed to integrate its largely Turkish Muslim population into Germany society. Germany's large Turkish population generally lives in isolated ghettos and the result is alienation and anger among Germany's large and youthful Muslim population, a trend witnessed throughout Europe. Moreover, the Muslim Brotherhood, with Saudi funding, has deeply penetrated Germany's large and increasingly hostile Muslim community with its radical agenda.

Because of their large Muslim populations, it should be no surprise that European politicians, especially in France and Germany, had difficulty supporting the United States in the Iraq war. What this means for the future of the European Union is alarming, but positive developments in the Middle East in 2005, coupled with the 2005 London bombings and French riots, increased European recognition that the Bush Doctrine of freedom and democracy can be the long-term antidote to Bin Ladenism. Europeans are now very sensitive to the fact that cells of young al Qaeda-Takfiris have embedded themselves into European societies, gulling their trusting infidel hosts while posing as moderate and mainstream Muslims, and waiting patiently to strike lethal and often fatal suicide blows against the heathen West.

French intellectuals are frequent critics of the United States and often receive disproportionate importance as a source of disinformation. Laurent Murawiec [2002] observed that it is popular in French intellectual circles to cite the "American way of life" as the greatest threat to civilization and to call "unbearable America" a totalitarian democracy that has "launched a war against the Old World." This is a popular theme with wide appeal among the French left-leaning intelligentsia and even some in the U.S., where the United States is often cited as the world's last empire, that it orchestrated the Asian financial crisis in 1998 to bring down its rival Japan, and that it uses NATO to control Europe against Europe's own interests. Wedded for years to utopian Marxism that failed to achieve a communist utopia, many French intellectuals now support the goals of radical, militant Islamism, replacing their Marxist utopia with a transnational utopian Caliphate that governs under Islamic Sharia law. Most bizarre is the French claim that the CIA conspired with Saudi Arabian Wahhabis and their oil money in a "grand conspiracy" to secure the world's oil reserves for global capitalism in return for permitting Saudi Wahhabis and the Saudi royal family to establish and support dictatorships throughout the Arab-Muslim world [Murawiec].

But many in France understand that the problem of radical, militant Islamism in the heart of Western Europe is a sobering phenomenon, growing and festering in ways that spell trouble for the fledgling European Union that struggles to effectively address the threat. Meanwhile, new potential EU members like Muslim Turkey are knocking at the European Union door, hoping for membership and the benefits it can bring to a poor Muslim country like Turkey that sits astride Europe and Asia. Turkey is a special case because of its secular makeup that resulted from Kemal Ataturk's revolution following the breakup of the Ottoman Empire after the First World War, and because Turkey is also a long-standing and only Muslim member of

NATO. The United States government supports Turkey's desire to join the European Union, but not all European countries welcome a Muslim nation into the European Union because it is seen as a Muslim "Trojan horse." Even though Turkey is a non-Arab country and is highly Westernized, the world will have to wait until at least 2015 so to see how Turkey's prospects develop for EU membership and formal admittance into the elite European club.

But Turkey can be a key to securing peace and stability in the Middle East. While Europe's problems with its large and growing Muslim population will continue to grow, Turkey's strategic position in the Middle East and active membership in NATO, the world's longest lasting and most successful international security alliance in history, can provide a linchpin for logically extending NATO to the southeast into the countries of the Persian Gulf and the world's largest supply of oil. Such an initiative could create what might be called "SENATO," for Southeast NATO, extending NATO's security guarantees to the perennially unstable countries of the region and their oil fields that are vital to the world's economy.

AMERICA'S RESPONSE TO THE SAUDIS AND WAHHABISM

Over the last 60 years, since President Roosevelt met Ibn Saud in 1945, succeeding American administrations have reinforced America's policy of maintaining stability in the world's oil supply. Moreover, over the last 30 years, American energy security policy has utterly failed while former American ambassadors, retired generals, and international businesses have made millions of dollars working for the Saudis, or for institutions funded by the Saudis, or for American companies doing business or seeking to do business with the Saudis. For the most part, these are honorable people who understand the issues in the region and have an appreciation for the difficulty of doing business in Saudi Arabia—up to the limits of any Westerner's ability to know.

THE TRIUMPH OF DEMOCRACY OVER MILITANT ISLAMISM

Many are distinguished Americans who have registered as agents of a foreign government (Saudi Arabia) with the U.S. Justice Department and U.S. Congress as required by law. Many others have been bought out by the Saudis to either promote and lobby Saudi issues in Washington, DC and European capitals and refute criticism of the Saudi royal family. This type of collusion has been actively promoted by the Saudis as a deliberate pattern of "gulling" America over many years. Outside observers might call it just plain bribery.

The process of formally dealing with the Saudis while being openly "gulled" by Saudi leaders has continued unabated, as government bureaucrats and political appointees often looked to lucrative Saudi consulting jobs after retirement due to the huge volume of money available and the entrenched relationships that exist on both sides between people in government and the private sector. There has been a long-standing mutuality of interest between the United States and Saudi Arabia based on maintaining oil price stability for the sake of the global economy. The Saudis understand that oil demand is tied directly to the long-term health of the global economy and, to their credit, have been good oil partners over the years, reliably playing their role in the partnership as the world's largest oil supplier to the market of the world's largest oil consumer.

After the Roosevelt-Ibn Saud meeting in 1945, little attention was subsequently paid to American relations with Saudi Arabia until the Arab oil embargo following the October 1973 Arab-Israeli war. The oil embargo provided a windfall of hundreds of billions in Saudi oil income, the beginning of the oil bonanza. Because of Western dependence on Persian Gulf oil and concerns stemming from the fall of the Shah of Iran, President Jimmy Carter announced the "Carter Doctrine" to the world in 1980, declaring that the vast Persian Gulf oil reserves are vital to the United States and Western interests and that the United States would defend the Persian Gulf oil fields from aggression. Each succeeding president, Democrat and Republican administrations alike, has endorsed this presidential doctrine, culminating in the deployment of 550,000 American troops to Saudi Arabia during the First Gulf War in 1990-1991 when Saddam Hussein invaded Kuwait and threatened Saudi Arabia.

Since the 1973 Arab oil embargo, the American government has worked diligently with Saudi Arabia as the supplier of last resort, and the other principal suppliers of crude oil to the world market, to keep the global supply of crude oil in balance with constantly rising global demand. The primary basis for America's relationship with Saudi Arabia through successive administrations in Washington has been to ensure stable and relatively low energy costs to support global economic growth. But 9/11 created a new and overriding issue—combating terrorism and its ideological sources—and Saudi-American relationships became more complex and even more vital.

After 9/11, Saudi-American relationships changed dramatically and the United States government finally began to comprehend the serious impact of American gullibility and culpability over the years as well as the complexities of Saudi Arabia as a 21st century nation just emerging from the Middle Ages. With great wealth from an underground treasure that the world desperately needs, the complex Saudi-American post-9/11 relationship developed an added dimension in addition to freely flowing oil and reduced pricing volatility—a new dimension that questions whether the two long-time allies really share a common goal of winning the war against radical, militant Islamism.

For over 30 years the West consistently failed to respond credibly to critical events in the Middle East, even in the face of increasingly violent terrorist attacks against American facilities in the Muslim world. Radical Islamist extremists concluded that the United States was a paper tiger as a result of its experience in Vietnam and long record of retreat in the Middle East. Successive bombings of American targets in Lebanon, Saudi Arabia, Somalia, Africa, and Yemen emboldened Osama bin Laden and in the twisted logic of Wahhabi-Bin Ladenism, al Qaeda arrogantly declared war against Saudi Arabia, the "the Great Satan" United States, and Western civilization.

America, the Paper Tiger

Until 9/11, the American response to repeated terrorist attacks had been grossly ineffective, generally employing police investigations as the preferred means of response. The United States had lost a number of diplomats in isolated Middle Eastern terrorist incidents in the 1970s, but the first significant attack on the West by violent radical Islamists was by Ayatollah Khomeini's Iranian Shiite Muslims who seized 52 Americans in the American Embassy in Tehran in 1979. Held as prisoners for 444 days, the Carter administration lost credibility in the eyes of the world with its failed rescue attempt. Fearful of Reagan's threats during the presidential election campaign, the Iranian mullahs released the American hostages on January 20, 1981, the day Ronald Reagan was inaugurated. The United States suffered serious loss of face in the Muslim world by its failed rescue attempt and inability to free its embassy staff.

Two years later in 1983, Hezbollah, an Iranian-sponsored Shiite militant group, launched two suicide bombing attacks on Americans in Lebanon, first on the American Embassy in Beirut, killing 63 embassy employees and wounding 120, and then on the U.S. Marine barracks at the Beirut airport, killing 241 marines and wounding 81. President Reagan did not retaliate because his Defense Secretary, Caspar Weinberger, expressed concern about damaging American relations in the Middle East. Instead, Reagan withdrew the remaining American troops from Lebanon and the terrorists achieved their objective for the attack. The Beirut airport suicide bombings were followed by the bombing of the U.S. Embassy in Kuwait in December 1983 and the kidnapping and killing of the CIA station chief in Beirut the following March, again without any response from the United States. However, in September 1984, when Hezbollah bombed the annex to the American embassy in Beirut, the United States authorized Lebanese agents to assassinate an Islamic cleric thought to be the Hezbollah leader, killing 80 in the attack.

In December 1984, Hezbollah changed tactics by hijacking airliners and killing American passengers on the flights. The first hijacking was a Kuwaiti airliner with two Americans killed; the kidnappers escaped punishment after the plane landed in Tehran. The Reagan administration offered a $250,000 reward for information that would lead to the arrest of the kidnappers without success. The next kidnapping was TWA flight 847 in June 1985 that landed in Beirut, where it was held more than two weeks. An American naval officer was shot and his body thrown onto the tarmac, and the Israelis agreed to trade hundreds of jailed terrorists for release of the passengers. The kidnappers escaped but four were later captured in Germany where one was tried and jailed.

Later, in October 1985, Libyan terrorists tried to hijack the cruise ship, Achille Lauro, and threw a crippled Jewish-American passenger, Leon Klinghoffer, overboard. That attack was followed by Libyan terrorists bombing airports in Rome and Vienna in December 1985, and a West Berlin discotheque frequented by American service members in April 1986. President Reagan ordered an F-111 air attack from bases in England on one of Muammar Qaddafi's Libyan residences. Qaddafi was nearly killed which caused Libya to withdraw from terrorism until December 1988, when Libyan agents planted a bomb on Pan Am flight 103 that exploded over Lockerbie, Scotland, killing all passengers and several people on the ground, 270 in all. Two Libyan intelligence agents were subsequently tried for the crime and one was convicted in 2001. Qaddafi escaped further punishment except for sanctions imposed on his country that were lifted only when Libya agreed to terminate its nuclear program in June 2003 shortly after the start of the Iraq invasion, having been sufficiently alarmed by a post 9/11 American ultimatum to either join the American effort in the war on terrorism or expect regime change.

By the late 1980s, Osama bin Laden was fighting in Afghanistan against the Soviet occupation. He correctly noted that nearly all Islamist terrorist attacks against American targets and the West had successfully achieved terrorist objectives at very little cost politically, financially, or in Muslim lives. Bin Laden's successful jihad in liberating Afghanistan from the Soviet Union and establishing the Taliban as Afghanistan's government, coupled with his observations regarding the success of the Islamist terrorist attacks, strengthened his embryonic radical terrorist movement. Moreover, bin Laden and his Saudi supporters had successfully "gulled" the infidel CIA into supplying weapons and money for his Afghan Arab warriors, and bin Laden had been able to use the cause of Muslim liberation from Western domination as a successful recruiting tool to bring thousands of young Muslims to Afghanistan for indoctrination and training in terrorist tactics. From this springboard, bin Laden then sent hundreds of young jihadists into the Balkans and Somalia in the 1990s in the cause of radical, militant Islamism.

Bin Laden's nihilistic jihadists were less welcome assisting Muslims in Kosovo and Bosnia where the European Muslims found the Wahhabis far too violent. In typical Wahhabi fashion, they led brutal attacks on nonbelievers, obliterated magnificent, centuries-old frescoes on the walls of ancient mosques, and destroyed cemeteries and statues. However, bin Laden's apparent success in driving the United States from Somalia in 1993 by downing two Black Hawk helicopters with American surface-to-air missiles left over from Afghanistan, and killing a few elite Army Rangers, caused him to develop an exaggerated view of al Qaeda's capabilities. He also underestimated American resolve and the difficulty of driving the Americans from the Middle East. With the end of the First Gulf War in 1991, bin Laden obsessively focused on removing American infidel forces from the holy lands of Saudi Arabia. He believed that the United States had become a soft "paper tiger" since Vietnam without the courage, determination, political will, or perseverance as a nation to succeed in prolonged and bloody military conflict. It was from this psychological orientation that bin Laden planned a series of escalating and bolder attacks on American interests in the Middle East, and ultimately on the American homeland itself in 2001.

In February 1993, a massive explosion from a truck bomb in the parking garage of the World Trade Center in New York killed six people and injured over 1,000; this was one of the few instances in which terrorists were captured and six were successfully prosecuted for the crime and received long sentences. The target, as on 9/11, was a symbol of America's global economic might. Even though CIA director James Woolsey suspected that the terrorists were a part of a larger terror network operating from the Sudan and called "al Qaeda," the Clinton administration believed that justice had prevailed through criminal prosecution of the terrorists and that the bombing was a law enforcement problem rather than a military matter.

The first World Trade Center bombing was followed by the shooting of two American diplomats in Karachi, Pakistan in March 1995 and the killing of five Americans with a car bomb in Riyadh, Saudi Arabia in December 1995. On June 25, 1996 a large truck bomb destroyed the U.S. Air Force Khobar Towers dormitory in Dhahran, Saudi Arabia in the Shiite Eastern Province near the oil fields, killing 19 American airmen and wounding 240 others, including civilians of several nationalities. The goal of the attacks in Saudi Arabia was to drive the Americans out of the country. Again, the Clinton administration sought justice for these crimes against Americans through law enforcement action and the intervention of the FBI rather than military action but with very limited success due to lack of support from Saudi authorities [Freeh, 32-33]. Al Qaeda stepped up its anti-American campaign in 1998 with simultaneous bombings of U.S. embassies in Kenya and Tanzania, killing over 200 people, mostly Africans. Distracted by impeachment hearings stemming from sex scandals that shocked the Muslim world, President Clinton at last identified bin Laden as the perpetrator and authorized the Pentagon to fire several cruise missiles at an al Qaeda training camp in Afghanistan and destroy a building in Sudan that was believed to be an al Qaeda weapons factory. The American president also launched covert CIA counterterrorist operations against bin Laden's operations but failed to make any significant progress against al Qaeda.

Bin Laden realized that he had now gained the attention of the United States, but this recognition and his success made him even more aggressive. In October 2000 he dispatched a team of suicide bombers against the U.S. Navy destroyer USS Cole, which had docked in Yemen's port of Aden for refueling. Seventeen American sailors were killed and 39 were wounded in the attack on the USS Cole. President Clinton was involved in Israeli-Palestinian peace talks at Camp David at the time of the Cole attack and failed to condemn al Qaeda for its direct assault on U.S. military operations or take any action against bin Laden. Nor did the incoming Bush administration take any action when it took office in January 2001 and bin Laden was once again left with the perception of a resonant victory against the infidels with no retaliation from the American "paper tiger." A summary of important militant Islamist attacks against the U.S. and the impotent pre-9/11 American responses are shown in Table 3.3 below.

Table 3.3
Summary of Significant Militant Islamist Attacks Against America

Event	Year	Result	American Response
Iranian Shiite Revolution	1979	52 American hostages held for 444 days	Failed US rescue attempt
Bombing of U.S. Embassy & Marine Barracks in Lebanon	1983	Killed 241 Marines & 63 employees, wounded 201	US withdrew troops from Lebanon
Bombing of US Embassy in Kuwait	1983	Killed 6	No action
Bombing of US Embassy Annex in Beirut, Lebanon	1984	Killed 80	No action
Aircraft & Cruise Ship Hijackings	1984-85	Several Americans killed	No action
Loss of 2 Black Hawk helicopters in Somalia	1992	18 Americans killed	US withdrew troops from Somalia
Bombing of World Trade Center in NYC	1993	Killed 6, wounded over 1,000	Arrested & convicted Islamist ringleader & others
American diplomats shot in Karachi, Pakistan	1995	Killed 5 Americans	Investigation, no action
Bombing of US Air Force dormitory in Saudi Arabia	1996	Killed 19 American airmen & wounded 240	FBI investigation, no action
Bombings of US Embassies in Africa	1998	Killed over 200, mostly Africans	Fired several cruise missiles at bin Laden
Bombing of USS Cole in Yemen	2000	17 killed, 39 wounded	FBI investigation, no action
Attacks against American Homeland	9/11/2001	Nearly 3,000 killed, thousands wounded	US launched Global War on Terrorism (GWOT)

Al Qaeda's repeated attacks on the United States were low-cost propaganda victories for bin Laden that echoed loudly throughout the Muslim world. Osama bin Laden soon became sufficiently encouraged to bring a devastating attack directly to the Great Satan's homeland as he did on September 11, 2001 in one of the most brazen and sophisticated terrorist operations in history. Nearly 3,000 innocent people died when al Qaeda martyrs hijacked four airliners and flew them at high speed into the Twin Towers of the World Trade Center in New York City, the Pentagon in Washington, DC, and into the ground in central Pennsylvania, apparently targeting the United States Capitol or White House. For nearly 25 years, the United States endured repeated attacks from radical, militant, Islamists but U.S. retaliatory responses were ineffective and futile, providing motivation for the attackers to raise the ante and strike once more, as they did on 9/11.

Not since Pearl Harbor, nearly 60 years before, had the United States been so shocked. In addition to hatred of infidels that is a root belief of Wahhabi-Bin Ladenism, an even more important reason for this daring attack on the world's greatest power was to advance Osama bin Laden's dream of consolidating his influence and power in the Muslim world. By appealing to the biases and hopes of millions of disaffected young Muslims, bin Laden hoped to restore Islam to its previous glory and prominence before Islam's armies were turned away from Europe in 1683. Despite moral qualms in much of the Muslim community about the loss of innocent life, the events of 9/11 established bin Laden and his radical Islamists as true Muslim warriors in centuries' old jihad against the infidel West. And with rhetoric especially appealing to the Arab-Muslim world, bin Laden claimed that all former Muslim lands such as Spain must be reconverted to Islam and restored to their former glory.

The Saudi Perspective on America

In 1979, when the Saudis faced multiple crises and the world seemed to be spinning out of control, American president Jimmy Carter appeared weak and ineffective and the Saudis openly questioned America's reliability as an ally to stand up to the Iranian revolutionary leaders, let alone the atheistic Soviets. This attitude was reinforced by the inability of the Carter administration to resolve the Iranian hostage crisis and respond effectively to Saudi security concerns. And when Carter ordered two AWACS command and control aircraft and six unarmed American F-15 fighter aircraft into Saudi Arabia in 1980 in response to a Yemeni border incursion, the Saudis openly ridiculed President Carter for the futile American response and Carter's failure to comprehend the seriousness of Saudi security concerns.

Fear of Shiite Iran has always been a primary Saudi security issue, made even more alarming to the Saudi ruling family in 1979 because of the large Shiite population in the oil-rich Eastern Province where Shiite loyalty to the Saudi government was questionable in the face of the Iranian Shiite revolution that ousted the ruling Reza Pahlavi family from Iranian power. Wahhabi hatred of Shiites is extreme and stems from the schism following the death of the Prophet Mohammed. A majority of the world's Shiites live in Iran and in the southern half of present-day Iraq where the two holiest Shiite cities, Karbala and Najaf, are located. During an anti-Shiite rampage in 1802, an Ikhwan force of 12,000 Saudi Wahhabis attacked and massacred approximately 4,000 Shiites in Karbala, Iraq and destroyed holy Shiite shrines, including the tomb of Hussein, the sainted Shiite grandson of the Prophet Mohammed. The following year, Wahhabi Ikhwan forces, already allied with the al Saud clan, attacked and desecrated the holy Shiite city of Najaf, Iraq, the burial site of the sainted and highly revered Ali, son-in-law of the Prophet Mohammed.

With support and encouragement from the American government following the Soviet Union invasion of Afghanistan, the Saudis began pouring hundreds of millions of dollars of their newly acquired oil wealth into Pakistan, Afghanistan, and North Africa for anti-Soviet and anti Iranian Wahhabi propaganda, Islamist schools, and Wahhabi mosques. This was a desperate effort to counter the threat of the spread of Iran's violent, revolutionary Shiite fundamentalism throughout the region, and especially in Saudi Arabia's own backyard with its large Shiite minority living along the Persian Gulf oil fields—as many as 2-3 million potentially unstable Saudi Shiites who suffered decades of Wahhabi discrimination, persecution, and second class status. Saudi government funding for Islamist schools in Western Pakistan and the subsequent formation of bin Laden's Arab brigade to fight against Soviet atheism in Afghanistan later gave rise to al Qaeda in the late 1980s and early 1990s and a new wave of extremely violent Islamist terrorism exploded upon the world based on Wahhabi-Muslim Brotherhood ideology and its totalitarian objectives.

Four subsequent events erupted during the waning years of the late 20th century, starting with the end of the Iran-Iraq War that had lasted from 1980 to 1988. In rippling effect, the dramatic fall of the Berlin Wall in 1989, the Iraqi invasion of Kuwait in 1990, and the sudden demise of the Soviet Union and atheistic Communism in 1991, cascaded upon the world and bewildered the Saudis, causing joy in some quarters and great unsettlement in others. During the Iran-Iraq War, the Saudis provided direct support and aid to the secular Iraqi Sunni leader, Saddam Hussein, against the Iranian theocratic Shiite regime, but the Saudis were surprised and bewildered by Saddam Hussein's invasion of Kuwait in 1990, only a year after the long and bloody Iran-Iraq War ended. The subsequent 1991 First Gulf War against Iraq and the demise of the Soviet Union in the same year ended a decade of international and regional tumult that set in motion a renewed bid by the Saudis to use their massive oil wealth with devastating effect to spread Wahhabi-Salafism around the world. With the use of Saudi oil money, a rekindling of Islamist fundamentalism and a fueling of rampant anti-Americanism and anti-Semitism raged relatively unnoticed through the last two decades of the 20th century.

The 1990s witnessed other problems relating to the rapid globalization of the world economy and from excesses brought on by the computer-telecommunications revolution, growth of the internet, and the U.S. stock market bubble that finally burst in the crash of early 2000. In the Muslim world, and especially among Saudi Arabia's conservative population, these unprecedented economic events were underscored by President Clinton's sex scandals that confirmed America's decadence to conservative Muslims and served to deflect the attention of the American administration away from al Qaeda and bin Laden. These factors, coupled with a general lack of concern for foreign affairs by the American public and the Clinton administration in the 1990s, convinced militant Islamist terrorists such as Osama bin laden and his emerging al Qaeda global terrorist organization that the United States and other Western democracies were decadent, immoral, corrupt, and ultimately impotent.

Then came September 11, 2001 and al Qaeda's terrorist attacks against the World Trade Center in New York and the Pentagon in Washington, DC. The attacks on 9/11 were a direct result of perceived

THE TRIUMPH OF DEMOCRACY OVER MILITANT ISLAMISM

American weakness in the Arab-Muslim world because of consistent American failure to respond vigorously to militant Islamist attacks against American facilities and interests going back some 30 years. The American public did not understand the nature of the militant Islamist enemy and the seriousness of the Saudi-Wahhabi threat to Western civilization and many remained in the dark nearly five years later.

The hijackers on September 11, 2001 were a new brand of ruthless terrorists that came from Saudi Arabia and were profoundly influenced by the teachings of the Muslim Brotherhood theorist, Sayyid Qutb, and newly virulent Saudi Arabian Wahhabi-Salafism. The Saudi government, wealthy Saudi individuals, and members of the Saudi ruling family supported international terrorism with large cash grants through multi-layered networks of Islamic charities around the world and directly to global terrorist organizations such as al Qaeda, the Palestinian Liberation Organization (PLO), and Hamas. It has been well documented in the international press that wealthy Saudis and members of the Saudi royal family financed al Qaeda before September 11th and that many wealthy Saudis continued to support and finance al Qaeda well after 9/11. Senior members of the Saudi royal family openly praised Palestinian suicide bombers and rewarded their families with cash grants and the former Saudi ambassador to Britain even published a poem eulogizing 9/11 and Palestinian suicide bombers. Speaking about Saudi Arabia, Senator Jon Kyl, Republican from Arizona and Chairman of the Senate Judiciary Subcommittee on Technology, Terrorism and Homeland Security, stated in 2003:

> The problem we are looking at today is the state-sponsored doctrine and funding of an extremist ideology [Saudi Wahhabism] that provides the recruiting grounds, support infrastructure and monetary lifeblood to today's international terrorists.

Today a monumental struggle is taking place for the heart, mind, and soul of Islam. This struggle is being waged by bin Laden's radical, militant Islamist forces dedicated to reactionary Wahhabi-Salafist goals of turning back the clock to the 7th century and the early days of Mohammed when Islam was supposedly "pure" and untainted. The struggle for the heart and soul of Islam is between militant Islamist forces of darkness with their hate-filled ideology and moderate Muslims who embrace Western values of secularism, pluralism, openness, tolerance, freedom, and democracy. The struggle for the soul of Islam is the most significant ideological battle taking place in the world today and one that profoundly impacts the lives of nearly everyone in the world because of the intensity of the issues and the billions of people involved. Senator Charles Schumer, Democrat from New York, was even more direct in condemning the Saudi government in a 2003 press release:

> This week's attacks [in Saudi Arabia] should underscore a very important point to the Saudi royal family: It's that playing both sides of the coin won't work when it comes to fighting terrorism," Schumer said. "The Saudis need to get over this Syndrome where they tell the US and the West what we want to hear but then tell the Arab street something else. If they don't get serious, there are going to be more attacks. The Administration needs to make that point forcefully to the Crown Prince. The first step in that effort is shutting down these Madrassa schools...while Islam is a peaceful religion the madrassas distort this message by preaching hate, violence and intolerance toward the Judeo-Christian world. These teachings have created a 'lost generation' in Saudi Arabia, where thousands of young Saudis are being indoctrinated with the idea that terrorism is an acceptable way to articulate their Islamic beliefs. In order for your government to be a true partner in the war on terror, it must stop funding those schools which preach extremism and to denounce their teachings."

THE TRIUMPH OF DEMOCRACY OVER MILITANT ISLAMISM

Inscrutable Saudis—Gullible Americans

The analogy of a desert mirage accurately portrays Saudi Arabia as a country that is ever changing and different from what it appears to be, populated with delightful, often incomprehensible, and always inscrutable desert people. The Saudis are ethnic Arabs, mostly from Bedouin origins and nomadic tribes that wandered the vast Arabian Desert for centuries, moving from oasis to oasis with caravans of goats and camels. Tribal culture, family and clan loyalty, and the incessant demands of the harsh desert heat and blowing sands have deeply marked the people of the Arabian Peninsula who proudly call themselves "Saudis" and defenders of Islam's holiest places.

Cities of Salt by the late Abdul Rahman Munif [1987] is a revealing and moving novel about the people of the desert that provides a thinly veiled description of the desert kingdom, addresses the impact of development in the early days of oil exploration, and tells of the tribulations of adapting to massive change and a turbulent new world. To Westerners who have lived in Saudi Arabia and even to some native Saudis, the kingdom remains an enigma because of deeply rooted social taboos and tight control by a royal family that rarely reveals itself to outsiders while having close marriage and business ties to thousands of Saudi citizens. Westerners who have lived in the desert kingdom agree that the people of Saudi Arabia are gracious, proud, and generous and make lavish displays of hospitality to their guests. In striking contrast, fanatical Wahhabi-Salafist believers and ultra-conservative Wahhabi clerics captured the country's foreign aid and missionary program in the 1980s and spawned a global resurgence of militant, reactionary Muslim fundamentalism upon the world.

The Saudi government has a long history of "double-dealing" with the West—"gulling the infidel"—beginning with the clever old king trading oil for security and buying patronage while spreading Wahhabism with its hatred of the West and calls for death to nonbelievers, including non-Wahhabi Muslims, Christians, Jews and even other Muslims. The desert kingdom is inscrutable and enigmatic because the inner workings among senior members of the royal family are very closely guarded, while senior Saudi princes and wealthy Saudi businessmen have secretly made regular payments to bin Laden and the al Qaeda network for many years and many allegedly continue to do so today.

From the beginning, the Saudi royal family believed their American friends would be easy to "gull" or "manage," especially with money. A distinct pattern of deceptive Saudi behavior has continued from the early days of Wahhabism in the 18th century all the way to the present as a deliberate way of deceiving the West. For years, the Saudi rulers have played both sides in a strategic game of deception and duplicity, a process that experienced Saudi observers call the "two faces" of the sphinx-like Saudis. The former Saudi ambassador to the United States, Prince Bandar bin Sultan, stated publicly that the Saudis have successfully cultivated (bought off) nearly every senior United States government official who could help the Saudi cause with lucrative consulting contracts after their government service was finished.

Saudi money and Saudi lobbying effectiveness have resulted in muted responses by the United States government when it comes to criticism of Saudi behavior for failing to take actions against funding for terrorism, as was the case for over two years following 9/11. As Saudi oil wealth continued to accumulate in the 1980s beyond the wildest dream of older generations, well-placed Saudi businessmen and members of the royal family amassed fantastic fortunes in just a few years. Illegal commissions from government contracts using complex off-shore corporate schemes are still common, and lucrative franchises have been granted to well-positioned Saudis to distribute American products throughout Saudi Arabia and the region. While all this was developing, an international Wahhabi terror network inspired by Egyptian and Syrian Muslim Brotherhood radicals and the philosophy of Sayyid Qutb was slowly but deliberately unleashed upon the world and funded with Saudi oil revenue. Regrettably, few in the West paid attention to the emerging Saudi Wahhabi threat until the events of 9/11 forced the United States to implement a bold, new strategy with the invasion and liberation of Afghanistan and Iraq and the antidote freedom and democracy to counter radical, militant Islamism.

Gerald Posner [2003] summarized the failures of the United States to prevent 9/11 and exposed alarming relationships between al Qaeda, the Pakistani government, and members of the Saudi royal family. Posner stated in *Why America Slept: The Failure to Prevent 9/11,* that when American Special Forces captured Abu Zubaydah, bin Laden's operations coordinator and a key member of al Qaeda, on March 28, 2002 in western Pakistan, Zubaydah was wounded in the shootout and subsequently provided detailed information to his interrogators about bin Laden's support from members of the Saudi royal family and the Pakistani government. Posner stated that the Saudis had made a typical deal with Osama bin Laden, using millions in Saudi oil money to bribe bin Laden into permanently leaving the kingdom following the defeat of the Soviet Union in Afghanistan. In return, the Saudis would finance bin Laden's terrorist training camps in Afghanistan while bin Laden agreed not to turn his fighters against the Saudi kingdom or the royal family. According to Posner, this account comes directly from American interrogations of Abu Zubaydah when he also provided names of members of the Saudi royal family who had provided funding to al Qaeda. When his American interrogators accused Zubaydah of lying, he identified direct links between Saudi Arabia, Pakistan, and bin Laden, at no surprise to the Americans. According to Posner, Abu Zubaydah said the Saudi connection came through Prince Turki bin Faisal ibn Abdul Aziz, son of King Faisal and the kingdom's longtime chief of intelligence and new Saudi Ambassador to the United States, replacing Prince Bandar bin Sultan in 2005. Zubaydah said that bin Laden personally told him of a meeting in 1991 when Prince Turki agreed to let bin Laden leave Saudi Arabia in exchange for providing secret funds if al Qaeda would not promote jihad against the kingdom and the royal family. The Pakistani contact was a top-ranking air force officer named Mushaf Ali Mir and bin Laden was able to strike a deal with him to obtain arms and supplies for al Qaeda, a deal that Zubaydah said was "blessed" by the Saudis.

Other Saudi princes identified by Abu Zubaydah were Prince Ahmed bin Salman bin Abdul Aziz (nephew of King Fahd and owner of the 2002 Kentucky Derby winner, "War Emblem"); his cousin Prince Sultan bin Faisal bin Turki al Saud; and another relative, Prince

Fahd bin Turki bin Saud al Kabir. Denying Abu Zubaydah's allegations, Prince Turki won a libel suit in London in 2004 [BBC, 12/6/2004], but within months of Abu Zubaydah's revelations, according to Posner, all three young Saudi princes and the Pakistani Air Marshall died mysteriously, apparently killed on orders from the Saudi royal family and Prince Turki was removed from his intelligence post and reassigned as Saudi ambassador in London.

In addition to support from the Saudi royal family and other wealthy Saudis, al Qaeda and related Islamist terrorist groups have received generous support through international Muslim charities managed and funded by Saudi Arabia. One of the five pillars of Islam is charitable giving and over the past 25 years government charities have funneled billions of dollars around the world to propagate the country's strict Wahabbi faith. Since the 1990s, many of the kingdom's most militant young men have been dispatched overseas to proselytize and work as Wahhabi missionaries for militant activities abroad while holding diplomatic passports. The government of Saudi Arabia and its ultraconservative Wahhabi religious leaders funded Osama bin Laden and the Taliban in Afghanistan as well as large international charities such as the Al Haramain Charitable Foundation, the Muslim World League, and the World Assembly of Muslim Youth (WAMY). Only in late 2004 did the Saudis reluctantly announce that they had reorganized the Al Haramain Charitable Foundation but even that announcement remains suspect in the face of conflicting Saudi statements and the enormity of the international web of charities that the Saudis have extravagantly deployed throughout the world. The parent organization of WAMY is the International Islamic Relief Organization (IIRO) and it is a part of the Saudi government. It has also been widely reported that Saudi funding continues to support organizations such as the Council on American-Islamic Relations (CAIR), an active and militant Islamist political organization with chapters in nearly 30 American cities [Levitt]. According to reliable press reports, several other Muslim organizations in the United States such as the Islamic Society of North America and the Islamic Council of North America are led by extremists and funded directly or indirectly by the government of Saudi Arabia [Jacoby and Brink].

Even though the Saudis have demonstrated greater cooperation with the United States in the war on terrorism since 9/11, Saudi charities still pay the salaries of Wahhabi missionaries around the world and still promote Wahhabi-Salafism as a fundamental part the government's foreign policy. This type of Saudi behavior is evidenced by the recent expulsion of a Saudi religious affairs diplomat from Germany following investigations stemming from 9/11 planning activities in Germany and is a deliberate Saudi attempt to "gull" the West, especially the United States and Europe, into believing that Saudi missionary work is simply benign religious proselytizing that should be tolerated under the West's freedom of religion privileges.

The "Gulling" of America

The process of "gulling" America started when the old king met President Roosevelt in 1945 and the duping process soon involved the major oil producers and nearly the entire oil industry, as well as the United States government and hundreds of international firms desiring to do business in Saudi Arabia. For years, the only information available on Saudi Arabia in the West was provided by ARAMCO. Even the United States government (including the CIA) was dependent on ARAMCO for information and intelligence on the royal family, but ARAMCO rarely criticized their hosts or commented on the emerging dangers of Wahhabism and Islamist fundamentalism or the infiltration of Saudi universities by radical, militant members of the Muslim Brotherhood from Egypt and Syria.

The "gulling" of America, or how the United States has been consistently hoodwinked by its Saudi friends, began many years before, in the early days of the old king, Ibn Saud. As President Roosevelt first learned, the Saudis are fierce anti-Zionists determined to use their strategic oil resource as a weapon against Israel and the West if necessary. That was best exemplified by King Faisal's oil embargo against the West in 1973-74 in retaliation for American last-minute military support of Israel in the 1973 Yom Kippur war.

King Abdullah has tried to maintain reasonably good relations with the United States since 9/11 while faced with growing internal disaffection and terrorist threats at home. But in a veiled threat of a renewed oil embargo during his April 2002 meeting with President Bush in Crawford, Texas, then Crown Prince Abdullah warned that the President should tread carefully in defending Israel. Soon after that visit, George W. Bush became the first American president to announce American support for recognizing an independent Palestinian state. Abdullah has walked a careful tightrope with Wahhabi fundamentalists in the kingdom and Saudi supporters of al Qaeda who have attacked and killed over 200 Saudis, Americans, and other foreigners, even beheading an American employee of the Lockheed Martin Corporation in 2004.

Abdullah survived a serious succession dilemma in 2005 when King Fahd died by accepting his aging and partially paralyzed half brother, Prince Sultan, as the next in line to the throne. As the aging sons of Ibn Saud pass away, resolution of the continuing succession dilemma will soon become a day of reckoning for the kingdom: Will the next generation monarch be a Western-leaning member of the royal family like Prince Bandar and his Western-educated cousins or an ultra-conservative, reactionary Wahhabi-Salafist like one of Bandar's many other cousins? Either alternative could well lead to a fierce internal struggle or civil war, especially if a charismatic, arch-fundamentalist cleric were to emerge, similar to Iran in 1979 when the Shah was deposed, and with the world's oil reserves held in the balance. Or, if the world is fortunate, perhaps an enlightened member of the royal family will emerge from the younger generation of well-educated princes who can transform the country into a modern constitutional monarchy with democratic checks and balances, while preserving traditional Saudi culture and mainstream Islamic values.

While the United States and its allies possess the military capabilities to secure the Saudi oil fields in a crisis, the global war on militant Islamist terrorism would become much more complex and dangerous if the Saudi royal family is overthrown or falls under the control of a conservative Wahhabi cleric or member of the royal family loyal to radical, militant

Islamists. The Saudis created the bin Laden problem by letting radical Egyptian, Syrian and Palestinian members of the Muslim Brotherhood poison their universities and by their consistent behavior in buying influence to gull critics into silence with money.

Meanwhile, many American politicians, retired ambassadors, retired generals, and more recently, academicians, have been placed on the Saudi payroll directly or indirectly, selling their professional credibility by defending the desert kingdom in Washington and European capitals and at prestigious American and European universities. The "gulling" of the academic community, especially Middle East Studies departments in the United States and Europe, is particularly alarming. Just as King Abdul Aziz Ibn Saud first bribed Egyptian academicians at Al-Azhar University in Cairo for their support, many of the most prestigious colleges and universities in the United States and Europe have now also accepted tens of millions of dollars in Saudi endowment funding for international Islamic Centers resulting in loss of academic freedom, objectivity, and independence. In the early 1990s, the Saudis funded a special $20 million gift in honor of President Clinton for an Islamic studies department at the University of Arkansas; $5 million for the University of California at Berkeley; $2.5 million for Harvard University; and more than $30 million to dozens of other prestigious colleges and universities willing to take foreign money and not criticize Saudi Arabia, the ruling royal family, or its form of Islam [Kaplin]. And in December 2005 Harvard and Georgetown each received $20 million gifts from the Saudis, amidst some muted student outcries, but American schools were not the only recipients. Oxford University received a $30 million gift from King Fahd for an Islamic Studies Center and virtually every country in Western Europe has been the beneficiary of Saudi largesse, but with troubling strings attached. The effect of these large Saudi handouts has been to silence critics and buy the support of academicians who routinely denounce Israel and the West and refuse to criticize the Palestinians, Saudi Arabia, or other autocratic Arab states. The result is an unfortunate abdication of long-standing and venerable academic principles, with the following failures of the academy:

- No full-length, objective academic study of Osama bin Laden
- Factual, analytical errors, serious academic mistakes, and intolerance of opposing points of view
- Unwillingness to confront oppression of women and repression in the Arab world
- No objective examination of violent global Jihad and Muslim anti-Semitism
- Obvious extremism, and openly expressed hostility toward the United States and Israel

Millions in direct Saudi government funding were funneled either directly or through Saudi charities for Islamic Centers at major American universities to buy academic influence. Funds from one of the world's wealthiest individuals and more enlightened members of the Saudi royal family, Prince Al Waleed ibn Talal ibn Abdul Aziz, number five on Forbes rich list, have been provided for international centers of Islamic and American studies. Shortly after 9/11, New York Mayor Rudy Giuliani rejected Al Waleed's $10 million donation for his bigoted statements critical of American Middle East policy and Israel as a condition of providing the gift.

The Saudis have been especially adept at assembling and maintaining a large and strong team of paid supporters in the United States and Europe, and were astutely led in Washington, DC for over 20 years by Prince Bandar bin Sultan. But Bandar's ambassadorship bore a striking similarity to that of the son-in-law of the Shah of Iran, Ardeshir Zahedi, who commanded the spotlight of Washington diplomacy for many years before the Shah was overthrown by radical, militant Islamist Shiites in 1979. Like Bandar, Zahedi had nearly unlimited power in Washington and enjoyed full access to the White House, State Department, Congress, and senior levels in the private sector. Zahedi now lives in exile in Switzerland. But even more ominously, the gerontocracy that currently rules Saudi Arabia, and its corrupt and debilitating system of royal patronage, mirrors the aging Soviet Union Politburo leadership in the last days before its collapse in

1991. It is critical for everyone, Saudis and the West alike, to understand if such a medieval system can survive in the 21st century.

DETERIORATING SAUDI-AMERICAN RELATIONS

The United States has paid a substantial price for ignoring Saudi Arabia and the events that have unfolded for over thirty years in the Arab-Muslim world. Not only did Americans pay a heavy price in the increased cost of oil, but they failed to recognize the growth of Islamist fundamentalism and its increasing threat to global peace and prosperity. As that threat increased, Saudi-American relations have remained stable on the surface, but behind that façade is a growing discomfort on both sides. The events of 9/11 marked an end to American acceptance of Saudi gulling, but, as we shall see, the reassessment of future relations was concealed by both sides.

For over 25 years, Saudi Wahhabism has been spread around the world using billions in Saudi wealth coming from its vast oil reserves along the shores of the Persian Gulf in the Eastern Province. While the world's economy has rapidly globalized over the last 25 years and trading nations have become more interdependent, Saudi Arabian Wahhabism has had free rein to use the most modern technology paid for by its oil wealth to spread its hate-filled dogma with little or no competition in the struggle for the heart and soul of Islam.

The first three chapters summarized the origin of this Islamist threat to Western values and its linkage to the monarchy of Saudi Arabia. In the next chapter, the development of American foreign policy following 9/11 and its response to the Saudi challenge is described and evaluated.

CHAPTER FOUR

The Bush Doctrine: Raising the Cost of Terrorism and Providing an Antidote

This chapter discusses Middle East developments in the context of the foreign policy of the United States and Western security arrangements in the post-Cold War era. Many of the early Islamist terrorist attacks in the 1970s and 1980s occurred while the United States was still preoccupied with the Soviet Union and were considered trivial in the context of the Cold War. When the Cold War ended in 1989 with the fall of the Berlin Wall, and Iraq strayed from acceptable limits by invading Kuwait in 1990, the full attention of the United States was finally directed to the Middle East. The U.S. foreign policy standard for dealing with Iraq's breach of acceptable behavior was the Truman Doctrine of containment through collective security alliances developed in the aftermath of World War II.

Following the precepts of the Truman Doctrine in the First Gulf War, President George H. W. Bush organized a vast alliance to counter

THE TRIUMPH OF DEMOCRACY OVER MILITANT ISLAMISM

Iraq's invasion of Kuwait and restore the legitimate government, returning the region to status quo ante bellum as the United States had done so well in following the containment doctrine in its struggle with the Soviet Union. The first President Bush was so successful in pushing Saddam Hussein out of Kuwait in 1991 with his "new world order" alliance that the "Powell Doctrine" of overwhelming force coupled with alliances became standard procedure for military planning and American responses to crises in Haiti, Rwanda, Bosnia, and Kosovo.

During the 43 years the United States followed the Truman Doctrine of communist containment, moral values in diplomacy were undercut by the stark realism of the serious threat posed by the free world's intransigent communist enemy. The United States had become uncomfortably tolerant of totalitarian states, as long as those states were on the American side in the Cold War. It supported many varieties of dictators as long as they were friendly to the United States in the war against communism. When the Cold War finally ended in 1991 with the collapse of the Soviet Union, American support for these dictators also ended and, without implying causality, the number of democracies blossomed throughout the world. In the last half of the 20th century, the number of countries with democratic governance increased from 22 to 120, "an astonishing 63 percent of the people on the planet" [Koh, 147]. The exception to this remarkable growth of democratic governments was the Middle East where, because of the West's dependence on oil, the United States sought stability and was reluctant to advocate democratization or regime change. The price for such advocacy was thought to be too high because the disruption of oil supplies could cause too much turmoil in the West's market economies. America's tolerance for unacceptable behavior was especially true of its relations with Saudi Arabia. But tolerance for despots and America's timidity toward the Middle East would soon be a thing of the past.

The disintegration of the Soviet Union also freed five Muslim nations (former Soviet provinces) in Central Asia from direct Russian control—Azerbaijan, Kyrgyzstan, Tajikistan, Turkmenistan, and Uzbekistan. These nations, with more than 50 million residents, are more than 87 percent Islamic and, because of their location near Afghanistan, would become pivotal in the war against Osama bin Laden as well as also targets for al Qaeda. The end of the Cold War, without a new foreign policy to replace the Truman Doctrine, left these countries out in the cold.

FORMULATING AND INITIATING A NEW FOREIGN POLICY

The violent attacks of September 11th on the Pentagon and the Twin Towers of the World Trade Center meant that the United States desperately needed to redirect its foreign policy toward a new and unconventional enemy in the post-Cold War era. For the first time since the early 19th century, the United States was fighting an undeclared war against religious zealots who were not part of a sovereign state. Truman's containment policy had evolved over nine years after 1939 when George Kennan wrote the first of his two famous memoranda, this one from the Riga outpost in Latvia outlining the threat to the West from the revolutionary nature of the Soviet Union's communist ideology [Yergin]. In President Truman's near-final statement of the containment doctrine in an address before a joint session of Congress on March 17, 1948, the President said:

> We have reached a point at which the position of the United States should be made clear…There are times in world history when it is far wiser to act than to hesitate. There is some risk involved in action—there always is. But there is far more risk in failure to act.

The Extension of Sovereignty

In September 2001, the United States reached another such point in its history, requiring a new formulation of American foreign policy. Only eleven days after the al Qaeda attack, on September 20th,

President Bush's address to another joint session of Congress began that reformulation by stating:

> Our response involves far more than instant retaliation and isolated strikes. Americans should not expect one battle, but a lengthy campaign, unlike any other we have seen. It may include dramatic strikes, visible on TV, and covert operations, secret even in success. We will starve terrorists of funding, turn them one against another, drive them from place to place, until there is no refuge or rest. *And we will pursue nations that provide aid or safe haven to terrorism. Every nation, in every region, now has a decision to make. From this day forward, any nation that continues to harbor or support terrorists will be regarded by the United States as a hostile regime...* [emphasis added]

In one paragraph of a 41-minute speech to a joint session of Congress and the American people less than two weeks after 9/11, President Bush laid out enough new policy, one of redefining the meaning of a nation's sovereignty to encompass nongovernmental actions taken by other parties on or from its sovereign territory, to outline his administration's immediate response to al Qaeda for the remainder of 2001. He also warned Americans that the country's first response would only be the beginning of a "lengthy campaign" in a war that would be like no other the United States had ever waged.

Although most Americans were struck with the rapidity of the Bush administration's response, the new definition of sovereignty, like Truman's policy of containment, had a similar nine-year gestation period. The origins of the new Bush Doctrine had been established in 1992 late in the first President Bush's term in office by Paul Wolfowitz, who had earlier served as head of the State Department policy planning staff during the Reagan administration, the same position George Kennan had held after the Second World War when he inspired the containment policy. Wolfowitz, a University of Chicago Ph.D. in political science and a neo-conservative (one of two or three in the

Bush administration holding a key national security policy position), in many respects had some Kennan-like characteristics. He was an intellectual who never seemed to fit at the top in a cabinet-level position, but who exerted great influence in determining policy for the new Bush administration, serving both Cheney in the Reagan administration and later Rumsfeld as the undersecretary of defense for policy. His 1992 draft Defense Planning Guidance policy paper, which was leaked to the press and withdrawn by the more cautious first President Bush, stated:

> '...that in dealing with this [the spread of weapons of mass destruction] threat, America should not rely upon the strategies of deterrence and containment that had worked against the Soviet Union but should contemplate the possibility of offensive military action. There might be a need,' the draft statement said, for 'preempting an impending action with nuclear, chemical or biological weapons' [Mann, 200].

The new principle of preemption would have to gestate for a year following 9/11, but the redefinition of a nation's sovereignty was needed to cope with al Qaeda's lack of sovereignty and the logical difficulty of incorporating such a stateless group into the framework of international jurisprudence, and the new shape of a world in which the United States was the sole superpower. Bush's answer was straightforward and revolutionary. Wherever al Qaeda existed or received support, that community had to be a part of some sovereign state and he proposed to hold that nation responsible for "harboring and supporting" a terrorist group that was violating all reasonable sanctions of international law.

Therefore, the United States would, henceforth, hold all such nations as being hostile to its legitimate interests and subject to retribution for al Qaeda's crimes against humanity. He offered all nations a choice of whether to support al Qaeda and become an enemy of the United States or join America and be an ally in the war that had been declared on the United States and Western civilization. America's defense would no longer be bound solely by collective security arrangements, or actions of the United Nations Security Council. The United States was now strong enough and sufficiently committed to act unilaterally and intended to do everything possible to safeguard its national security. The term "unilateral," unthinkable in the legacy of Franklin Delano Roosevelt and Harry Truman, was now an applicable description of America's new foreign policy, as would become clearer in Bush's subsequent addresses that unfolded the Bush Doctrine.

Application in Afghanistan—A Learning Experience
Not only did President Bush quickly enunciate a major plank in his foreign policy, but the United States brought the full force of American power against those responsible for the September 11th attack by launching an invasion of the al Qaeda headquarters in Afghanistan less than one month later on October 7, 2001. The timetable was quite remarkable in light of the remoteness of Afghanistan, the lack of access treaties with the six surrounding countries (Iran, Turkmenistan, Uzbekistan, Tajikistan, Pakistan and China), and the lack of any prior military planning to establish satisfactory arrangements with these nations to deploy sufficient military personnel, supplies and equipment. And in addition to diplomacy and planning, there was also the sheer physical difficulty of moving the manpower, munitions, and supplies far away into the rugged mountains of remote Afghanistan.

By coincidence, the head of the Pakistani Inter-Services Intelligence agency, General Mahmoud Ahmad, happened to be in Washington on 9/11. The next day Richard Armitage, the burly American undersecretary of state and colleague of Secretary Powell, called General Ahmad to his office to lay out the administration's needs with the admonition: "History starts today," followed by, "Are you with us or against us?" [Mann, 298-9]. Ahmad wired the American requirements outlined by Armitage to President Musharraf who agreed to:

(1) a secret American presence on its side of the Afghan border but no U.S. troops were officially allowed to be stationed within its borders;
(2) U.S. planes could use Pakistani airspace but not its air bases, except for emergencies; and
(3) the Pakistani military would increase border patrols to reduce al Qaeda escape avenues into Pakistan, but with no promises to capture and turn over would-be escapees.

Indeed, Musharraf went so far as to request that the United States not invade Afghanistan and instead tried to negotiate with the Taliban regime to turn over Osama bin Laden, but to whom was never made clear [Friedman, 185-6]. Needless to say, Musharraf's negotiations proved fruitless, and Americans moved into Afghanistan in late September 2001.

Because three of the nations adjacent to Afghanistan (Turkmenistan, Uzbekistan and Tajikistan) were former members of the Soviet Union and Muslim states, the first set of access negotiations had to be with Russia, which still considered these nations part of its sphere of influence. Armitage flew to Moscow the week after 9/11 to seek Russian assistance from Prime Minister Putin. By September 22nd the Russians agreed to help the United States in exchange for American agreement to eliminate public criticism of Russian actions in Chechnya and provide assistance in stopping arms smuggling to the Chechen rebels through Georgia where the U.S. had substantial influence. Bases in Uzbekistan and Tajikistan were thus made available to American forces and, for the first time, men and materials began moving into Central Asia. Covert American agents, veterans of the Afghan-Russian war 20 years earlier, were dropped into northern Afghanistan as quickly as possible with $70 million in hundred dollar bills to buy loyalty among the anti-Taliban mujahadeen forces and an instant American-supported Afghan army was formed, paid for, and deployed.

Another set of highly sensitive negotiations began in late September with Iran. The British Foreign Minister Jack Straw traveled to Tehran to begin discussions about cooperation with the Afghan invasion. The British had been on board in the Afghan operation from the beginning [Woodward, 2003] and maintained a long history of working closely with the U.S. in the Persian Gulf region since the First Gulf War; it was American and British fliers that enforced the "no fly" provisions of the U.N. resolutions to protect the Kurds and the Shiites in Iraq. In addition, direct discussions between the United States and Iran took place secretly in Geneva under a multi-nation umbrella. Iran agreed to cooperate with American efforts to topple the Taliban and agreed to close its border against escaping al Qaeda members in exchange for America's guarantee of the rights of the Shiite population in Afghanistan in a new Afghan government.

After the United States issued an ultimatum to the Taliban government to surrender bin Laden and his fellow terrorists and to close down al Qaeda's training camps, or suffer the consequences, the U.S. initiated a softening-up bombing operation of the few known targets in Afghanistan and announced the support of Great Britain and Australia in its military campaign to overthrow the Taliban regime. The United States received other offers of military assistance from several European nations, including France, but with the type of operation the U.S. was planning in Afghanistan, other forces would have been a distraction, as they had been in Bosnia with combined NATO operations.

America's experience with covert support for Afghan guerrillas in the earlier anti-Soviet campaign meant that its CIA covert agents and Special Forces personnel were well-informed about the Afghan groups that would oppose the Taliban government. The veterans of the previous operation were in Afghanistan a week before the commencement of bombing on October 7, 2001. Those few Americans served as forward air controllers—on-the-ground spotters—for America's high tech, close air support that was launched by the Air Force from Uzbekistan and Tajikistan and from Navy planes off carriers in the Indian Ocean in support of native Afghan opposition against al Qaeda and Taliban forces. The forward air controllers, in combination with the pinpoint accuracy of American air-launched guided weapons, were deadly as the terrorist forces were drawn into combat in the countryside, where the Afghans had earlier defeated the Soviets. This time it was the al Qaeda-Taliban forces that were picked to pieces by precision attacks called in by American forward air controllers armed with laser designators and riding horseback in the Afghan mountains.

Bin Laden had hoped that the 9/11 attack against the United States homeland would lure American forces into a quagmire in Afghanistan where he believed his al Qaeda forces could rout them using the same tactics that had been so successful against the Soviets. Instead, it was the Taliban and al Qaeda forces who failed to learn from those experiences while the United States took advantage of the lessons of the earlier war. With a minimum of American troops, the U.S.-supported forces routed the Taliban government by the end of November 2001 and seized all of the major Afghan cities by December 7th, less than three months after the initial al Qaeda attack on the United States mainland. Although Osama bin Laden escaped, presumably into northwest Pakistan, retribution had been swift indeed, and the first safe haven for his terrorist organization was neutralized. The breathless pursuit of al Qaeda that President Bush had promised on September 20th had started with blitzkrieg-like success.

The United States had learned in pursuing al Qaeda that it could lean on its allies and even nations such as Iran, which initially were considered in the enemy camp, to obtain assistance as long as it was willing to listen to the concerns of other countries to negotiate a satisfactory response. The United States also learned that it had been mistaken to assume that it could simply hunt down terrorists in a nation without assuming some responsibility for restoring order to the chaos its military operations would create in the process. Colin Powell's admonition in the run-up to the Iraq war, "...if you break it, you own it and must fix it," did not require the destruction of a so-called enemy state for the United States to recognize its obligation. The United States had a long record of rebuilding countries, like Germany and other European countries, Japan, and Korea, even when the destruction did not come directly from U.S. actions. Furthermore, restoring order could achieve America's ancillary goal of democratizing poorly governed, autocratic Muslim nations. Indeed, the latter lesson became a fundamental objective in Bush's new American foreign policy. No more "status quo ante bellum" as a basic principle in America's new military intervention policy; future military operations would have to do much more than simply win military battles—they must win the war, which meant restoring order, rebuilding damaged infrastructure, and providing the structures needed for democratic reform.

The United States also learned that the United Nations, even with all of its problems from dysfunction to corruption, had an important role to play in organizing and giving credibility to a new Afghan government. The United States asked for and received U.N. assistance in organizing an interim Afghan government and elections for a permanent government. A U.N. team worked through the fall of 2001 in identifying and choosing representatives from the various Afghan ethnic and tribal groups for a December conference in Bonn, Germany to elect an interim authority until U.N. organized elections could be held in October of 2004. In Bonn, Hamid Karzai was chosen by the delegates as the interim leader. Karzai was a tribal leader of the Pashtuns, the largest ethnic group in the country, which controlled the southern and eastern portions of Afghanistan and overlapped into western Pakistan. Pashtu is spoken by about half of the Afghans, who are 99 percent Sunni Muslims. Karzai, over the objections of the Pakistani intelligence service, had effectively led a small Pashtun fighting force against the Taliban that successfully negotiated the surrender of towns around Kandahar, the last major city held by the Taliban until December 7, 2001. Karzai had demonstrated his leadership qualities and was the choice of the Americans to lead the new republic [Friedman, 182-8]. The conference sponsored by the United Nations legitimatized their choice and NATO organized 6,000 troops for the International Security Assistance Force initially staffed with general officers from Germany, The Netherlands, and Turkey to provide security in the capital, Kabul. The war in Afghanistan had progressed extremely well, and the prospects for a successful peace process for this ancient, war-torn country were excellent. By early 2006

NATO had expanded its role and added additional troops under an overall NATO command for Afghanistan, allowing a small reduction in American troop levels.

COMPLETING THE BUSH DOCTRINE AND CONTINUING THE PURSUIT

After 9/11, both the President and his constituency believed that, for a former governor with little foreign policy experience, George W. Bush had stepped into the role of commander-in-chief under wartime conditions smoothly and with few missteps. Candidate Bush had no previous foreign policy experience but surrounded himself with smart, experienced people, and studied hard to prepare himself in foreign affairs. He made it clear during the 2000 election campaign that Colin Powell would be his choice for secretary of state and he employed a group of highly experienced advisors during the campaign called the Vulcans, as detailed by Daalder and Lindsay [22-34]. Eight Vulcans consisted of three advisors who would play prominent roles in his foreign policy team:

- **Condoleezza Rice**, former provost at Stanford University, expert on Russia in the first Bush administration, became Director of National Security.
- **Paul Wolfowitz**, dean of the Johns Hopkins School of Advanced International Studies, former foreign policy advisor in the Nixon, Ford, Carter, Reagan, and first Bush administrations, became Undersecretary of Defense for Policy.
- **Richard Armitage**, assistant secretary of defense in the Reagan administration, became senior Undersecretary of State.

The other five members were: Robert Blackwell, Stephen Hadley, Dov Zakheim, Robert Zoellick, and Richard Perle. Of this group of eight, only Wolfowitz, now a Republican, and Perle, still a Democrat, were card-carrying neo-conservatives, but all eight advisers were generally acceptable to neo-conservatives, a political movement that claimed members from both American political parties.

As Mann's book [251-2] indicates, both the presidential candidate and his cadre of advisers took seriously the responsibility of educating George W. Bush in the fundamentals and intricacies of American foreign policy, and these advisers contributed significantly to the development of America's new foreign policy in the first administration of George W. Bush.

Expanding the Definition of Hostile Action

With the initial success invading Afghanistan and ousting the Taliban government, President Bush continued public exposition of a new foreign policy in his State of the Union address on January 29, 2002. This speech became known as his "axis-of-evil" speech for the following paragraphs:

> Our second goal is to prevent regimes that sponsor terror from threatening America or our friends and allies with weapons of mass destruction. Some of these regimes have been pretty quiet since September the 11th. But we know their true nature. North Korea is a regime arming with missiles and weapons of mass destruction, while starving its citizens.
>
> Iran aggressively pursues these weapons and exports terror, while an unelected few repress the Iranian people's hope for freedom.
>
> Iraq continues to flaunt its hostility toward America and to support terror. The Iraq regime has plotted to develop anthrax, and nerve gas, and nuclear weapons for over a decade. This is a regime that has already used poison gas to murder thousands of its own citizens—leaving bodies of mothers huddled over their dead children. This is a regime that has something to hide from the civilized world.
>
> States like these, and their terrorist allies, constitute an *axis of evil*, arming to threaten the peace of the world. By

seeking weapons of mass destruction, these regimes pose a grave threat and a grave danger. They could provide these arms to terrorists, giving them the means to match their hatred. They could attack allies or attempt to blackmail the United States. In any of these cases, the price of indifference would be catastrophic.

We will work closely with our coalition to deny terrorists and state sponsors the materials, technology, and expertise to make and deliver weapons of mass destruction. We will develop and deploy effective missile defense to protect America and our allies from sudden attack. *And all nations should know: America will do whatever is necessary to ensure our nation's security.* [emphasis added]

The definition of aiding and supporting terrorists had been extended to include the provision of weapons of mass destruction to terrorist organizations. This speech was accompanied by some frank discussions, directly or indirectly, with these and other countries possessing weapons of mass destruction, especially nuclear weapons. The most significant change in moving from the Cold War to the war on terror was to void the fundamental defensive strategy of mutual deterrence. In the Cold War, each side believed the other was rational and would not attack, knowing that it would be destroyed in a counterattack. However, such a strategy would not work against religious zealots who believe that death in battle against infidels leads to martyrdom. Islamist militants willing and eager to die killing infidels are immune to such deterrence theory. Thus, it was necessary to warn countries possessing nuclear weapons that the new U.S. foreign policy meant that the United States would hold those nations responsible for ensuring that nuclear weapons would not fall into the hands of religious extremists. The list of enemy nations was expanded to include North Korea, as well as Muslim nations with actual or potential nuclear capabilities and who were currently accommodating Islamist militants, excluding, of course, America's special Muslim ally, Pakistan.

As Pakistan would learn shortly, the last line of the "axis-of-evil" speech was addressed to all nations, friend and foe alike. The United States, in the future, "will do whatever is necessary to ensure our nation's security." That passage suggested that the United States of America, the world's only superpower, would act unilaterally whenever its security is threatened or whenever it believes that its security is threatened. The passage only referred to one collective security organization, an ambiguous and undefined "America's coalition;" it did not refer to the United Nations, NATO, or the host of other mutual security pacts that the United States created during the many decades of the Cold War. Only the United States at the start of the 21st century had sufficient military might to make such a provocative and unilateral declaration.

Nevertheless, the world's reaction to the speech centered on the "axis-of-evil" metaphor and the implication of good versus evil morality judgments that were the operational elements of the new American foreign policy. Most of America's allies did not criticize the United States for declaring that it was prepared to act unilaterally in its own defense until later, when it did so by invading Iraq without a clear U.N. Security Council mandate. Perhaps President Bush's well-deserved reputation for being plain spoken and ineloquent gave him some cover, but those who listened carefully to his major addresses and studied the written words learned that the President's plain speaking conveyed precisely what he meant.

Application to "Allied" Enemy Governments

The lesson of studying what Bush said was made clear to two of the three nations in the world (the other being the United Arab Emirates) that had recognized the former Taliban Afghan government: Pakistan and Saudi Arabia, both presumed allies of the United States. American efforts in the war on terror throughout December of 2001 and much of 2002 were directed quietly toward these two "friendly" countries. Diplomatic pressures bordering on extortion were forcefully exerted on Pakistan. It had also become increasingly clear that the Saudis had likely funded the nuclear weapons programs of Pakistan and Iraq to the tune of $7 billion and that Pakistan had also sold its nuclear weapon technology to North Korea, Iran and Libya with further proliferation coming from North Korea and China. Pakistan's nuclear weapons are directed at India but are capable of reaching virtually any target in the Middle East, and both Iran and Saudi Arabia have shown interest in pursuing independent nuclear capabilities, ostensibly to counter Israel as well as each other. America's most immediate concern was that Pakistan's nuclear weapons, the most mature nuclear program in the Muslim world, might fall into al Qaeda hands, especially because many Pakistanis were sympathetic to al Qaeda, including senior members of the military. Americans knew that the government of President Musharraf did not have complete control of the nation's intelligence service and Saudi Wahhabi missionaries were active in the country, especially in remote and inaccessible areas along the Afghanistan border.

To make matters worse, for the past three decades American intelligence agents had been clandestinely following Dr. A.Q. Khan, the architect of the Pakistani nuclear weapons program, in his travels throughout the world, even reportedly protecting him from arrest by Dutch investigators [Broad and Sanger]. American agents naively thought that Khan was under control as a result of their surveillance, but the real effects of Khan's efforts to develop an international black market in secret nuclear weapons is still unfolding, though it was known he had started selling secrets to Iran as early as the late 1980s. What the CIA did not know until very recently is that Khan had obtained a small bomb design from the Chinese in the early 1980s that became the prototype for Pakistan's bomb, which could be launched with the smaller missiles Pakistan already had in its arsenal. The May 1998 atomic testing chess match between India and Pakistan, when Pakistan exploded five separate nuclear devices in a single day, much to the dismay of the world, had taken the CIA completely by surprise.

To avoid future surprises, George Friedman [211-230] reported that Pakistan, Russia, and Iran were notified that the Bush administration's new U.S. policy of preemption had a special application for nuclear weapons: in the absence of any alternative solution, the United States would in the future consider employment of nuclear weapons to destroy unsecured nuclear storage sites. Again, according to Friedman, Russia cooperated fully in making its nuclear facilities available for U.S. inspection, and Pakistan, which in early 2002 was facing a diplomatic crisis with India, now found itself confronted by two nuclear threats—India and the United States. Faced with possible catastrophe, Pakistan gave in. Musharraf permitted U.S. inspectors from the military and CIA to deploy scientists in all Pakistani nuclear facilities. The documents and records in these facilities led to the conclusion that certain Pakistani scientists, in addition to Kahn, and certain intelligence service agents had to be purged from their respective weapons programs for permitting leaks of classified nuclear secrets. After securing the Pakistan nuclear weapons program, the United States then successfully mediated the dispute between Pakistan and India.

The Saudis could not be coerced or managed in this way, but they too had to be dealt with to stop the flow of Saudi funds and other material support to al Qaeda and to obtain information on al Qaeda cells throughout the world. There were other problems, such as: (1) Saudi failure to cooperate with American investigators of the al Khobar bombing; (2) the unexpected firing right after 9/11 of the seemingly cooperative head of Saudi intelligence, Prince Turki al Faisal, who had been the CIA's primary source of information about the Saudis and al Qaeda's network in Saudi society; (3) the January 2002 Saudi demand to remove U.S. forces from the country; and (4) Saudi failure to provide requested information about financial contributions to al Qaeda. The Saudi demand that U.S. forces leave the country was handled expeditiously by moving the U.S. Air Force Air Control Center at the al Kharj Prince Sultan Air Base to Central Command's new headquarters in Doha, Qatar on the Persian Gulf. In response to these "unfriendly" Saudi initiatives, U.S. Special Forces arranged to conduct training exercises in Yemen, just south of the Saudi border where al Qaeda had some training camps. The U.S. military, with naval forces in the Persian Gulf, Indian Ocean, and Red Sea and ground troops in

Yemen, Oman, Qatar, Bahrain, and Kuwait and a friendly government in Jordan had virtually surrounded Saudi Arabia. The exception was Iraq.

Feeling U.S. pressure, the Saudis launched an ambitious public relations program, blaming Jewish neo-conservatives in the Defense Department for the worsening problems in the long-standing U.S.-Saudi relationship. Saudi statements threatened the cessation of all U.S. negotiations until a satisfactory peace agreement between Israel and Palestine could be reached. Even though the Saudis had never before made such an overture, Saudi Crown Prince Abdullah, through an interview with Tom Friedman of *The New York Times*, proposed an unprecedented Saudi peace plan for the Palestine-Israeli dispute. This campaign was the final straw in convincing the U.S. government that the usual Saudi gulling tactics were simply a delaying technique to avoid responding to its request for cooperation against al Qaeda. The Saudis had to be squeezed and convinced that the United States was a greater danger to the Saudi kingdom than al Qaeda. George Friedman [233] argued that:

> The United States realized it could defeat Al Qaeda only by taking its bases of support—financial, logistical, and personnel systems. That meant that the U.S. had to hit the arteries—had to deal with Saudi Arabia ... Al Qaeda was, in fundamental ways, a Saudi phenomenon. Its leaders and members were Saudis, its ideology was Wahhabi, and its financing drew on Saudi citizens.

In truth, the Saudis, like bin Laden and most in the Muslim world, did not respect the military power of the United States. They had observed, as had bin Laden, the American retreat in the face of successive terrorist attacks and came to the same conclusion that the United States was unable, politically, to fight seriously in extended conflicts, especially in the Middle East. America's success in ousting the Taliban in Afghanistan was also seen as incomplete and America's staying power was questioned.

America's Dilemma

Thus far, the United States had instinctively responded to the 9/11 attack by first "stopping the bleeding" through immediately beefing up homeland security and launching a longer-term investigation into 9/11; second, "stopping the enemy from making another strike" through the disruption of its command and control center in Afghanistan; and, third, "stopping the flow of funds to the enemy terrorist organization" through the elimination of financial support. America's dilemma arose at the third step: it knew who had been supporting al Qaeda and how the support had been channeled through Saudi Arabian charities and direct contributions of wealthy Saudi citizens, but it could not get the Saudis to admit knowledge of these financial arrangements or to provide U.S. intelligence with other information about al Qaeda. What could the United States do in response to Saudi stonewalling? Here is a list, not in necessarily in priority order, of possible U.S. policy options available in late 2001 and early 2002:

1. Do nothing more and declare victory while continuing to monitor al Qaeda operations in Pakistan and the flow of funds from Saudi Arabia to al Qaeda.
2. Devote a significant effort to safeguarding existing supplies of weapons of mass destruction (WMD) held by countries outside the direct American sphere of influence to ensure that these weapons did not fall into al Qaeda's hands.
3. A multilateral peace option—coupled with options #1 and 2, a major diplomatic effort to negotiate a peace agreement between the Israelis and Palestinians.
4. Pursue Osama bin Laden into Pakistan, despite Pakistani unwillingness to permit U.S. forces to enter its sovereign territory and thus risk war with Pakistan, an inherently unstable Muslim government with nuclear weapons.
5. Invade Saudi Arabia to stop further financial support to al Qaeda and safeguard Saudi oil fields from al Qaeda.
6. Invade Iraq and depose Saddam Hussein, partially in

recognition of the validity of al Qaeda's charge made against the United States for its past support of totalitarian Muslim states, to eliminate Iraq's presumed WMD arsenal, and to demonstrate to terrorists that America was no paper tiger.

But, to chose among the options, the Bush administration first needed to complete the development of its foreign policy. The containment policy of the Cold War was no longer an appropriate basis for evaluating the likely alternatives available to United States in December of 2001. Consequently, before the President could decide further action in the war on terror, the reformulation of American foreign policy had to be completed.

Putting the New Bush Doctrine Together
Of the goals outlined as immediate American responses following the 9/11 attack, two of the three goals had been accomplished—the bleeding had been stopped with a beefed up homeland security program and an investigation into 9/11 had commenced. Moreover, the enemy had been prevented from launching another strike against the United States. The American invasion of Afghanistan had totally disrupted the al Qaeda command and control system and diplomatic initiatives launched against Pakistan, Iran, and Russia minimized the danger of weapons of mass destruction falling into al Qaeda's hands. However, the third goal of stopping the flow of funds to al Qaeda had not been accomplished due to Saudi Arabia's defiance and recalcitrance.

The United States had gone as far it could in carrying out the war on terror without reformulating its foreign policy to select from among the alternatives for continuing the war on terror. The development of a new foreign policy had started and through a series of iterations would be completed about a year after 9/11.

On June 1, 2002, speaking at the graduation exercises at the United States Military Academy at West Point, President Bush defended the most controversial portion of his State of the Union Address, the role of moral judgments in America's foreign policy. After reiterating the many dangers and uncertainties of the war on terror, especially his concern about weapons of mass destruction, he broke new ground by saying:

> Because the war on terror will require resolve and patience, it will also require firm moral purpose. In this way our struggle is similar to the Cold War. Now, as then, our enemies are totalitarians, holding a creed of power with no place for human dignity. Now, as then, they seek to impose joyless conformity, to control everyone and all of life.
> America confronted imperial communism in many different ways—diplomatic, economic, and military. Yet moral clarity was essential to our victory in the Cold War. When leaders like John F. Kennedy and Ronald Reagan refused to gloss over brutality of tyrants, they gave hope to prisoners and dissidents and exiles, and rallied free nations to a great cause.
> Some worry that it is somehow undiplomatic or impolite to speak the language of right and wrong. I disagree. Different circumstances require different methods, but not different moralities. Moral truth is the same in every culture, in every time, and in every place. Targeting innocent civilians for murder is always and everywhere wrong. There can be no neutrality between justice and cruelty, between the innocent and the guilty. We are in a conflict between good and evil, and America will call evil by its name. By confronting evil and lawless regimes, we do not create a problem, we reveal a problem. And we will lead the world in opposing it.

President Bush's three policy statements, in little more than 250 days, contained hints of all of the major principles and premises of the new Bush Doctrine. For those who still had not gotten the message, the National Security Council, with President George W. Bush's letter of transmittal, issued a clearly worded 20-page document to the world on September 17, 2002, entitled "The National Security Strategy of the United States of America," that fully summarized President Bush's new foreign policy. Bush's transmittal letter laid out the basic premises, first explaining that the United States "enjoys a position of unparalleled military strength and great economic and political influence...we do not use our strength to press for unilateral advantage." That is, the United States proclaimed that it had world hegemony, predominant influence over the entire world, which it will not utilize for national gain. Second, the United States would, however, use that power and influence to defeat:

> ...shadowy networks of individuals [that] can bring great chaos and suffering to our shores for less cost than it costs to purchase a tank... To defeat this threat we must make use of every tool in our arsenal—military power, better homeland defenses, law enforcement, intelligence, and vigorous efforts to cut off financing... We defend America and our friends by hoping for the best. So we must be prepared to defeat our enemies' plans, using the best intelligence and proceeding with deliberation. History will judge harshly those who saw this danger coming but failed to act. In the new world we have entered the only path to peace and security is the path of action. [That action, the strategy went on to explain, will be taken,] "by constantly striv[ing] to enlist the support of the international community, [but] *we will not hesitate to **act alone**, if necessary, to exercise our right of self defense by **acting preemptively** against terrorists, to prevent them from doing harm against our people and country*" [emphasis added].

That is, the United States in the war on terror will act both preemptively and unilaterally. The world had not seen such a declaration in the 20th century with its configuration of multi-powers fighting to maintain a balance of power among shifting coalitions. Only a nation with hegemony over the world in the new post-Cold War era could issue such a stark declaration.

Although the new U.S. National Security Strategy used the term "preemptive war," the Bush administration's incursion into Iraq was really a preventive war, as Gaddis [2005] makes clear. He defines preemption as "taking military action against a state that was about to launch an attack;" whereas prevention means "starting a war against a state that might, at some future point, pose such risks." It is the immediacy of the adverse action that differentiates preventive war from preemption. Iraq did not represent an immediate challenge, but it certainly could have been a threat in the future as it slipped out from under the U.N.-sanctioned disarmament controls.

Both the 1992 document, when first suggested by Paul Wolfowitz, and 10 years later in 2002 when enunciated by President Bush as America's new foreign policy, seemed at first to be out of line with America's heritage. However, as John Lewis Gaddis [2004] noted, John Quincy Adams, perhaps the greatest American secretary of state, who served from 1817 to 1824, developed a foreign policy based on three principles: (1) preemption, (2) unilateralism and (3) American hegemony over the Western Hemisphere, as stated in the Monroe Doctrine. Adams' foreign policy served as the basis of America's foreign relations until President McKinley added an imperialistic dimension that gained prominence at the end of the 19th century. Bush's foreign policy in the first year of the war on terror argued for acceptance of American world hegemony based on American military and economic superiority. Adams' more narrowly defined hemispheric hegemony, without military strength, was dependent solely on Great Britain's willingness to employ its navy against other European powers who periodically threatened nations in the hemisphere, especially during the Civil War. Bush's 21st century foreign policy was not so different, reflecting America's extensive growth in military, economic, and diplomatic power in the 185 years since Adams became secretary of state.

In 2002 the United States was the world's only superpower and its urgent need to aggressively fight the war on terror had made it act accordingly. The Bush Doctrine did one other thing that Adams could not have imagined in the 1820s when the United States was only one of three nations in the world that democratically elected its government. Bush's policy included the promotion of freedom and democracy as a key element of American foreign policy by promising that the United States would:

> (1) Speak out honestly about violations of the nonnegotiable demands of human dignity using our voice and vote in international institutions to advance freedom.
> (2) Use foreign aid to promote freedom and support those who struggle nonviolently for it, ensuring that nations moving toward democracy are rewarded (in proportion) to the steps they take.
> (3) Make freedom and the development of democratic institutions key themes in our bilateral relations, seeking solidarity and cooperation from other democracies while we press governments that deny human rights to move toward a better future.
> (4) Take special efforts to promote freedom of religion and conscience and defend it from encroachment by repressive governments.

None of these programs sound too bold or threatening to undemocratic states, but when grander language was employed by the President is his Second Inaugural Address to describe these programs and efforts as "ending tyranny in our world," critics were frightened into believing that the United States would henceforth embark upon an aggressive foreign policy that would threaten all totalitarian states. Comparing the Bush Doctrine with the Truman Doctrine in which a country's attitude toward communism was central to America's diplomatic relations with that country is to suggest that now the democratic behavior of a country would be a controlling factor in U.S. relations toward it.

No other president since Woodrow Wilson had ever proposed to employ a strategy of democratization as a central plank in America's national security policy. Franklin Delano Roosevelt worked pragmatically to create democratic institutions in the post-Second World War era, which he did not live to see, but his vision was much more guarded than the optimistic and sweeping view President Bush took as a result of the growth of democratic countries in the second half of the 20th century. It certainly represented a completely different approach than the Cold War when the United States rigorously denied any appetite to liberate oppressed peoples in Iron Curtain countries and failed to support popular uprisings as in the Hungarian revolt of 1956.

Even Roosevelt's more limited support for democratization was lost during the Cold War as the United States entered into a myriad of security and economic relationships with authoritarian governments opposing the interests of the Soviet Union. Paradoxically, it was American support for the autocratic government in Saudi Arabia that was one of the principal reasons that prompted Osama bin Laden to launch his terrorist attacks against the United States. With the new Bush Doctrine, it appeared that bin Laden and the United States shared the goal of overthrowing or modifying the behavior of the Saudi monarchy, but differed on what type of government should replace it. The United States, in the context of the Bush Doctrine, saw the theocracy that bin Laden proposed for the Arabian Peninsula as even more tyrannical than the Saudi autocracy, which Americans hope can evolve into a 21st century constitutional monarchy.

As we shall see later in discussing the conduct of Bush's foreign policy, how the Bush Doctrine is characterized does affect judgments that are made about America's actions. Gaddis found precedents for the principles of the new Bush Doctrine in prior American policies of Secretary of State John Quincy Adams and President Woodrow Wilson. The United States carefully outlined the conditions in which it would act preemptively, but what about the rights of other states, when in their own self-interest, they attempt to preemptively take action against other states? Is there a hierarchy of nations that allows only the more powerful or most democratic to have and to employ this right? The Bush Doctrine is silent on this issue, implying that only a nation holding world hegemony has such a power.

Gaddis' world hegemony, unilateralism, and preemptivism are three principles that follow from Bush's determination to make America's new foreign policy proactive, not reactive, and to exercise the rights of the world's only superpower to take all necessary actions to protect America's security. Indeed, one can argue that it is the unique and predominant position of the United States in the world that makes it the number one target of Islamist militants in their battle to gain prominence in the Islamic world. Consequently, the United States must employ all of its resources, including its pre-eminence, to defend itself and its citizens from the irrational and potentially devastating attacks of Islamist militants dedicated to destroying Western civilization. Thus, America's status as the number one target for extremists justifies its exclusive right to preemption or prevention. Later, in his Second Inaugural Address, President Bush made this abundantly clear when he declared to the world:

> We have seen our vulnerability—and we have seen its deepest source. For as long as whole regions of the world simmer in resentment and tyranny—prone to ideologies that feed hatred and excuse murder—violence will gather, and multiply in destructive power, and cross the most defended borders, and raise a moral threat. *There is only one force of history that can break the reign of hatred and resentment, and expose the pretensions of tyrants, and reward the hopes of the decent and tolerant, and that is the force of human freedom.* [emphasis added]

Gaddis' model lists only three basic principles for Bush's policy, but here we have added democratization as the fourth factor because that is Bush's antidote to bin Laden's tyrannical terrorism. It seems clear that the National Security Strategy of the United States suggests that the Bush administration believes that Wilsonian democracy offers the only possible means of rectifying bin Laden's one legitimate complaint of injustice and autocratic rule in much of the Muslim world. Moreover, the new Bush Doctrine reinforced the fundamental point that the only credible, long-term antidote for nihilistic Bin Ladenism is freedom and democracy.

In summary, Gaddis' interpretation of the Bush Doctrine, with his three principles of world hegemony, unilateralism and the right to pre-emptive action, together with the addition of freedom and democratization as the antidote to Middle East autocracy, is a reasonable model for explaining America's new foreign policy. The Saudis and other critics of the Bush Doctrine are wrong to characterize and discredit the policies as the product of narrow Jewish neo-conservatives—Wolfowitz may have been the principal architect going back to 1992, but the resulting doctrine reflected much broader thinking than just neo-conservatism philosophy.

Republican foreign policy had supported democratization for nearly 20 years with Reagan's 1985 support of dissident Corazon Aquino for the ouster of Ferdinand Marcos, the long-time Philippine dictator. The major role for democratization in the foreign policy of a Republican president was a complete reversal of the party's support for friendly dictators. This revolution in thinking occurred, not as a result of neo-conservatism as Halper and Clarke allege, but of a pragmatic secretary of state, George Shultz, who finally convinced Reagan that "by clinging to Marcos's dictatorship…the United States might strengthen the insurgency against his regime and thus open the way for a Communist victory in the Philippines" [Mann, 133]. Significantly, the two American emissaries to the Philippines who were involved in carrying out Shultz's new initiative were Paul Wolfowitz and Richard Armitage.

James Mann [329] concurred with two of the four Gaddis principles, omitting unilateralism and adding the Wilsonian ideal of employing democratization as central to America's national security. Three policy analysts expressed similar terms in describing the revolutionary nature of the new policy. Mann described it as "breathtaking," while Gaddis found it "breathtakingly simple" and yet paradoxically "grand," and Podhoretz, a chief spokesman for neoconservatives, was ecstatic in praising the doctrine as an extension to a new set of dangers of the Kennan vision of the United States, "the responsibilities of moral and political leadership that history plainly intended us to bear" [Podhoretz, 2004].

Despite their praise, all three agreed that the final judgment on the ultimate success of the Bush Doctrine would have to wait for evidence to unfold in the brittle and languid domain of the "axis of oil"—the Middle East, where oil and democracy have rarely mixed.

IMPLEMENTATION OF THE BUSH DOCTRINE

Although the process for designing an American response to al Qaeda's 9/11 attack suggested the development of a new foreign policy for selecting among a set of equally unattractive alternatives as the next step or steps in fighting the war on terror, in actual practice the process proceeded in parallel. President Bush very much favored an aggressive strategy that would keep the United States and its allies on the offensive, preferring the war option over the peace or multilateral options.

We believe that the president's offensive strategy was largely driven by his overriding concern that U.S. homeland security would probably always be inadequate to the job of protecting American citizens from the myriad of possible new al Qaeda attacks. As a consequence, the President emphasized a strong offense as the best defense against further homeland attacks and dismissed the less aggressive options, such as declaring victory and doing nothing, or only pursuing bin Laden into Pakistan. Instead, he focused on safeguarding weapons of mass destruction held by countries outside the American sphere of influence and on direct and influential military action in the Middle East. By choosing to continue on the offense, President Bush rejected the option of doing nothing more after Afghanistan and simply declaring victory, which would have been the safest political choice for a president facing re-election in two years.

Shortly before the release of the full statement of the Bush Doctrine on

THE TRIUMPH OF DEMOCRACY OVER MILITANT ISLAMISM

September 20, 2002, President Bush addressed the United Nations General Assembly on September 12th to appeal to the international organization to enforce its own resolutions concerning Iraq's disregard of the conditions of the 1991 Gulf War cease-fire. The President argued that:

> The conduct of the Iraqi regime is a threat to the authority of the United Nations and a threat to peace. Iraq has answered a decade of U.N. demands with a decade of defiance. All the world now faces a test, the United Nations a difficult and defining moment. Are the Security Council resolutions to be honored and enforced, or cast aside without consequence? Will the United Nations serve the purpose of its founding, or will it be irrelevant?

Even though Bush had asked Secretary Rumsfeld about American invasion plans for Iraq as early as November 21, 2001, it was not until the week after Bush's State of the Union address in January 2002 that Secretary Rumsfeld was asked formally by the President to begin preparing plans for the invasion of Iraq. Even before the full statement of the Bush Doctrine had been formalized, the United States was proceeding to develop a plan to implement the new doctrine. Because Bush had promised to vigorously pursue war against al Qaeda, it was essential that the United States not lose momentum in that struggle.

The United States had to move to a second target in the war on terror after the successful liberation of Afghanistan to keep pressure on bin Laden, but more importantly, to eliminate safe havens for al Qaeda and get to the source of radical, militant Islamism in the heart of the Arab-Muslim world. Why Iraq was chosen as the preferred second best alternative in the war on terror is a much more complicated issue and one with politically significant and long-lasting consequences for President Bush and the United States.

Why Iraq?

The question might better be asked: Why not Saudi Arabia? For, as George Friedman and we have argued, al Qaeda was and is very much a Saudi phenomenon. Al Qaeda was largely managed by Saudi nationals and financed by both Saudi private and public contributions that funded radical militant Islamist activities for years. As a radical Islamist movement, al Qaeda was an ideological off-shoot of Wahhabi-Salafism, the state religion of Saudi Arabia. It was the Saudis who had all but broken off relations with the United States when the Arab monarchy had been pressed to provide sensitive intelligence information about al Qaeda and to stop the flow of Saudi funds to the terrorist organization and the Saudi global network of Islamic charities. Certainly the links between Saudi Arabia and al Qaeda were much stronger than any case for Saddam Hussein's support of al Qaeda. Without disclosing the Saudi connection, it was hard for President Bush in the 2004 reelection campaign to answer charges that the Iraq invasion had been anything but a diversion from the war on terror. Our analysis and understanding led us to conclude that the invasion of Iraq was the next best way to get the Saudis to stop funding al Qaeda and provide the United States with information about al Qaeda's operations, while beginning the long overdue process of transforming the Middle East.

Indeed, if the United States was determined to take military action in the Middle East in continuing its pursuit of al Qaeda, it had but two options: either invade Saudi Arabia directly or invade another major country in the region to convince the Saudis of America's military strength and determination to rid the world of al Qaeda and the source of its ideology and funding. In July of 2002, the Bush administration leaked a story to *The Washington Post* [Ricks] about a Pentagon briefing in the summer of 2002 in which a Rand Corporation consultant proposed that the United States seize the Saudi Arabian oil fields and its financial assets unless it stops supporting al Qaeda. Although this story was thought to be a part of the tough negotiations that were going on between the Saudis and Americans, the alternative of invading Saudi Arabia was under serious consideration. However, the problems of invading Saudi Arabia would have been Herculean, making military action against the Saudis highly improbable: (1) no case against the Saudis had been made publicly or diplomatically; (2) the Muslim world would have been inflamed because of the holy cities of Mecca and Medina; (3) the effect on American relations with its other allies would have been disastrous by destroying faith in America's promises; and, (4) if world oil production had been disrupted during an invasion of Saudi Arabia, the United States would have had to shoulder the blame for worldwide economic calamity.

The other perfect country was, of course, Iraq, which shares a long 500-mile border with Saudi Arabia and could in a relatively short-term, with investment in its decaying infrastructure, become a disruptive competitive force in the Saudi-dominated oil market. Iraq had other advantages: (1) Shiite Iran, the arch enemy of Saddam Hussein, would look favorably on deposing the militant Sunni and Baathist tyrant and could become an ally in the war against al Qaeda by supplying valuable intelligence information; (2) Syria, another Baathist-ruled autocratic government and consistent supporter of terrorist organizations, would be squeezed between pro-American Iraq, Turkey, and Israel; and, most important, (3) Saudi Arabia desperately wanted Saddam Hussein kept in power as a shield against Shiite Iran and as a counter to majority rule by Iraqi Shiites, the hated enemy of Sunni Wahhabis.

The winner, hands down, as the next U.S. target in the war against al Qaeda was Iraq. Though not necessarily the optimal target, Iraq was the most logical and readily available choice for pursuing al Qaeda and simultaneously influencing change in Saudi Arabia and the broader Middle East. Invading Iraq was almost like "killing two birds with one stone." First, Saddam Hussein was unquestionably evil and for years had stood as a malevolent symbol for all that was wrong in the Arab-Muslim world, making all other Arab autocrats look good by comparison. Second, the principals in the President's war council had been very much aware of how the Saudis would view another war with Iraq, completing the job that was started in the First Gulf War by toppling Saddam Hussein and instituting a democratic republic that was likely to be dominated by the Shiite majority. When Bush's laconic vice president was defense secretary in the first Bush administration, he was asked by a defense department consultant why we did not simply finish off Saddam while we had him on the ropes, and Cheney responded, "The Saudis won't like it" [Mann, 192]. They still did not like it, as Prince Bandar, the long-time Saudi ambassador to the United States through four presidencies and who was privy to virtually all of America's state secrets about its Middle Eastern policies, made clear after learning of U.S. intentions to invade Iraq and right up to the moment on March 19, 2003 when President Bush alerted the American public that the invasion had been launched. Bandar consistently argued that it would be much better to take out Saddam covertly, which the Saudis had been promising to help with since 1994 [Woodward, 2004, 229]. But like so many of the past Saudi promises that failed to materialize, this seemed like simply another round of gulling the Americans again. This time, however, President Bush refused to let the United States be fooled.

We do not yet know whether this explanation for the invasion of Iraq represents the complete thinking of the Bush administration war council or whether the decision was simply carried by those in the administration who had favored regime change in Iraq since the First Gulf War, such as Cheney, Rumsfeld, Wolfowitz, and others. Packer [2005, 46-7] quotes Richard Haass, Director of Planning in the State Department as saying, "'Why did the United States invade Iraq? It still isn't possible to be sure—this remains the most remarkable thing about the Iraq War.'" Nevertheless, we believe that a sound case can be made that the invasion and liberation of Iraq were an integral, perhaps even the main event, in the overall strategy for defeating al Qaeda, regardless of why the Bush administration actually decided to act.

A Surrogate War in Iraq

Until the decision to invade Iraq was finally made in September 2002, the Bush Doctrine and its execution in the war on terror were immensely popular at home and abroad. Bush's approval job rating was as high as 86 percent after 9/11 and remained at 60 percent through August 2002; most nations in the world were pleased with the dramatic and swift overthrow of the despicable Taliban regime as evidenced by NATO's willingness to join the coalition in Afghanistan in the postwar peacekeeping mission. But that was all about to change as a result of the

March 2003 invasion of Iraq and Bush's approval rating dropped to 52 percent by the time of the 2004 American presidential elections. The Bush administration has done an extremely poor job of explaining the Iraq invasion as an integral part of its strategy in the war on terror, partly because it could not tell the public all the reasons for the invasion. The Catch-22 of the Iraq option was the need to maintain total secrecy about one significant objective. If it went public with the Bush administration's dissatisfaction with the Saudis and the shadowy nature of the Saudi relationship with al Qaeda, it would have been impossible to obtain Saudi cooperation in fighting al Qaeda and risks of further disruptions in the Middle East could escalate.

If we are right, however, it was the United States that was gulling the Saudis, and not vice versa. Bush resolutely stuck to his increasingly unpopular war in Iraq without revealing all the complex reasons for the invasion and subsequently was reelected by a narrow 3 percent margin in November 2004. Part of the reason for the President's difficulties was the success of the Saudi propaganda campaign in Europe and the United States, attributing the invasion to Jewish neo-conservative attempts to eliminate Iraq, Israel's arch enemy in the Middle East. Other critics argued that President Bush, a reckless and naïve Texas gunslinger, was simply seeking revenge for Saddam Hussein's attempted assassination of his father. Ironically, these allegations could be viewed as a cover story to conceal the real link between the Saudis and al Qaeda that should have been a major reason for the invasion.

Part of the difficulty in making a good case to the American people for the Iraq invasion was, we believe, the pivotal role that misleading information played in selecting Iraq as a theater of operations, but there were, however, valid reasons for choosing Iraq as the second theater in the war on terror. In light of Saddam's past crimes against his people, Iraq was certainly a suitable candidate for Bush's policy of democratization of outlaw states through regime change, which had been official U.S. policy since October 31, 1998 when a weakened President Clinton signed the Iraq Liberation Act into law. Some Iraqi links to Islamist terrorists could be made in its harboring of al Qaeda members and paying $25,000 bounties to the families of Palestinian suicide bombers. Iraq had also achieved outlaw status by ignoring for over a decade U.N. resolutions for the elimination of its weapons of mass destruction, and, as was later learned, Iraq was guilty of bribing some Western nations and their representatives through the corrupt U.N. oil-for-food program to ease weapons importation sanctions and divert cash for weapons and Saddam's personal use.

In making the public case for invading Iraq, the Bush administration's principal justification was that Iraq's presumed possession of weapons of mass destruction (WMD) that could fall into terrorists' hands made Iraq a menacing and looming threat to the United States, which would have future political ramifications. At the time, intelligence agencies in Europe and the Middle East, as well as the CIA, all believed that Saddam Hussein had hidden stockpiles of biological and chemical weapons and planned to develop a nuclear device as quickly as possible after U.N. sanctions were lifted. Saddam did little to counter this belief, for why else would he throw out the U.N. inspectors in 1998? Few could realize at the time that it was megalomania or perhaps the paranoia of a tyrant who refused to recognize publicly what he considered would be humiliation and weakness in the eyes of Iraqi citizens and his Middle East rivals that prevented Saddam Hussein from openly proving to the world that no such stockpile of WMD existed. Everyone knew that Saddam was a liar, but no one understood that the "Mother of all Lies" would lead to his downfall, for his only defense, in the final analysis, would have been the truth, but that he refused to admit. Another possibility, of course, was that Saddam did, indeed, have WMD stockpiles that were moved to secret underground locations in Syria with Russian assistance in the days before the American-led invasion. This is still the position of the usually reliable Israeli intelligence service and other independent observers; only time and the fall of the autocratic Assad regime in Syria will tell.

Nevertheless, President Bush would later pay a very high price for the lack of full disclosure to the American people about all of the reasons for invading Iraq. When weapons inspectors failed to find WMD in Iraq, critics of the war were able to charge the president with misleading the people, others of going to war under false pretenses, and some of even deliberately lying. Although the president had simply been misled along with many others, as Podhoretz [2005] has made abundantly clear, the consequences of not justifying the Iraq war in terms of fighting the overall war on terror would become significant when the war did not go as well as expected. Beginning in the summer of 2005, political pressure for pulling American troops out of Iraq became intense, especially after the president was weakened politically by the Hurricane Katrina disaster in the American Gulf coast and high gasoline prices.

U.S. Diplomacy and Multilateralism

When the United States began to talk publicly about its plans for invading Iraq in the summer of 2002, worldwide opinion that had been so supportive of the United States after 9/11 and throughout the Afghan campaign broke solidly against President Bush and favorable opinions about the United States were soon a fading memory. Antiwar protests occurred in major European capitals and in American cities. With such adverse public reaction, foreign leaders found difficulty stepping forward to the defense of the United States, and it would take real courage for a politician to agree to join the United States in its effort to unseat Saddam.

Many Americans asked why so many nations opposed America's incursion into Iraq. Americans were, after all, accustomed to having their policies supported and popular overseas. First, it was far easier and politically rewarding for European leaders like Germany's Gerhard Schroeder to campaign for reelection by running against the American war in Iraq because of strong antiwar feelings among their people. Second, many nations, like France, Germany, and Russia, had economic reasons through favorable trade arrangements and arms sales for opposing the removal of Saddam Hussein, and the corrupt U.N. oil-for-food program added to those economic advantages. And third and most important, as Robert Kagan [11] has pointed out:

> For along with these natural consequences of the transatlantic disparity of power, there has also opened a

> broad ideological gap. Europeans, because of their unique historical experience of the past century—culminating in the creation of the European Union—have developed a set of ideals and principles regarding the utility and morality of power different from the ideals and principles of Americans, who have not shared that experience. [And furthermore on page 33] The differing threat perceptions in the United States and Europe are not just matters of psychology, however. They are also grounded in a practical realty that is another product of the disparity of power and the structure of the present international order.

While Europe receded under U.S. protection during the Cold War, the United States became involved more broadly in the rest of the world, among other things incurring the wrath of Islamist terrorists that the Europeans had been slow to appreciate.

The domestic political problem for President Bush was that many Americans, remembering the Roosevelt and Truman standards of international conduct, were more comfortable with the European model of collective behavior, and preferred an alliance with America's traditional allies. And, after remembering the first President Bush's great success with a grand alliance in the First Gulf War, large American-led military coalitions became the politically expected norm for international interventions. There was comfort in numbers but failure to bring other nations into Bush's war with Iraq would create credibility problems with the American public. Despite the President's expressions of willingness to go it alone in pursuit of al Qaeda, administration officials agreed that a multinational alliance would be politically and militarily useful. Unilateralism, with its rapidity of action, has both advantages and limitations.

Another nagging question for Americans, one that the Saudis helped to raise, was the question of America's role in settling the seemingly irresolvable Israeli-Palestinian dispute. Many Americans and hundreds of Europeans asked: Wouldn't the U.S. win more friends in the Muslim world if it resolved that dispute rather than change the regime in Iraq? This is another issue in which the Arab public and authoritarian Arab governments differed; the plight of the Palestinian refugees was a vital issue among many Muslim people, but their governments, aside from trying to eliminate the Jewish state through war or through support of terrorist groups, did not seem to care about the Palestinian people and offered very little support for the refugees. The Bush policy, in light of Yasser Arafat's rejection of President Clinton's peace proposal in 2000, was based on the belief that there was no hope for a realistic peace agreement until the Palestinians straightened out their own government with free elections and reined in its terrorist factions. After 9/11, it would have been extremely difficult for any American government to be unsympathetic to mounting terrorist attacks on innocent Israelis. The death of Yasser Arafat, the avowed terrorist leader of the Palestine Liberation Organization, was one of the most hopeful events in the war on terror in 2004. If the newly elected Palestinian leader, Mahmoud Abbas, can gain control over Hamas and other militant factions, the world will be the beneficiary not only of a reengaged Israeli-Palestinian peace process and the establishment of an independent Palestinian state, but of genuine peace in the region as well.

In spite of these sources of doubt about American policies, there were, fortunately, a few real allies of the United States that chose to come to the aid of the United States in the run-up to the Iraq war. First and foremost, British Prime Minister Tony Blair, over the objections of many members in his own Labor party and at great personal political risk, eloquently and courageously supported the American cause for unseating Saddam Hussein, promising 20,000 troops for the invasion. In addition, Australian Prime Minister John Howard signed up and offered 2,000 troops. Its former Dominion compatriot and long-time ally of the United States, Canada, however, opposed the invasion from the time it was first publicly considered and remained a critic as the war progressed. Poland, Spain, Italy, Ukraine, South Korea, and even Japan became part of the "coalition of the willing," to use President Bush's term.

A host of other nations also signed on, but few provided material assistance. Vital basing support and access in the region were provided by Turkey, Saudi Arabia, Kuwait, Bahrain, Qatar, United Arab Republic, and Oman. One public relations disaster of the Bush administration was the claim that, by including countries like Macedonia, Micronesia, the Marshall Islands, Palau, and Tonga, the second President Bush's coalition was actually larger than his father's in the First Gulf War, an alliance that contributed materially to paying the war costs, but the fact remained that about 85 percent of the forces in the March 2003 invasion of Iraq were American.

Allies can be comforting, but they also create obligations. Partially to repay the administration's great debt to Tony Blair, the Bush administration agreed to seek additional U.N. Security Council sanctions for Iraq and approval of the invasion. The issue divided the president's war council, but President Bush finally sided with Blair and Secretary Powell, giving the secretary the assignment of rounding up enough votes in the Security Council to support America's armed intervention in Iraq. After eight weeks of intensive diplomatic discussion and debate, the secretary achieved a major diplomatic victory. On November 8, 2002 the United Nations Security Council voted unanimously (15 to 0) to approve Resolution 1441 warning Saddam Hussein that, if he "continued to violate his disarmament obligations, he would face 'serious consequences'" [Woodward 2004, 226].

The American diplomatic victory in the United Nations, though temporary, gave the Bush administration the legitimacy it needed to proceed with the invasion, for it had been preceded on October 10th and 11th with the passage, by a wider margin than in the First Gulf War, of a Congressional resolution to use the U.S. armed forces in Iraq "as he [the President] deems to be necessary and appropriate." However, the U.N. action was less of a victory than an exposure of the hypocrisy of international diplomacy as practiced in the 21st century. The Security Council consisted of 15 countries that were both for and against war in Iraq, and all had approved the U.N. Security Council resolution with the intent of later using it against their opponents' position. As a direct result of the resolution, Saddam Hussein permitted the U.N.

inspection teams back into Iraq and issued a mangled 12,000-word report on its weapons programs "that everyone believed was full of omissions and based on old materials" [Woodward 2004, 349].

Nevertheless, the major opponents of war (France, Russia, China, and Germany) did not view this action by Iraq as "a material breach" of the U.N. mandate. Instead, they asked for more inspections and more time, and the diplomatic war at the United Nations continued, right up to the time of the March 19, 2003 invasion. Powell went back to the Security Council on February 5th to give the Council a now discredited overview of U.S. intelligence supporting the view that Iraq still had weapons of mass destruction, but opponents of the war, led by the French, refused to budge. A second Powell effort to win another Security Council resolution, again at the behest of America's British allies, did not get off the ground for lack of supportive votes.

The question of invading Iraq remained a diplomatic stalemate, requiring the United States, Great Britain, Spain, Poland, Italy, and the rest of the "coalition of the willing" to invade and liberate Iraq on the basis of Resolution 1441. Both sides claimed that legal right was on their side. In answer to the question that President Bush had used to frame the debate, it is clear that the United Nations was unable to serve the purpose of its founding and was willing to risk its relevance. In addition, the hypocritical debates at the U.N. strengthened the case for the wisdom of building America's security on the Bush Doctrine's policies of hegemony, unilateralism, and pre-emption rather than multilateralism through tangled, aging and bureaucratic international organizations designed for another era.

Immediate Benefits of Invading Iraq

Because of American efforts since World War II to cover up the sins of the Saudis, it would have been much more difficult to prove outlaw status for Saudi Arabia than it was to indict Iraq, an already convicted felon, in the court of world opinion. Nevertheless, there was a much stronger and more direct link between the 9/11 terrorists and Saudi Arabia, with its militant state religion of Wahhabi-Salafism, as the primary source of ideology and funding for bin Laden and other Islamist extremists throughout the world. Even though, based on the merits, Saudi Arabia could have logically been the second target of America's war against militant Islamists, Iraq provided an adequate and suitable surrogate and an effective means of communicating America's great dissatisfaction with continuing Saudi support for militant Islamist terrorism.

On the other hand, the invasion of Iraq put the United States and the global economy at some risk of a possible disruption in the supply of Middle East oil. And there were other risks. Retired Air Force Lieutenant General Brent Scowcroft [8/16/2002], National Security advisor in the first Bush administration, in his *Wall Street Journal* essay, "Don't Attack Iraq," warned that:

> If we were seen to be turning our backs on that bitter [Israeli-Palestine] conflict…in order to go after Iraq, there would be an explosion of outrage against us. We would be seen as ignoring a key interest of the Muslim world in order to satisfy what is seen to be a narrower American interest.

Scowcroft was correct that the reaction to the invasion on the Arab street was greeted heatedly as another example of Western colonialism, but it was hardly an "explosion of outrage." However, the reaction of Islamic governments was quite different, much more subdued and even supportive in Iran. After all, the United States was removing the greatest threat to Middle East stability by ousting the region's most ruthless dictator, who by his actions and statements everyone believed was stockpiling weapons of mass destruction that could be as easily provided to terrorist organizations or directed at other Arab states, Israel, or the West.

Even before the first bombs landed on Baghdad or coalition forces had advanced north from Kuwait, outlaw states, as well as Saudi Arabia and Pakistan, got the message of America's new intolerance for harboring terrorists and the husbanding of weapons of mass destruction. Libya was the first to fold in late June 2003, shortly after the Iraq war started, and immediately ceased its nuclear development program and welcomed international inspection teams, prompting the United States to drop long-standing sanctions against the renegade country and its unpredictable and autocratic leader. Pakistan the year before had confessed its sins of selling nuclear secrets and started to reform its intelligence service.

The Saudis even became more open about their role in financing international terrorism, including al Qaeda, and began shutting down Wahhabi charities and other sources of funds. Saudi Arabia also expanded oil production to meet rising global demand, declared a women's rights convention and limited municipal elections for regional councils in early 2005, and was formally admitted into the World Trade Organization (WTO) with new international responsibilities and increased governmental transparency as a result.

For a new American foreign policy that only first partially emerged on September 20, 2001, progress had been substantial and swift, with the potential democratization of Iraq and the greater Middle East as a special bonus to support the Bush administration's view that freedom and democracy would be the ultimate catharsis for Middle Eastern totalitarianism and autocracy.

DEMOCRATIZATION OF THE ARAB-MUSLIM WORLD

For a candidate who first campaigned for president by declaring his opposition to President Clinton's nation-building efforts in Haiti, Bosnia, and Kosovo, President George W. Bush, to use a term he made famous in attacking his opponent in the 2004 presidential campaign, certainly "flip-flopped" on the issue of democratization. That remarkable change in policy perspective between the candidate for president and the elected president resulted from the education that he had received from the Vulcans and a sobering evolution in the President's thinking. Traditionally, Republican internationalists had opposed advocating regime change in countries friendly to the United

States, but George Shultz and Ronald Reagan had changed all that—George Bush the candidate simply hadn't gotten the message yet. Instead, the new president brought expectations about the possibilities for nation-building to new heights by incorporating it into the bedrock of America's national security policy and made it the principal long-term antidote to radical militant Islam that redefined American relationships with autocratic governments all over the world.

Democracy was much more than the mere trapping of elections with the establishment of a government acceptable to the United States. America would establish a process, preferably under the auspices of the United Nations, for a democratic constitution and free elections of a national assembly, and then take its chances on the preferences of Muslim voters. The Bush administration was truly committed to the principle that freedom and democracy could take hold and prosper in the Muslim world, even though the history of democracy in the Middle East was limited to the 80-year checkered experience of the Republic of Turkey. A new way started to emerge in the Arab-Muslim world and for the first time since the end of the First World War, democracy, freedom, human rights, and open markets signaled the prospect for a new era of enlightenment and openness that could guide the Arab-Muslim world into a better future.

The Afghan Experience

The first test of Bush's democratization policy was in Afghanistan, and the early stages of forming an elected government proceeded quite well. Six months after the December 2001 U.N. conference appointing the interim authority, a second conference, a grand one called the Loya Jirga, was convened in Kabul for 1,500 elected delegates from throughout the country to decide the structure of the future government, appoint a group to prepare a draft of a new constitution for Afghanistan, arrange for general elections, and ratify the election of Hamid Karzai as the interim president. A draft constitution providing for a strong presidential system of government was approved at a meeting of the Grand Assembly with 502 delegates during the period from December 14th to January 4, 2004. Karzai signed into law the

Afghan constitution on January 26, 2004. Originally, the Assembly had hoped to hold elections for the first permanent president during that summer, but they were postponed because of a slow voter registration process.

By October 9, 2004, 10.5 million Afghans had registered to vote and about 8 million exercised that right with Karzai receiving 55.4 percent of their votes. Such a high turnout ratio (76.2 percent) in the country's first presidential election was indeed remarkable. Even more remarkable was the fact that the recently vanquished Taliban and al Qaeda forces were unable to cause any serious mischief or security challenges during the elections. Although a higher percentage of men than women voted, it was a dramatic about-face for 40 percent of the registered female voters to vote in less than "three years after the downfall of misogynist Taliban regime" [Qayash]. Hamid Karzai was sworn in on December 7, 2004 as Afghanistan's first elected president in the country's nearly 260-year history, exactly three years to the day after the fall of the Taliban. The next step in the democratization process was the election of a new parliament on September 18, 2005. Although the turnout for the parliamentary election was lower than the presidential election due to confusion about the large number of candidates (more than 10 candidates for every seat), more than 50 percent of the Afghans voted and the elections were judged a success. A final goal for the completion of a strong national government was the creation of a 70,000 troop national army to wrestle control from the local tribal chieftains and by the fall of 2005 the army had already recruited 26,000.

Since 9/11, everything about Afghanistan moved at fast-forward speed, but the struggle there, and in western Pakistan, has not ended. Much remains to be done to restore Afghan infrastructure after more than 25 years of warfare throughout the country, to find a means of stopping the poppy crop while developing alternative ways of earning a living in this barren mountainous region of the world, and to overcome the deep-rooted ethnic antipathy that has been so prominent throughout Afghanistan's history. The rapid pace of developing a democratic government portends well for both Afghanistan and the success of President Bush's democratization policy as the antidote to

Islamist militancy. In September 2001, no one could have predicted such remarkable progress in this remote and ungovernable state, let alone the removal of the Taliban government in only two months. With much more yet to do, Afghanistan is nevertheless a success story for the Bush administration and NATO, and that success played well in the battle with al Qaeda for the hearts and minds of the Muslim world.

The Iraqi Experience

The description of the war in Iraq is the subject of the next chapter, but here, in a discussion of America's foreign policy in the war on terror, the effect of democratic politics is addressed in settling the war between the American "occupiers" and the Baathist-Islamist militant insurgency in Iraq. Originally, the Americans had hoped to hold free elections in June 2004, but the efforts of the Iraqi insurgents made earlier elections impossible due to the lack of security in the Sunni Triangle northwest of Baghdad and the unwillingness of the United Nations to conduct early elections. As a result, the first Iraq elections were postponed until January 30, 2005 and even then there were debates right up to the last moment about the advisability of holding elections in the face of vicious terrorist attacks and a possible Sunni boycott.

The first election in Iraq on January 30, 2005 was the most important step in developing political support for the Bush concept of democratization as the antidote to Islamist terrorism. It was, however, followed by two other elections in 2005; the first on October 15th ratified the new Iraq Constitution and the second on December 15th elected a new permanent, four-year Council of Representatives. Each of these elections was crucial to winning the war in Iraq and will be discussed in Chapter 5, but the January 30th election was vitally important to the eventual success of the Bush Doctrine because of the reaction of other Middle East Muslim nations to the progress being made in Iraq, notwithstanding troubling and fiercely determined Iraqi insurgents.

The successful Iraqi election in January 2005 served as a powerful inspiration throughout the Middle East and broader Muslim world and helped set the stage by providing momentum for the political process in Iraq, for many critics on both sides of the Atlantic had held little hope for a successful election process in Iraq. A positive trend started first in December 2004 with events in Ukraine, a former Soviet republic, when free democratic elections ousted a former strong-arm autocrat. Then shortly after the New Year, the Iraqi elections received another boost from an unexpected source—the Palestinians. On January 9th Palestinian voters freely elected Mahmoud Abbas following the death of the Palestinian dictator Yasser Arafat, and Abbas went on to proclaim his intent to end the armed Palestinian struggle against Israel. On January 30th eight million Iraqi voters braved bombs and bullets to cast their ballots, and on February 10th Saudi Arabia held its first-ever municipal elections, only for men and only for half the seats at that, but the beginning of a possible fracture in the royal family's absolute rule. The Saudi government also hosted a government conference on terrorism and a conference on women's rights, suggesting that the Saudis had taken steps to get on board the liberalization bandwagon while at the same time fighting al Qaeda at home.

More events unfolded within 30 days of the Iraqi election in January 2005. On February 26, 2005, Egypt's president, aging military dictator Hosni Mubarak, announced that in the forthcoming presidential election his government would permit other candidates to run in addition to Mubarak, although the fact that Mubarak received 88.6 percent of the September 7th vote, with less than a 25 percent voter turnout, somewhat diminished the enthusiasm for democracy in Egypt, but later parliamentary elections restored some of that enthusiasm.

On February 28th tens of thousands of demonstrators in Beirut forced the resignation of the pro-Syrian government, and President Bush, with support from the French government, demanded that Syria immediately remove all of its 15,000 troops and intelligence agents from Lebanon. The Syrians, after American and U.N. demands, totally pulled out of Lebanon before the Lebanese elections in May 2005, with a hint that Lebanese independence might signal an end to the autocratic Baathist regime in Syria. Further pressures were exerted on the Assad government by the U.N. investigation into the assassination of former Lebanese prime minister, Rafik Hariri, allegedly by high officials in the Syrian government.

On March 7, 2005, hundreds of Kuwaiti women demonstrated outside the Kuwaiti parliament, demanding political rights including the right to vote and be nominated in elections. They stated that their demands do not contradict Islamic law and Kuwait's parliament agreed to address their issues as the UAE announced reforms and the Bahrain government announced that courses in democracy will be taught in the Bahrain schools. And as Muslim Kyrgyzstan threw off vestiges of autocratic leadership from its Soviet past in March 2005, hundreds of Iranian women were seen on the streets of Tehran wearing pink scarves and pink coats in defiance of the autocratic Islamist mullahs who seized power from the Shah in 1979.

From Lebanon to Palestine, Saudi Arabia, Syria, and Egypt, dramatic events unfolded following the January 2005 elections in Iraq, holding out the possibility of a true Arab spring that might begin to bloom, all because of the events surrounding free elections in Iraq which seemed to create a snowball effect, with more democratic countries supporting the American call for freedom and democracy in the Middle East. Moreover, Libya had changed its colors and gave up its nuclear weapons as people throughout the region began to sense the possibility of change. In early 2006, dozens of brave Arab democrats met in Doha, Qatar where they signed the "Doha Declaration of Democratic Principles," an eloquent and revolutionary statement of democratic principles, equality for all, and religious tolerance. And in Washington, DC, Saudi exile Ali Alyami courageously led the Center for Democracy and Human Rights in Saudi Arabia (www.cdhr.info) in developing a "Blueprint" for a peaceful transition to democratic rule in Saudi Arabia, while communicating daily by email and the internet with hundreds of fellow Saudi dissidents and supporters in Europe, the United States and the Middle East.

The rapid pace of development in the Middle East surprised many people in the U.S. and in Europe, leading Germans and French newspapers to publicly ask, "Could Bush have been right," when he stated in his Second Inaugural Address America's goal of "ending tyranny in our world"? Truly, the paradigm in Iraq and the Middle East had totally changed, as Tom Friedman [2005] concluded in a recent column:

> [W]hatever you thought about this war, it's not about Mr. Bush anymore. It's about the aspirations of the Iraqi majority to build an alternative to Saddamism. By voting the way they did, in the face of real danger, Iraqis have earned the right to ask everyone now to put aside their squabbles and focus on what is no longer just a pipe dream but a real opportunity to implement decent consensual government in the heart of the Arab Muslim world.

That many difficulties lie ahead is obvious, but seeds of progress and hope have been planted and Middle East autocrats now ponder an uncertain future for themselves. It is possible that radical Islamist ideologues could replace autocrats as they did in Iran in 1979 when the Shah fell and cause further problems as Iran has done recently by daring the world to challenge its right to nuclear arms. And as Hamas proved in early 2006, it is also possible that Islamists can win democratic elections and lead governments dominated by anti-American extremists, but that is one of the risks inherent in freedom and democracy. The Middle East has been frozen in rigid autocracy for centuries, but that is now set to change because people understand that the aspirations of the Iraqi people are ultimately the aspirations of oppressed people around the world, especially in the Middle East, where the Bush Doctrine of using democracy as an antidote to radical Islamist militarism was first tested.

CONCLUSION ABOUT THE BUSH DOCTRINE

Perhaps the best way to judge the effectiveness of the Bush Doctrine of freedom and democracy as the antidote to Bin Ladenism is to ask the following questions:

- How would the war on terror have differed if the United States had continued to pursue al Qaeda following its Cold War rules of engagement?
- What would the Middle East be like today with Saddam Hussein still in power?
- What would have been accomplished if the United States pursued multilateral (neither unilateral nor hegemonic), non-preemptive, and non-regime-change policies that existed prior to 9/11?
- Could the United States have escaped additional al Qaeda attacks on its homeland solely by raising its defensive fences around its borders while the pursuit of al Qaeda proceeded more slowly than the breathtaking pace the Bush administration elected to employ?

Answering these questions is, of course, highly speculative, but enough reasonable approximations can be made to demonstrate the wisdom and efficacy of the Bush Doctrine.

First, the United States would have been able to oust the Taliban from Afghanistan and destroy the al Qaeda training camps in the country with a United Nations sanctioned coalition of NATO, Russia, Japan, China, and many other nations, providing such a coalition could have responded quickly enough. World sympathy for the United States after sustaining such an uncivilized attack on 9/11 in which so many innocent civilian lives were taken would have supported a unanimous Security Council resolution (1378) asking the Taliban to surrender Osama bin Laden and to close his training camps or face an invasion to capture and destroy.

On the Palestinian-Israeli front, few can criticize the Bush administration for failure to advance the cause of peace, even if the other American wartime activities crowded the issue off its agenda, for as long as Yasser Arafat remained in charge, no progress in negotiations with Israel could be expected. The 2005 Palestinian elections and a new cooperative spirit on both sides created renewed hope for a viable Palestinian state and a long-term solution to the Israeli-Palestinian conflict, providing Hamas could be peacefully integrated into the democratic process.

The invasion of Iraq was much more problematic and became the issue that made the Bush Doctrine so controversial in the United States and especially in Europe. Some believe that the United States, behaving more deferentially toward Europe, could have persuaded the Security Council to sanction the invasion of Iraq and overthrow of Saddam Hussein with a much larger coalition force that would have provided funding support for both the military and rebuilding operations in Europe. Such an outcome is, however, extremely unlikely given the strength of the anti-war movement in Europe and lack of independent European statesmen who would have taken on public opinion in their countries as Tony Blair did in the U.K. It is easy to forget how difficult it was for Tony Blair to challenge his own Labor Party on the Iraq issue, risking his political career in a cause for which at a minimum 75 percent of the British electorate disagreed [See Stothard]. Can anyone imagine Jacques Chirac of France or Gerhard Schroeder of Germany having the political fortitude to challenge such a majority opinion, even if it had not been in their countries' (and Russia's) economic interests to keep Saddam Hussein in office and maintain the status quo in Iraq? There would not have been an invasion of Iraq without the Bush Doctrine that called for the United States to act unilaterally and preemptively—preventively—in its own interests to defend the United States and the world from Islamist militantcy.

And without the Iraq invasion, would America have received any cooperation from the Saudis in cutting off the flow of funds to al Qaeda and radical clerics around the world? Probably not. The Pakistanis and Libyans may have become more cooperative with a U.N. resolution and coalition in Afghanistan, but it is unlikely that Saudi behavior would have changed. In all likelihood, they would have continued to stall American efforts to stop their funding of al Qaeda. Without changing Saudi behavior, the danger of further al Qaeda attacks on the United States would have been significantly greater. However, what about the increased number of jihadist recruits that joined the insurgency in Iraq? Most of these recruits were used as suicide bombers and most came from Saudi Arabia [Nordland et al., 29]. Although that number may have been increased, even substantially, there is merit, from the standpoint of defending the United States, in drawing these extremists into an arena away from the American homeland where they could be killed or captured without threatening innocent American lives.

There can be little question that the Bush Doctrine and its aggressive implementation put Osama bin Laden back on his heels and he became the reactor, no longer the aggressor. Bush's goal of taking the offensive and putting al Qaeda on the defensive certainly had been accomplished and there had been no more attacks on the American homeland since 9/11.

However, it was not until the January 30, 2005 elections in Iraq that the world and, especially the Arab-Muslim world, saw the power and wisdom of the Bush Doctrine and the proposed antidote to radical Islamist militarism fully unveiled. The Afghan experience with its earlier election had been illuminating, but the pride that so many Iraqis showed in their fearless march to the polls kindled the fires for freedom and democracy that Bush believed would lead to real reform in the Middle East. Whether democracy spreads and takes root in the Arab-Muslim world will be the essential and final test of the long-term effectiveness of the Bush Doctrine.

The next chapter examines the difficulty the allied coalition faced in creating the climate that permitted the January 2005 Iraq elections. The foreign policy of the Bush Doctrine may have been sound, but its execution, as we shall see, left much to be desired for a number of reasons.

CHAPTER FIVE

The Iraq War—Where Nothing Met Expectations

    Military history often takes years to be accurately researched, understood, digested, and properly written, so this account, prepared largely from contemporary reports, must be interpreted for what it is—an initial assessment and reaction from open sources. The Bush administration's successes in rapidly developing a new and comprehensive national security policy and its quick triumph in Afghanistan unfortunately did not carry over into Iraq for a number of reasons.
    Going into Iraq was quite different from the Afghan campaign. From the start, U.S. intelligence agencies had more valid information about Afghanistan than they did about Iraq. At the outset, the agencies were not aware of the extent of the deficiencies in their Iraqi intelligence, which was too often based on a few covert agents on the ground in the friendly Kurdish portion of the north and the word of Iraqi exiles, whose primary objective was convincing the United States about the ease of invasion. Secretary Rumsfeld and the Joint Staff in

the Pentagon accepted the "rosy" picture in large part, no doubt, because it fit preconceived notions and because the CIA had so little information and so few agents in Iraq. As a consequence of the lack of good intelligence and because of misleading information, the early months of the invasion produced many surprises. This led to many unanticipated difficulties as American forces were required to operate largely in the dark, with the exception of sketchy outlines provided by overhead satellite pictures and other electronic intelligence sources.

The most disappointing aspect of American military performance in Iraq was the lack of an adequate postwar plan which led to indecisiveness and lack of spontaneity by commanders in responding to actual conditions on the ground due to the lack of an understanding of the enemy and lack of an adequate strategy that could adapt to changing circumstances. Americans have historically succeeded because of ingenuity and the ability to adapt to the unexpected. In the past, even though there might have been huge discrepancies between what commanders had been told and what actually existed, American forces had always taken great pride in being flexible and inventive in encountering the unexpected. Not so in this case.

The problems of poor intelligence mushroomed into even worse tactical decision-making, as the failures to respond to actual conditions led to momentary paralysis, followed by another round of mistaken tactics. The war seemed to be governed by Murphy's Law: not only did everything seem to go wrong that could, but when it did, the U.S. military made the wrong corrections, magnifying the ill-effects of previous errors. The generals in the war zone and their Defense Department managers safely back home were out-strategized in fighting what soon became an out-of-control war against determined insurgents consisting of remnants of the defeated ex-Baathists, Sunni tribal leaders and their loyal tribesmen, Iraqi Wahhabis, and foreign jihadists from Saudi Arabia and surrounding countries.

PHASE 1: OFF TO AN APPARENTLY GOOD START

On March 17, 2003, President Bush issued his final ultimatum: "Saddam Hussein and his sons must leave Iraq within 48 hours. Their refusal to go will result in military conflict commenced at a time of our choosing." The war got off to what seemed to be a good start on March 19, 2003 when a covert CIA agent reported that he knew where Saddam Hussein would be that evening in the south of Baghdad. The invasion was clandestinely launched as planned that afternoon with the introduction of Special Operations Forces into the west and north of Iraq; Polish forces were to capture an oil platform in the Persian Gulf and Australian forces were to safeguard a dam. At 7:12 p.m. EST, after a conference with his war council members, the President departed from original plans and ordered some 40 Tomahawk cruise missiles and two bunker-busting 2,000 pound bombs from two F-117 stealth single-seat fighter jets to be dropped on the Dora Farm where Saddam was supposedly sleeping. At 9:30 p.m. reports came into Washington that air raid sirens in Baghdad had gone off, and at 9:45 the White House press secretary announced that the President would address the nation at 10:15 that night. The President's address was brief and without detail, simply saying that the early stages of the military campaign against Saddam Hussein had started, mentioning the fact that 35 nations were giving crucial support, and suggesting that the campaign could be longer and more perilous than some predicted [Woodward, 398]. Whether or not it was true, reports from the covert agents at the Dora Farm site reported that, although Saddam had not been killed, he was at least injured and shaken up in the initial assault. These reports were subsequently found to be totally incorrect, as Saddam Hussein hadn't been at the Dora Farms since 1995 [Gordon and Trainor, 3/12/2006].

Two hours later, however, Saddam Hussein, looking "pale and drawn...appeared on television to deliver a rambling, defiant speech full of exhortations to his people to resist the attackers" [Walker, 24].

Again, instant analysis proved to be in error, as the real reason for Saddam's glasses was the unavailability of a printer for his large-type cue cards [Gordon and Trainor, 3/12/2006]. Nevertheless, the Americans scored a victory of sorts by playing into the paranoid fears of the Iraqi dictator who looked uncomfortable and unsure of himself reading his speech with glasses that made him look old and uncommanding. Although Saddam delivered several additional speeches in the next few days, beginning first on April 4th while walking through neighborhood streets of Baghdad and continuing right up to April 9th, he had already turned over command of the Iraqi defense force to his two sons, Uday and Qusay, and soon went into hiding for fear of being overthrown by his own army. The war had started and the coalition forces had made a good start, improvising a direct attack on the head of the Iraqi government in the grand style of the American "can-do" military tradition. The failure to continue this style of adaptive warfare would prove to be much to the disadvantage of the Coalition Forces.

The Easy Part

The next day, March 20, 2003, the invasion commenced as originally planned with Special Operations Forces partially controlling the vast western desert area to prevent Scud missile firings and the southern oil fields to prevent the burning of the oil wells as had occurred in Kuwait in the First Gulf War. The major ground invasion started at 10:00 p.m. on the 20th because the planned nine hours of "shock and awe" bombing did not begin until 1:00 p.m. on the 21st as originally planned, reversing the normally predictable schedule of softening-up bombing that preceded American ground attacks, as in the First Gulf War and more recently in Afghanistan. This time the Pentagon even launched a discomforting public relations effort claiming a "shock and awe" air campaign, which in fact was much lighter than in the First Gulf War because the U.S. did not want to kill innocent civilians or destroy too much Iraqi infrastructure. Baghdad's electric power system, for example, had been taken out in the First Gulf War but was protected this time around so electricity might be readily available to the victorious allied army after the fall of Baghdad.

THE TRIUMPH OF DEMOCRACY OVER MILITANT ISLAMISM

The American invasion plan, honed to perfection by many months of planning and incessant questioning by Secretary Rumsfeld, had been to strike quickly with a small, mobile, well-coordinated and integrated military force. General Franks' plan was for the U.S. Army's V Corps to quickly cross the Iraq-Kuwait border and attack Baghdad west of the Euphrates. The U.S. Marine Corps would make a swift, parallel advance and attack east of the river by heading toward Nasiriya and crossing the Euphrates at that point. The British, with support from U.S. Marines, would secure Basra, Iraq's second largest city, and Iraq's port in the south.

By Saturday, March 22nd, the lead column of the U.S. 3rd Infantry Division was already 150 miles deep into Iraq. While the British troops advancing on Basra in southern Iraq encountered heavier than expected resistance from unconventional Iraqi forces, the British were able to secure the Rumaylah Oil Fields after the initial U.S. Marine incursion, preventing catastrophic oil fires that had been so problematic in Kuwait in the First Gulf War. After safeguarding the oil fields, the British made progress toward Umm Qasr, the Iraqi port south of Basra on the Persian Gulf, which would be vital as a key saltwater port for bringing in humanitarian relief supplies, as well as additional military personnel and equipment.

The advance forces wore hot and heavy chemical defense equipment and gas masks in fear of Saddam's use of chemical or biological weapons that U.S. and British intelligence believed had been stockpiled to counter the invasion forces. Over time, the American soldiers ceased to wear the hot, bulky suits and gas masks, but the troops were ordered to keep them readily available at all times. The leading American forces met very little resistance as they moved around various Iraqi cities in their path, while succeeding troops behind the front line forces faced a few pockets of Iraqi resistance willing to fight for their homeland. The British troops invading Basra in the south met more organized resistance and faced tougher fighting and, after the Iraqis were routed, only polite acceptance from the Shiite population, not the welcoming celebrations for the liberators that the Iraqi exiles had promised the planners in Doha, Tampa and Washington.

On the fifth day of the invasion, March 24th, U.S. forward troops met stubborn resistance along the Euphrates River near Nasiriyah, Samawa, and Najaf, and later in the holy Shiite city Karbala. Embedded reporters had become accustomed to the Coalition's rapid success thus far, and these anticipated combat delays caused them to challenge the administration's war plans which had only sustained minor setback and delay. The American solution was to bring in close air support and hammer the Iraqi troops that were dug in, but that took time due to bad weather caused by a severe three-day sandstorm throughout southern Iraq. The press came to believe that the American invasion plan was in real trouble, and for the first time reports even started to emerge from retired generals back in the United States, saying that Coalition Forces did not have enough troops on the ground in Iraq. Indeed, American ground troops were taken aback by the intensity of fighting by the Saddam Fedayeen, paramilitary fighters organized by Saddam to guard against a Shiite uprising in southern Iraq. However, when Lieutenant General William S. Wallace, commander of the Army's V Corps, suggested to reporters that the American advance might have to be delayed "to suppress the Fedayeen threat in the rear" [Gordon and Trainor, 3/13/2006], General Franks even threatened to fire Wallace, as an indication of Franks' strong commitment to his battle plan and his unwillingness to deviate from the approved schedule.

General Tommy Franks may be one of the first army officers in history since Stonewall Jackson to believe that smaller, faster forces were to be preferred to larger numbers of soldiers, and he wasn't about to back down from that strategy. He certainly differed from former JCS Chairman, General Colin Powell, who planned the First Gulf War with overwhelming force that came to be known as the "Powell Doctrine," although Powell did not raise serious objections when the president's war council approved Franks' final war plan [Woodward, 125-6]. Private contractors were used to supplement traditional military logistics support functions like supply and food management that were normally operated by the military, thus explaining some of the diminished size of the invading forces who were for the most part all combatants due to the logistics "outsourcing." The United States, indeed, had a sufficient number of troops to defeat the Iraqi army, but not enough fighting troops to occupy and rebuild Iraq and it did not have an adequate postwar stabilization plan or enough good intelligence to deploy its combat forces effectively after the fall of Baghdad and overthrow of Saddam Hussein. Nor did the United States understand Saddam Hussein's guerrilla warfare strategy and what the Coalition Forces were to face in the Sunni Triangle after the fall of Baghdad.

When the sandstorms finally abated and the bad weather gave way to clear desert skies in late March, U.S. Air Force and Navy pilots started flying as many as two thousand sorties a day, comparable to the level in the First Gulf War. "Something quite strange began happening; Iraqi forces that had been plotted carefully on the maps started to disappear. Iraqi forces that were thought to be there one day simply weren't there the next" [Friedman, 298]. And so far there had been no chemical or biological attacks. By April 5th, American troops, proceeding cautiously, had reached the southern edge of Baghdad and reconnaissance probes into the city were ordered. No significant fire was drawn from these probes and commanders still did not know how much resistance could be expected in a full-scale attack on the Iraqi capital. Still not certain on the 7th of April, American forces sent a missile into a restaurant in the Mansour district of Baghdad in a diversionary attempt to kill Saddam and disrupt Iraqi resistance. Finally, on April 9th, American forces entered Baghdad and began formal occupation without meeting any organized resistance. On that day a large statue of Saddam was dramatically toppled by American troops and the world, watching live on television, thought the war was over, just three weeks after the American liberation commenced. Nevertheless, the American invasion forces in Baghdad had every reason to be apprehensive, for nothing so far had gone exactly as expected or planned.

Allied forces had been aware as early as October 2002 that Saddam had freed nearly all criminals from his bleak Iraqi prisons, so the initial American reaction to the massive looting that occurred throughout

Baghdad from the moment the city was captured was to place blame on freed criminals. Regardless of the cause, the systematic destruction and looting of government office buildings and facilities should have been a warning to U.S. commanders on the ground that this was not just random chaos, but might have been pre-planned and well-orchestrated anarchy. The Baathist insurgency aided by small numbers of al Qaeda-inspired foreign jihadists started immediately, but Secretary Rumsfeld dismissed these lawless activities with the explanation that "freedom is untidy," a totally mistaken and erroneous understanding of what was happening. Even the Baghdad electrical grid and pipelines from the oil fields that the Coalition had so carefully protected from bombing attacks were now victims of insurgent sabotage, leaving the defeated Iraqis literally in the dark and in the heat without fresh electricity, drinking water, or gasoline for their cars. While U.S. troops held the bridges over the Tigris River in Baghdad, looting in the city was confined to the east side of the river but as soon as the troops abandoned the bridges, looting moved across the river. If the U.S. occupation forces were ever to gain control over the looters, they should have held the bridges until they were ready to patrol the area west of the Tigris, but the "fog of war" at the time clouded what was really happening as Saddam's guerrilla warfare plans unfolded. The Coalition Forces were off to a terrible start, from which it took nearly three years to recover.

Failures to Adjust to New Realities

Despite the Coalition's success in meeting or exceeding its timelines for capturing Iraq and toppling its evil and infamous dictator, Saddam Hussein, nothing about the war had gone according to the assumptions upon which the invasion plans had been built. No chemical or biological weapons had been unleashed against coalition forces, nor were any of the expected stockpiles of weapons of mass destruction (WMD) found as the Coalition Forces raced headlong into Baghdad. The expected barrage of Scud missiles on the coalition's reserve forces in Kuwait never fully materialized—only a dozen homemade Iraqi missiles, with just one hit, and that an empty theater building—and there were no Scud missile attacks on Israel as had been expected and as had actually occurred in the First Gulf War. Indeed, except for pockets of resistance by irregular Iraqi forces behind the front lines and the regular army defense around the holy city of Karbala, the Iraqi army did not engage the invading coalition forces in any significant way. Nor did they surrender in large numbers, as they had in the First Gulf War; they just seemed to disappear into nowhere as the Coalition Forces approached, and as they did in Baghdad where brutal house-to-house urban combat had been expected. Indeed, the end of formal hostilities failed to measure up to Secretary Rumsfeld's expectations for there was no formal surrender or military coup ousting Saddam Hussein and his two sons. Hostilities simply ended, much to Rumsfeld's dismay, creating a vacuum that led to serious security problems for the Allies.

The reality of the war should have become apparent to American commanders by late March when an Iraqi civilian killed four American soldiers at a checkpoint in Najaf by blowing up his car. Other suicide bombers soon attacked and killed American soldiers during fighting around Baghdad. On April 12th a resistance group surfaced that called itself "The National Front for the Liberation of Iraq," which should have removed all doubt when the group issued a statement to a number of European governments proclaiming its intention to launch armed resistance and invite Arab volunteers from outside Iraq to join in overturning the American occupation. Prior to the invasion, Saddam had started importing Arab jihadists from Saudi Arabia, Jordan, and Syria. Several journalists covering the war were aware of this development but American commanders paid little or no heed. [e.g., Anderson, 261]. It was as if no one wanted to believe American forces would be facing Islamist jihadists from adjacent Arab countries, but the signs were already there. There were other signs that Saddam's loyal Sunni Baathists had never intended a stout defense, but rather planned to melt away and then wage protracted guerrilla warfare against the occupiers, like General Washington did against the British in the American Revolution. Centered in the Sunni Triangle north and west of Baghdad, Saddam had deployed a heavy concentration of Iraqi troops that had never been involved in any fighting against the invaders.

The real surprise was that in defending Baghdad the Iraqis didn't fight house-to-house, where the advantage of American technical and armament superiority would have been substantially diminished. It was subsequently learned that Saddam's war plan called for such resistance, which the Iraqis thought could delay the inevitable defeat by months, but Saddam's troops were apparently unwilling to make such a suicidal effort for what they believed was a lost cause [Nordland et al., 25]. Even without a stout defense of Baghdad, Saddam's retreating forces created enough chaos and sabotage to seriously disrupt the planned American liberation of Iraq and convert it into an arduous and bloody occupation.

In the central Sunni section of the country, the problem was wartime turmoil, confusion, and chaos, but south of Baghdad where the Shiite majority resided, the occupiers found something equally unexpected but far less troublesome—stability and order. The towns had been organized prior to the invasion by local Shiite religious leaders in charge of well-established administrative structures that were capable of governing their communities. These leaders simply went about their business without recognizing control from the occupying military authorities, and without any armed resistance. Because the CIA had so few operatives inside Iraq before the war, American intelligence had no means to detect the activities of neighboring Iranian forces that were in Iraq before the invasion, as they organized and prepared southern Iraqi communities for the anticipated American defeat of Saddam's Baathist regime. The Shiites did not revolt against the Allied invasion as the Sunnis did in the north because, as the majority religious group, they were ready and anxious to assume leadership for the first time in the history of the country in a permanent, democratic government. Truly, nothing in Iraq was quite as it seemed.

PHASE 2: THE OCCUPATION

The military victory over the Iraqis was won quickly in five or six weeks and with minimal allied casualties. From the start of the war through April 24th when most of the mopping up operations north of Baghdad had been completed, the Americans and British lost 175 soldiers and sustained 635 wounded, while the Australians had no casualties. The Americans estimated that 2,230 Iraqi soldiers had been killed and 7,400 Iraqis had been taken prisoner, while civilian deaths were estimated between 1,930 and 2,377 [Walker, 211]. The Allied bombing campaign was considered the most accurate aerial bombardment in the history of warfare, with most of the damage confined to Saddam Hussein's palaces and discreet military installations.

Except for the occasional misdirected bomb or missile due to faulty intelligence or questionable attempts to assassinate Saddam Hussein, the civilian population had been spared severe damage and casualties. Many Iraqi people may even have believed that the costs in human lives were worth the benefit of getting rid of Saddam Hussein's totalitarian regime. Unfortunately, the occupation rapidly turned into a nightmare with no end in sight for the Coalition and the war-fighting phase was remembered as the high point of the Iraqi operation.

Failure to Plan

When asked why the D-Day planning process was taking so long, Eisenhower remarked to Churchill that "a plan is nothing but lack of a plan is everything." The most telling reason for the ensuing nightmare in Iraq was the lack of a good plan, which to Eisenhower was "everything," and to the Third Infantry Division in Iraq, its lack of a plan was also "everything," as noted in:

> "...the extraordinary words in the 'after-action report'... [which] reads: 'Higher headquarters did not provide the Third Infantry Division (Mechanized) with a plan for

Phase IV [the postwar phase]. As a result, Third Infantry Division transitioned into Phase IV in the absence of guidance'" [Zakaria].

Planning the occupation was the responsibility of Secretary Rumsfeld, the Joint Staff, and the commander of Central Command, General Tommy Franks, and his staff. Franks was tired and had worked extremely hard since 9/11, planning and executing the successful invasion of Afghanistan and had submitted his request for retirement from the U.S. Army in late April 2003, shortly after Coalition Forces were launched into Iraq. For whatever reasons, Franks failed to creatively devise occupation plans as he had done in fighting earlier campaigns, but the ultimate failure belongs to Rumsfeld and his civilian cadre in the Pentagon, not Franks. Notwithstanding the deplorable lack of good, actionable intelligence information, failure to provide American occupation forces with a well thought out plan for the occupation can only be considered gross dereliction of duty because of the lives put at risk and the conditions that developed in the Sunni sector of Iraq after active hostilities between the Coalition and Iraqi forces had ended.

Secretary Rumsfeld and his key advisors within the Department of Defense must accept responsibility for failure to develop a satisfactory U.S. occupation plan while rejecting inputs from other departments and agencies such as the detailed planning document developed by the State Department. It is doubtful if the State Department's plan for the occupation of Iraq would have avoided the pitfalls the military encountered after Saddam's Baghdad statute tumbled to the ground and the city erupted in chaos and looting, but this will be a task for historians to evaluate.

Past American postwar planning activities had also been meager, but earlier commanders had been generally luckier and more successful than the effort in Iraq. For instance, in the spring of 1945, four months before the Japanese surrender, the War Department finally got around to ask Ruth Benedict, a Columbia University cultural anthropologist, to write a report on Japan to assist U.S. military in its coming occupation. The report that later was published as *The Chrysanthemum and the Sword* became a bestseller,

> "but most importantly, her government work ended up becoming the 'Bible' for the American troops who undertook the occupation of Japan" [Stille].

American soldiers bringing democracy to Japan after centuries of militarism had some common understanding of the Japanese culture from Benedict's report and they were able to cope successfully. But such was not the case in Iraq in spite of the fact that the United States had hundreds of social scientists, journalists, and retired military officers with hands-on experience in Iraq and the Middle East, something Benedict did not have in Japan.

An even more relevant history for the occupation of Iraq was the experience of the British—the major U.S. partner in the Coalition—in 1920 when it had occupied and created the modern state of Iraq after the First World War. Iraq had been a part of the Ottoman Empire until the Treaty of Versailles broke up the empire and placed Iraq under British mandate until 1932. The early part of the 12 years of British occupation in Iraq was marked with insurrections led by both Sunni and Shiite religious groups that "soon transcended the country's ancient ethnic and sectarian divisions" [Ferguson]. The British were only able to quell the uprising by extremely harsh military action in which thousands of innocent civilians were massacred, something the Coalition was loath to repeat.

Instead of concerning themselves with Iraqi culture or its history, American forces prepared for the end of hostilities as if they were rescuing flood or earthquake victims. The Pentagon plan for the cessation of fighting called for retired U.S. Army Lieutenant General Jay Garner to serve as Director of Reconstruction and Humanitarian Assistance for Iraq. Garner was an expert in directing disaster assistance programs and had served admirably in northern Iraq with the Kurds in the 1990s following the First Gulf War. Clearly, the Defense Department believed that the principal postwar problem in

Iraq would be limited to providing food and shelter to the hungry and homeless. Through no fault of his own, General Garner lasted exactly one month in his impossible Baghdad role, coordinating unrealistic post-combat operations directly for the Pentagon, an almost assured disaster from the start.

Failing to understand Iraq's culture or history, among other things, led the American forces to underestimate the difficulties they would encounter. Insurgency was what the Americans found, but only in the Sunni areas of Iraq, with a single later exception. The Americans should have expected rebellion and insurgency led by the defeated Baathists of Saddam Hussein's regime, supplemented by Arab jihadists from neighboring countries, but the CIA unfortunately had only four agents on the ground in Iraq before the war and they were mostly from the oil sector and had limited knowledge of Saddam's military plans. If the Iraqis actually planned a war of retreat and insurgency, the Americans should have surmised that all the support systems for a guerrilla war, as the arms caches in Iraq indicated, had been in place in the Sunni Triangle northwest of Baghdad long before the invasion was launched and plans should have been adjusted accordingly. The Baathists were not about to fight the Americans in the open where superior U.S. armament and tactical air power would have picked them to pieces as they had in the First Gulf War. Instead of meeting the enemy head on, Saddam's Baathist strategy was to drag the Americans and its Coalition partners into a protracted quagmire of insurgent warfare like Vietnam, forcing the American population to eventually tire of war and demand retreat and withdrawal of U.S. forces from Iraq. While it had been al Qaeda that refused to alter its tactics during the American invasion of Afghanistan, it was now the Americans who refused initially to admit that they were facing a deadly insurgency of growing intensity.

Ironically, returning Shiite exiles were in large part responsible for the occupation forces' failure to provide necessary security, for they had insisted that Saddam's army and police force had to be totally dismantled immediately after hostilities ended and that all Baathists in government positions be removed from office. Although a retained

Iraqi army and police force could well have contained some of the clandestine Sunni Baathist insurrectionists, which would have taken some time to root out, a military police force and American combat soldiers on the ground were necessary to provide basic security for the protection of life and property. With as many as 30,000 released felons on the streets and no Iraqi police or military force, it is no surprise that chaos quickly spread and, without continued employment for any of the former security personnel and no future for Baathists in the reconstructed Iraq, the Sunni Baathist insurgency rapidly grew in numbers and strength.

The decision by Paul Bremer, the American-appointed administrator of the Coalition Provisional Authority who succeeded Jay Garner, to accept the Shiite demand and dismiss high ranking Baathists from the civil service and the Iraqi police and military, left the occupation forces in a catch-up mode throughout the remainder of 2003 and all of 2004. Bremer's endorsement of the Shiite demand ranks as the worst and most damaging American occupation decision. Bremer [2005] later defended his decision by arguing that "[t]he disbanding of Saddam's army signaled, to all Iraqis, the birth of a new nation," and that the army had already disbanded itself. However, had Bremer announced immediately that, after checking individual records for Baathist criminals, the Coalition was prepared to reestablish the Iraqi police and army forces, an effective security force could have been in place in much less time than later proved to be necessary by retraining new applicants. Because most former civil servants, police, and army forces were blameless and unemployed, many became recruiting candidates who later joined the Sunni Baathist insurgents.

We recognize the difficulties encountered in training a new Iraqi army—shortages of Arab linguists and military trainers, the hostile environment, or lack of the best qualified and motivated trainees—but the slowness of the program was a serious hindrance to release Coalition troops from duty in Iraq. And we now know that the rising strength of the Sunni insurgency made it that much more difficult to train and recruit qualified Iraqi security force candidates.

Over the succeeding months, the Baathists and Sunni Islamist jihadists fought a continuous and increasingly successful counterinsurgency from the Sunni Triangle. More recently foreign al Qaeda jihadist forces under the command of Abu Masab al Zarqawi caused many more American and innocent Iraqi casualties than occurred during the invasion. Although the al Qaeda jihadist group was by far the smaller force in the insurgency, it made up for its lack of size by a willingness to commit the most heinous acts, kidnapping foreigners and beheading the victims, and its willingness to kill more Shiite Iraqis than the Baathist Sunni insurgents were inclined to do.

However, the jihadist atrocities were indicative of weakness, not strength, because the acts were offensive to the broader Muslim community, which was al Qaeda's real target audience in Iraq. Al Qaeda's objective in Iraq was to prove that Americans are cowards who lack the political will to fight a protracted and bloody guerrilla war in the Middle East. American willingness to stay and fight meant that bin Laden's primary objective in Iraq could not be realized and that eventually Iraq, like Afghanistan, would enter into the American victory column. It also meant that, while al Qaeda had to allocate so many of its recruits to the Iraqi insurgency, the American homeland was less likely to be attacked—part of the Bush strategy of a strong offense as the best defense. Fear and intimidation spread among moderate Sunnis inside the Sunni Triangle as the insurgent forces continued to grow from both the inside—as many discouraged police and military personnel enlisted—and from the outside, as more young Arabs from Saudi Arabia and other nearby countries answered the call for jihad. Such fear made the U.S. intelligence job of identifying insurgents more difficult but gradually actionable intelligence information became more available and reliable. One significant intelligence breakthrough was the killing of Uday and Qusay Hussein, Saddam's sons, on July 22, 2003 in Mosul by the 101st Airborne troops using information received from a paid informant.

In contrast, few insurgent attacks took place in the Shiite or Kurdish areas of Iraq where the resident population refused to conceal and protect the rebels. The only guerrilla outbreak among the Shiites came in the spring of 2004 when a rebel Shiite cleric, Muqtada al Sadr, staged an uprising and moved his Mahdi Army to Najaf, one of the holiest cities in Shiite Islam. Without al Sadr's knowledge, Grand Ayatollah Ali al Sistani, the major Shiite religious leader in Iraq, actually staged al Sadr's attacks as part of a political strategy of persuading the Allied force that Iraqi Shiites were fully capable of waging an insurgency war against the occupiers if they did not follow al Sistani's plans for national elections to provide Shiite majority control in the permanent Iraqi government. Once al Sadr was informed that Shiites would no longer assist him, surrender was inevitable and al Sadr retreated to his stronghold in the slums of Baghdad to begin a peaceful campaign as a potential candidate in the January 2005 elections. However, al Sadr was not brought to justice for his alleged murders of Coalition Forces and fellow Iraqis, and he remained at large with limited authority to act independently, protesting from time-to-time in the streets of Baghdad, though gaining some seats in the National Assembly from the January 2005 elections. He continued to be a troubling pest in 2006 but failed in his attempt to influence selection of the leaders of the emerging government when Ibrahim al Jafari was forced to step down as Prime Minister designate in April 2006.

Further intelligence success followed, based on a collection of actionable intelligence information derived from questioning Saddam's former bodyguards and family members. In a routine military search, Saddam Hussein was captured on December 13, 2003 in a hole in the ground in the town of ad-Duar, 15 kilometers south of Tikrit, his hometown. Saddam had weapons in his possession and about $750,000 in U.S. $100 bills. He was in such an unkempt and confused condition when he climbed out of his underground hole that many Iraqis could not believe from the photos that this was the feared dictator who had killed and tortured hundreds of thousands of innocent Iraqis. DNA samples and dental records were used to positively identify Hussein, who soon after being shaved and cleaned up, resumed his defiant behavior, this time in a U.S. prison near the Baghdad airport and not in one of his many ostentatious palaces. Public opinion about the occupation received a brief but unsustainable bounce in popularity both in the United States and in Iraq but the insurgency continued to grow in violence and intensity and the Americans would face a disgraceful setback in one of their own Iraqi prisons.

The Abu Ghraib Prison Disaster

For decades, Saddam Hussein's secret police had tortured, abused, and killed innocent Iraqi citizens at the infamous Abu Ghraib Prison 20 miles west of Baghdad. The story of the torture of Iraqi prisoners by American soldiers at Abu Ghraib was broken by CBS on April 28, 2004 during its "60 Minutes II" program after the press failed to pick up on an innocuous one-paragraph press release from the U.S. Headquarters Command in Baghdad on January 16, 2004 announcing, "An investigation has been initiated into reported incidents of abuse at a Coalition Forces detention facility" [Ricchiardi]. In January, few newspapers even ran a story on the release. More than three months later, however, when CBS television ran videos filmed by the Abu Ghraib guards of taunting naked Iraqi prisoners with dogs, leashes, and female guards, making naked prisoners form human pyramids or chaining them outside their cells, a feeding frenzy of press reports exploded around the world.

Most damaging to the American cause were the Abu Ghraib videos aired by Al Jazeera and other Arab networks throughout the Muslim world, seriously offending Muslim sensitivities and sexual mores and superficially raising a question in their minds as to who was more evil, Saddam Hussein or depraved American infidel soldiers. Although Saddam's inhuman mistreatment of prisoners and Zarqawi's beheadings were far worse than anything the Americans did at Abu Ghraib or Guantanamo, the United States had experienced a huge setback in the ideological battle for the hearts and minds of the Muslim world. The story of American torture of Iraqi prisoners was bin Laden's greatest propaganda victory since 9/11 and it strengthened al Qaeda's call to Sunni Arab Muslims for jihadist death strikes and suicide attacks against the American infidels.

What had gone wrong? How could American military police have behaved in such an unprofessional and depraved manner? Two factors explain the disgraceful breach of behavior: (1) the deepening series of major intelligence failures that continued to plague U.S. forces and (2) an even more serious problem, the deplorable lack of military training and discipline in some of the Army's poorly-led reserve units. The disgrace of Abu Ghraib is really a microcosm of a far greater problem in the organization of American military forces and its "all-volunteer" Army consisting of active duty Army units, the Army National Guard, and the Army Reserve. In time, U.S. Army reserve forces in Iraq would reach nearly 40 percent of the total U.S. forces deployed there. As a backlash from the Vietnam War, the politically unpopular draft was ended under President Nixon and mandated service in the U.S. military stopped in 1973. The era of volunteer service had started and the active and reserve components of the U.S. military were sold to the public by the Nixon and subsequent administrations as complementary elements in the new "totally integrated" all volunteer force, a concept untested in sustained combat.

With some exceptions among the better trained Army National Guard units, experience in Iraq has shown that many of the Army's reserve units were poorly trained and even more poorly led. This was especially true of the Army Reserve units at Abu Ghraib Prison where the commander, Brigadier General Janis Karpinski, a reservist called to active duty from her civilian job for service in Iraq, was suspended, demoted, and reprimanded for failure to properly train and prepare her troops in the 800th Military Police Brigade she commanded. The Army charged that General Karpinski was responsible for prisoner abuses that were carried out by soldiers under her command and occurred when she commanded 16 prisons in Iraq. Poor intelligence was bad enough, but at least it was improving. The real dilemma the Army faced was with untrained, ill-disciplined, and poorly-led reserve forces and that situation continued to deteriorate. Neither the politicians in Washington nor the military leadership in the Pentagon desired to discuss the reservist problem because the alternative would be the politically unpopular draft, but the fact remained that the Army's so-called "total force" system was badly broken and required an immediate fix. In addition to the appalling situation at Abu Ghraib with the Army's reserve forces under General Karpinski's disgraceful leadership, poor Army intelligence and undue pressure on the CIA to obtain solid intelligence information also contributed to the conditions surrounding the Abu Ghraib prisoner abuse problem.

With the worsening insurgency, U.S. military intelligence forces were becoming increasingly desperate to ferret out information and captured Iraqi insurgents became the best prospects. The poorly-led and ill-disciplined American reservists at Abu Ghraib, operating without adequate supervision or directives, followed their worst instincts, and the lowest common denominator among their ranks, a sadistic army specialist named Charles Graner, was sentenced to 10 years in prison for his unpardonable actions. Six other guards received lesser sentences and all were courts-martialed and discharged from the United States Army. The Pentagon investigation headed by former Secretary of Defense James Schlesinger found no others guilty of any crimes, including General Karpinski. However, General Karpinski was relieved from command and the official Army investigation stated that she "understaffed the prison, exercised poor oversight, and failed to remind her soldiers of the Geneva Conventions' protections for detainees" [Copeland], implying culpability on her part for the lack of appropriate supervision of the guards.

Secretary Rumsfeld twice offered his resignation because of the scandal, but President Bush refused to accept it both times. From the standpoint of the war on terror, acceptance of Rumsfeld's resignation offers, for both the Abu Ghraib disaster and the deplorable lack of planning for postwar operations, would have clearly demonstrated to the world that such conduct is totally unacceptable by American ethical standards. But President Bush was in the midst of a hard-hitting presidential reelection campaign at that time in 2004 in which his strategy was to tough-out the bad news coming from the Iraq war without admitting any errors by his administration and force his Democratic opponent, John Kerry, to explain to the electorate what changes the Democrat would make in fighting the war that would improve the outcome. Surprisingly, Senator Kerry did not raise the prisoner abuse scandal during the presidential campaign and a majority of the electorate didn't accept Kerry's proposals as convincing solutions to the Iraq war problems. However, after the election, President Bush could have replaced Donald Rumsfeld for the Abu Ghraib scandal and the other strategic and tactical planning errors that had been made in fighting the Iraq war after its initial success in deposing Saddam Hussein. Personnel changes in the management of the occupation should have been made because a loud and clear American statement was needed denouncing the horrors of the Abu Ghraib disaster.

Another issue raised by the Abu Ghraib scandal was an ethical dilemma of how to treat terrorist prisoners in an unconventional war in which the enemy combatants, fanatical religious fanatics willing to die for their cause, did not subscribe to traditional Western standards for fighting a war under the terms of the Geneva Convention. As a consequence, the President sent mixed signals to the military security forces in establishing U.S. policy for the treatment of prisoners:

> As a matter of policy, the United States Armed Forces shall continue to treat detainees humanely and, to the extent appropriate and consistent with military necessity, in a manner consistent with the principles of *Geneva* [Sullivan and his italics].

Secretary Rumsfeld created further confusion among the ranks by issuing in December 2002 and then, six weeks later, rescinding an order that approved the expansion of interrogation techniques for questioning the prisoners of the Afghan war who were interned at the American detention center for terrorists at the U.S. Naval Base in Guantanamo Bay, Cuba. British interrogators were similarly found guilty of prisoner abuses in Iraq but America, because of its global preeminence and virtuous intentions, had created a huge bin Laden propaganda victory that severely detracted from America's ability to win the war on terror.

Despite the barbaric treatment that Coalition prisoners of war received at the hands of Islamist militants, the United States is always best served by observing and remaining true to American values. Winning the war on terror requires winning the heart and soul of the more than one billion mainstream Muslims around the world. Because the Abu Ghraib prisoner abuse scandal was such a monumental disaster for America's war efforts, Rumsfeld's offers to resign should have been accepted or, failing that, the senior general officers in the chain of command should have been fired and forced to resign from the Army. Anything short of that gave the appearance of a nation less honorable and less virtuous than its noble charters purport it to be.

Loss of Momentum and Confidence

From the moment American troops cautiously entered Baghdad in early April of 2003, the American high command and its soldiers seemed to lose confidence due to the lack of a comprehensive post-combat plan. Instead of taking charge of the captured capital city, American commanders seemed to stand back and watch as looters decimated government buildings and facilities. Only the Oil Ministry building was protected, leading to the impression among Iraqis that the sole asset the Americans cared about was oil. Western journalists in the city had to recruit soldiers to safeguard one last hospital that hadn't been looted, but otherwise chaos reigned supreme [Engel]. The organized sabotage of the electrical and water systems may have been difficult to stop but looters could have been driven off or captured and order could have been restored through the imposition of martial law. Instead, the American troops appeared to be concerned only with their own safety, not the safety of innocent Iraqis or their property. Indeed, additional troops were available to control the rioting; 16,000 soldiers in the First Cavalry Division had been available for deployment to Baghdad in mid-April, but Secretary of Defense Rumsfeld canceled their deployment and "General Franks eventually went along" [Gordon and Trainor, 3/13/2006]. It took nearly 21 months, until the Iraqi national elections at the end of January 2005, to recover from the appalling first impression created by the total breakdown in security.

The second major failure of the occupation of Iraq was the immediate lack of recognition that the Iraqi army had in fact not surrendered, but was instead waging a protracted insurgency or guerrilla war against the coalition forces. The evidence in Baghdad was all around: (1) extensive use of dedicated irregulars and martyrs as suicide bombers, rearguard forces in attacking the invaders, and disappearing armies in the field as the coalition forces approached them; (2) hidden caches of arms throughout the countryside and the city as supplies for an insurgent army; (3) lack of any formal surrender by the army leaders and (4) the most obvious evidence—the press releases in Europe as early as April 12, 2003 announcing the insurgency and the call to arms for a global Muslim jihad against the American infidels and their Allies. All of these indicators should have immediately alerted the Pentagon and the generals in Iraq to the kind of war Coalition forces faced. But instead of aggressively addressing the insurgency, American forces in Baghdad hunkered down and assumed defensive positions, allowing the insurgents to organize, assume the offensive against them, and disrupt allied efforts to create a stable environment for a new Iraqi government.

One brief attempt in the first year of occupation was made to break out of this defensive posture, but it quickly floundered on the rocks of indecision and lack of American political will during an election campaign. In April 2004 after four American security contractors were ambushed, burned, and their bodies dishonored in Fallujah, an Iraqi Wahhabi-influenced city in the Sunni Triangle about 40 miles west of Baghdad, the U.S. Marines:

> mounted an assault on the city, a punitive mission that outraged many Iraqis and was called to a halt before it achieved any of its goals. A compromise deal was cut in which former Baathists agreed to provide security. In fact, the town quickly became a haven for insurgents and terrorists [Nordland et al].

The results were disastrous with the entire Muslim population of Iraq rising up as one to protest the American incursion into Fallujah, which was hailed as a major victory for the insurgents and a defeat for the Americans. To turn over control of Fallujah to Sunni Baathist insurgents and foreign jihadists in the Sunni stronghold defies understanding. Indeed, after a year of fighting the growing insurgency, U.S. forces did not even know who the enemy was. It also suggests that during the 2004 presidential election campaign, no one in the Democratic Party was following the war closely enough to raise this issue, for Bush had been vulnerable on problems with the Iraq war, but he was never seriously challenged by Kerry, who seemed afraid to bring up Iraq. Most U.S. commanders apparently thought they were fighting foreign jihadist terrorists, al Qaeda, when in fact the real organizer of the overall insurgency and the principal supplier of insurgents were 12-15,000 members of Saddam's former Baathist party who had enlisted support from outside Arab jihadists, primarily young Saudi suicide bombers, even before the outbreak of hostilities. In fact, the insurgency was well-planned and the Baathists came out into the open from underground operations and became deadlier and more difficult to fight and reign in.

Following an innovative and imaginative initial battle plan, an almost complete American void in planning and adapting to postwar conditions is baffling to outside observers. Indeed, Packer [147] argues that:

> If there was never a coherent postwar plan, it was because the people in Washington who mattered never intended to stay in Iraq," and he quotes a Defense Department official as saying, "Rummy and Wolfowitz and Feith [Undersecretary for Planning] did not believe the U.S. would need to run postconflict Iraq.

The Iraqi exiles were evidently supposed to do it. Thus, the Pentagon bosses had been totally surprised by the Baathist insurgency and failed to have a proper contingency plan in place. Even the most naïve in the Pentagon and Central Command must have realized that the more time the Coalition gave the insurgency to organize and recruit, the stronger the insurgency would become as intimidation spread and new jihadist recruits joined the battlefield against the Americans. That is exactly what happened, as the number of insurgency incidents grew and the types of targets changed.

The immediate targets in the early days of the Iraq insurgency were the Coalition troops—the occupiers—and the message was: "Get out, you'll never successfully occupy Iraq." The United States had a reputation in the Muslim world as an impressive high-tech military force but with little political staying power—a true paper tiger. The Baathists thought that if they could convince the American public that they were facing another Vietnam quagmire that could not be won, the fickle American public would quickly lose faith and force a pullout as the United States did in Somalia in 1993 and Vietnam before that.

This was Saddam's plan from the beginning. A slightly more sophisticated Iraqi tactic on that same theme was to isolate the occupiers by attacking other organized entities indirectly supporting the Coalition by providing humanitarian assistance to Iraqis and lending credibility and legitimacy to the occupation. In July and August 2003, the Jordanian embassy and the United Nations headquarters buildings were destroyed by suicide bombers and prominent international aid workers were kidnapped and assassinated as part of this expanded campaign to isolate the occupiers. The U.N. and many aid groups promptly pulled out after being attacked, blaming the Americans for failing to provide security, and providing the insurgents with another easy victory.

Before the insurgents increased the intensity and broadened the scope of their attacks, the U.S. military was literally shooting itself in the foot by canceling on April 17, 2003 its order for body armor for its soldiers and vehicle armor for its Humvee vehicles [Moss]. When the insurgency started to look more serious by May 15th, the U.S. Army was unable to simply reopen the supply chain. The body armor supplier was unable to mass produce a stock of vests, leaving many soldiers unprotected for months and 10,000 armor plates for the Humvees were lost and arrived late. Coalition forces and private individuals, unconstrained by Pentagon purchasing procedures, were able to purchase body armor on the open market for their own protection. By January 2004, the 10,000 armor plates still hadn't been located, but all Humvees operating in the Iraqi theater were at last protected. It seems that, "The bulletproof vests had been labeled high priority, but in the ensuing chaos [of military procurement for the war], everything got treated as high priority, which meant that in fact nothing was" [Moss].

The scene in Iraq was going from bad to worse for the American forces, and even though many Iraqi citizens were pleased with the toppling of the despised dictator, Saddam Hussein's ultimate capture in late 2003 did not deflect the downward trend in morale, for many Iraqis were still without electricity, gasoline, or personal security. The only thing that the Iraqis never seemed to be short of was food, the one contingency the invading American force had been fully prepared to provide. U.S. soldiers who had bravely fought the Iraqi army were also getting demoralized, especially some of the untrained, ill-disciplined, and poorly-led Army Reserve units, as it appeared their government couldn't protect them from snipers, roadside bombs, and suicide bombers and didn't rotate them in and out of Kuwait for R&R where other reservists had been assigned full-time duty without the around-the-clock anxieties of daunting counterinsurgency duties in Iraq.

PHASE 3: AN INTERIM GOVERNMENT

In desperation, the Coalition Administrator, Paul Bremer, swore into office the new Iraqi interim government two days before its scheduled initiation date of June 30, 2004 in order to confuse the insurgents and not allow them to disrupt the ceremony. The Pentagon had hoped that turning over authority to Iraqis would slow down the insurgency by giving Iraqis ownership in the new government, and, by moving it up two days, it also permitted Mr. Bremer to get out of Iraq even earlier than planned. The Americans were now, in theory at least, supposed to be in Iraq at the request and direction of the new sovereign government. Most Iraqis didn't buy this, however, because they viewed the new interim government as American stooges or puppets. They were mostly returning exiles, many of whom had been or still were in the employ of the United States Central Intelligence Agency—the London-based "Gucci Guerrillas." The various religious sects and ethnic groups were all represented; they were all Iraqi citizens, but they had been chosen by the Americans, not by the Iraqi people. That difference would remain critical as American forces worked their way through an unintelligible and confusing Iraqi maze.

Inability to Bring Factions Together
Ayad Allawi, the interim prime minister, secular Shiite and former Baathist who went into exile in the 1970s, accepted as his first responsibility the task of reaching out to the Sunni moderates to engage them in the new government. He appointed a Sunni and another former Baathist, as his defense minister. Allawi, from the first moment he assumed leadership in the government, was concerned that efforts to create a unified Iraq would be shattered by those seeking revenge and retribution for past injustices. He was, however, unsuccessful in coming to any understanding with the Sunnis, partly because of American insistence that anyone who had waged a successful attack on the Americans or government forces, as well as any high-ranking, former Baathists, was automatically excluded from the political process. This excluded most politically active Sunnis and the conditions imposed on the negotiations made Allawi's job virtually impossible. But Allawi's efforts certainly put the Sunnis on notice that there was willingness among some Shiites to create a new federal government for all Iraqis that included Sunnis, Kurds, and Shiites.

With the best chance for compromise behind the interim government, the Sunni insurgency continued to grow in size and intensity and the number of Iraqi and American deaths continued to rise. Meanwhile, also joining the broader insurgency were newly radicalized Sunni Iraqis, many of them Wahhabis from the Shamar confederation in the Sunni Triangle and tribal "cousins" of northern Saudi Wahhabis, and Iraqi nationalists who hated the occupying force and were disenchanted by the economic turmoil and destruction caused by the endless fighting. Instead of compromising with the interim government, the Baathist insurgents established a closer working relationship with the foreign Arab jihadists led by Abu Musab al Zarqawi, a Jordanian Takfir Wal Hijra, the fierce Wahhabi-Salafist offshoot violently opposed to Shiites and the West. Zarqawi sent a letter to Osama bin Laden in January 2004 offering to serve as al Qaeda's representative in Iraq in the war against the infidel Americans and this closer working relationship between Zarqawi and the Iraqi Baathist insurgents formally brought al Qaeda into the picture as the jihadist enemy. Prior to this improved working relationship, the jihadists and the Baathists had bickered on numerous issues and started to go their separate ways; this new entente brought them closer together and heightened the effectiveness and brutality of the insurgency through better coordination, closer cooperation, and even more violent attacks against the Americans and Iraqi Shiites.

As a result, the number of suicide bombings increased markedly in the fall of 2004, rising from an average of about 1.5 bombings per week to more than that per day, as the al Qaeda forces combined their ability to recruit jihadists through the Baathist Party intelligence and financial network in Syria and other countries such as Saudi Arabia, where most of the young suicide bombers originated. Cars loaded with explosives and driven by young jihadist martyrs were almost as accurate as America's precision bombing attacks, but far more effective in spreading terror. The Baathist intelligence network, with allies in the Iraqi police and army either through political allegiance or intimidation, was vastly superior to the Coalition's intelligence capabilities. In addition, Saddam Hussein had provided the needed funds to finance an extended insurgency and it has now become increasingly clear that Syrian Baathists also provided extensive assistance to the Iraqi insurgents. With money, manpower, intelligence, and a cause to die for, the Baathist-led Sunni insurgency was winning the battle of the occupation in late 2004, and, even worse, the foreign Arab jihadists seemed to be gaining greater control of the insurgency. The Allies needed a miracle to turn the war of insurgency around and in their favor.

Fallujah—Round II

Recalling how the British had quelled the 1920 rebellion against the colonialists [Ferguson], the coalition forces decided, in desperation, to get tougher and more aggressive in their war against the insurgents. Meanwhile, in late October 2004 just weeks before the American election, U.S. forces announced their intention to end the terrorist safe haven in Fallujah, a city of 300,000 in the Sunni Triangle with an area of about 350 square miles, by bringing in 6,000 American troops—four marine battalions and two army battalions—together with 2,000 Iraqi troops as the assault element to clear the rebellious city of all insurgent forces. A nearly equal number of troops totally surrounded Fallujah to prevent insurgents from escaping during the attack. It was unfortunately necessary to give public notice of the impending assault so innocent civilians could leave before the attack, and many insurgents also fled the city. With surprise eliminated, the combined attack finally began on November 8th, less than a week after the presidential elections in the United States and before the end of Ramadan, the Muslim fasting holiday of prayer and charity.

As expected when American forces bring formable air and artillery power against an enemy, the outcome was never in doubt. However, house-to-house urban combat, which lasted for nearly 12 days, was a high casualty operation and Coalition forces sustained 51 Americans killed and 425 seriously wounded while 8 Iraqi soldiers were killed and 43 wounded. Although light for urban warfare, the American forces sustained an 8 percent casualty rate, "a low but not insignificant loss for less than two weeks' combat" [Keiler]. An estimated 2,000 to 3,000 insurgents were killed or captured, but probably an equal number, including virtually all its leadership including Zarqawi, escaped with the civilian population before hostilities began.

Historically, Fallujah has had a large Wahhabi population with Bedouin origins and was known as the "City of Mosques," which the insurgents fully utilized for defense. A U.S. Army report on the Fallujah fighting indicated that one out of every two mosques in Fallujah was used to hide fighters or weapons during the American offensive. One such mosque, the Muhammadia Mosque where fighting was especially heavy, took 16 hours of house-to-house urban combat to eventually capture. The American soldiers tried not to enter the mosques first and employed Iraqi soldiers for the inside fighting. Because of prior notice of the impending attack, almost all civilians had evacuated their homes and avoided injury. Disruption and chaos were high prices for so large a civilian population to pay to rid their city of the insurgents, especially when so many Iraqi Wahhabi Sunnis were sympathetic to the Baathist cause.

However, the Baathists and local Sunnis were less sympathetic to the foreign Arab jihadists who had commandeered much of the private property in the city and left behind substantial evidence of atrocities. Although the second battle of Fallujah was, at a minimum, a significant tactical victory for the Coalition, it was not the miracle that was needed to assure defeat of the insurgency. That would have to wait, but an opportunity to turn the tide was already underway.

Election Preparations

Because of the insistence of Grand Ayatollah Ali al Sistani that Iraqis would choose their first permanent legislative assembly from national slates determined by Iraqi political parties in free elections, the original plans of Paul Bremer to select legislators through regional caucuses held throughout the nation were revised. Fortunately, it was one of the few decisions in which the resolute President Bush, a vigorous advocate of free elections, was willing to change his mind, at least on how the legislators should be selected. Further, Sistani, the powerful Shiite cleric and advocate of Iraq's movement toward democracy, also insisted that free elections should come sooner rather later, finally agreeing on January 30, 2005, the earliest date U.N. election advisors would accept. This approach had the advantage of each Iraqi citizen being enfranchised without intermediaries selected in caucuses. However, it had the disadvantage of disenfranchising voters in most Sunni districts where the insurgency was strong and voters were intimidated.

The toppling of Saddam Hussein converted Grand Ayatollah Ali al Sistani from a devout, monastic, scholarly, and apolitical Shiite cleric into a wise and just politician who remained remote and above the fray, while from behind the scenes he put together the national Shiite political slate. His goal was clearly to ensure that the Shiite majority, after decades of Sunni-Baathist domination, received its opportunity to lead Iraq. He understood that the formula for political success and stability in Iraq required a secular democracy with power shared among the various ethnic and religious sects. Sistani, Iranian by birth and education, remained opposed to the Shiite theocracy in Iran because he believed that worldly political authority in the hands of religious clerics was inappropriate. Sistani and his Shiite followers, his aides assassinated and fellow Shiites massacred in their mosques, suffered deeply at the hands of the Sunni insurgents by refusing to tolerate revenge tactics by his followers but, "[i]n the face of incessant provocation he has marginalized men of violence" [Ignatieff].

Through the constant and reassuring power of Sistani's faith and the enthusiastic support of the Kurds in the north, who suffered years of deprivation and massacre under Saddam Hussein, the Iraqis moved resolutely toward the January 30th election date. Both the Shiites and the Kurds endured the painful increase in suicide bombings as the insurgents changed the focus of their attacks from the American occupiers to the likely victors in the upcoming elections. By revising the targets of their attacks, the insurgents made it clear to the Iraqi population and the greater Muslim world that the goal of the Sunni insurgency in Iraq was not to repel infidels from sacred Islamic lands, but rather to create chaos and misery among fellow Muslims as a means of obtaining political power for their own ends and their own goals. The attacks on the Shiites by the Islamist jihadists proved to everyone in Iraq and in the Arab world that the jihadists were not interested in anything other than achieving their own goals of installing an authoritarian Taliban-like reign of terror that would even exceed the depravity of Saddam Hussein's torture chambers.

As 100,000 Iraqis volunteered to set up and conduct the elections, it became increasingly apparent that the elections would be held on schedule. Both within and without Iraq, critics claimed that free and fair democratic elections could not be held until the entire country was secure and it was safe for all citizens to vote. But the protestors ignored the fact that postponement of the elections would only reward the insurgents for their violence and encourage their continued efforts at further disruption. Fortunately, American resolution on the issue of holding the January 30th elections on schedule changed the war's momentum, for the Iraqi election was truly the miracle the coalition needed to turn around the war effort in its favor.

The elections made it clear that the insurgency was only a threat in the predominantly Sunni areas of Iraq—four of 18 provinces—because the insurgency was led by Baathist party leaders who tolerated and protected the al Qaeda-led Islamist militants from other nearby Arab states. These outside militants, especially Saudi suicide bombers imbued with fanatical Wahhabi intolerance of Shiites, would occasionally venture into Shiite territory and unleash powerful suicide bombs as a means of fostering civil war, but their murderous efforts were largely unsuccessful in a strategic sense. The agents of al Qaeda had no protectors in the southern Shiite parts of Iraq, and the Grand Ayatollah Ali Sistanti counseled his fellow Shiites to "turn the other cheek" because he knew that the militants could not spread fear and intimidation among his followers.

It was quite a different story for the moderate Sunnis, who received leaflets from the Sunni Islamist militants that warned, "To those of you who think you can vote and then run away, we will shadow you and catch you, and we will cut off your heads and the heads of your children" [Filkins, 1/26/2005]. Intimidated, most Sunni political leaders advocated a boycott of the election, after calling for a postponement right up to January 30th. The perverse effect of this imbalance in security was to limit the participation of Sunnis in the election process while at the same time permitting the majority Shiites to go to the polls without intimidation. Thus, the majority position of the Shiites was further enhanced in the national election results.

The elections were extremely popular and the turnout, even with the threats of death to all voters, was 57.8 percent of all registered voters, with turnouts as high as 92 percent in the northern Kurdish province of Dohuk to as low as 2 percent in the western Sunni province of Anbar [Burns and Glanz]. The U.S. military played a low key and almost invisible role providing security around the polling places, while Iraqi military and police personnel were highly visible in protecting the election sites. The effect of voting, combined with the visible absence of American soldiers in the voting process, filtered out the American "occupier" image for many Iraqis and other Muslims watching the news on Al Jazeerah television, for Americans were now seen less as occupiers and more as enablers of a new Iraq. Prior to the election, Americans were blamed for all of Iraq's problems—the lack of electricity, gasoline, crumbling infrastructure, and security.

> All that seemed to have changed last Sunday [January 30th election day], when millions of Iraqis streamed to the polls...Suddenly empowered with the vote, Iraqis no longer seemed to view America as all-powerful, or themselves as unable to affect events. A result has been a suddenly more accepting view of the United States [Filkins, 2/6/2005].

> [Even the U.S. troops serving in Iraq were ennobled:] Soldiers ranging from privates to senior officers described last Sunday's national election as vindication for over a year of hard service. The unexpectedly strong turnout, they said, altered their perception about the willingness of Iraqis to embrace the American mission here and helped project a rare positive image of the U.S. military following such stains as the Abu Ghraib prisoner abuse scandal last year [Fainaru].

Although the Shiite slate created by Grand Ayatollah Ali Sistanti, the United Iraqi Alliance, won 48 percent of the total vote, it fell well short of the two-thirds vote required to organize the new government. That left the Kurdish Alliance, with 26 percent of the vote, in position to broker the structure of the new coalition government with the Shiites and Sunnis. Because the Kurds favored a secular government, the two-thirds vote requirement virtually guaranteed that the new government would be secular and not an Islamist theocracy like the Shiite government of Iran, even if the United Iraqi Alliance reneged on its secular-government campaign promises. The Iraqi List, a party put together by interim Prime Minister Ayad Allawi, gathered 14 percent of the vote, leaving 12 percent of the vote split among nine different minority parties. Even with the low Sunni voter turnout, 40 Sunnis were elected to the National Assembly (15 percent of the seats), slightly less than they would have been afforded on a proportional basis since the Sunnis represent about 20 percent of the total Iraqi population [Taheri, 2/19/2005].

Despite the low showing by the American-backed Allawi party, American interests were well served by the results of the election for the formation of a secular coalition promised to include Sunni representation in the new prime minister's cabinet. Soon after the elections, Shiite leaders made it clear to disenfranchised Sunnis that they were willing to find ways to include Sunni representation in the government through their powers to appoint members of the executive branch and to the powerful committee drafting the new Iraqi Constitution. "The Association of Muslim Scholars [an important Sunni political organization]...said it would abide by the results of the ballot, even if it viewed the government as lacking legitimacy" [Shadid and Struck].

The reasons for the Shiite generosity, after centuries of domination and ruthless persecution by Sunnis, resulted from the Grand Ayatollah's attitude of forgiveness and a pragmatic realization that ratification of the new Constitution would require approval by more than 15 of the 18 Iraqi provinces; i.e., the Sunnis by virtue of their majorities in four provinces had veto rights over the new Constitution according to the rules for the drafting of a new Constitution adopted by the coalition and its appointed interim government. Moreover, the Kurds in the north control three provinces and thereby had a constitutional "trump card" to play in negotiating seats in the new government. Forgiveness and the old-fashioned give-and-take of pragmatic politics provided the basis for establishing and maintaining the new democratic Republic of Iraq.

PHASE 4: PAINFUL POLITICAL LESSONS AND AN INTENSIFIED INSURGENCY

The insurgency Saddam Hussein planned for the defense of Iraq underwent several iterations after the Coalition invasion. Initially, it was based on hard line Baathists augmented by Islamist jihadists Saddam invited to Iraq before the invasion. These two groups were supplemented by reliable lower level Baathists, not included in the initial planning, who were forced out of their military and civilian jobs by the demand for the de-Baathification by the Shiite exiles. Additional devout fundamentalist Wahhabis, mostly from Saudi Arabia, provided the primary source of suicide bombers that were so effective in intimidating other Iraqis as well as in killing large numbers of Coalition soldiers. In addition, two other groups of Sunni Iraqis joined the insurgency either for religious or nationalistic motives. The first group consisted of Iraqi Wahhabis from the Shamar confederation who had been persecuted under Saddam but now stepped forward against the infidel invaders. The second group came from Sunni tribal leaders and their members who resented the American presence and sought revenge for the occupation.

Although the numbers of each of these groups varied substantially over the course of the insurgency, the best estimate of their relative numbers in early 2006 was: about 10,000 Saddam loyalists and ex-Baathists; 5,000 Sunni tribal leaders and loyal tribesmen; 1,500 Iraqi Wahhabis; and 1,000 foreign jihadists, with these latter two religious groups organized into a fierce fighting contingent under Abu Musab al Zarqawi, Osama bin Laden's al Qaeda agent in Iraq. The numbers suggest that only about 20 percent of the total membership of 17,500 insurgents at the beginning of 2006 were unwilling to consider political compromise for the future of Iraq—1,000 hard core and high ranking Baathists subject to arrest for past crimes and 2,500 religious zealots. There is also increasing evidence [Tavernise and Filkins] that the al

Qaeda-controlled forces have annoyed their less sectarian insurgent allies, just as they previously did in the Balkans.

The goal of the new Iraqi government and the Coalition was to split the insurgency through a political compromise with the 80 percent of the insurgents—to get them to turn against the Baathist criminals and the foreign-led Wahhabi Islamist insurgents. Because the insurgency did not have a single unifying purpose or goal, the new government was able to gradually exploit the differences among the insurgents, which is what came to pass as a result of the 2005 elections. After the arrival of U.S. Ambassador Zalmay Khalilzad, politics became the primary focus for finally winning the Iraq war, and democratic elections followed by negotiations among all three parties—Kurds, Shiites, and Sunnis—came to be the primary means for reaching a settlement, even as the insurgency strengthened.

Sharp Rise in Iraq Insurgency

The January 30th election results and the slow formation of the new elected government changed the direction of the war's tide, but it did not end the insurgency by any means. Indeed, the insurgents were even more strongly motivated to disrupt and derail the democratic process leading to the development of a new Iraqi Constitution. Although the nature of the insurgency in Iraq changed several times since the war began in 2003, the rate and intensity of attacks, and the number of Iraqis killed, rose substantially after the new government took over in May and continued through the remainder of 2005, but dipped again after the October referendum on the Constitution. Targets for the attacks tended to be Iraqi Shiites, members of the new government regardless of religious affiliation, and diplomatic representatives of friendly Muslim nations supporting the new Iraqi government. Iraqi citizens, Sunnis and Shiites alike, became weary of the violence and recognized that the Sunni insurgents and radical jihadists had nothing to offer except another Baathist dictatorship or a jihadist totalitarian theocracy. The soft targets attacked by the young suicide bombers were extremely difficult to protect, as police and army recruiting sites, open air markets, restaurants, bus stations, mosques, funerals, and even bank queues were hit without mercy. Weapons of choice were typically car bombs or suicide bombs, both on foot and in vehicles. Clearly, the insurgents were seeking to create political havoc and possibly civil war because many of the target groups were Iraqi Shiites in their places of worship.

The change in tactics by the insurgents to high frequency, direct suicide bombings of Iraqi citizens further reduced public confidence in the new Iraqi government, especially in the Baghdad area where more than 45 percent of the deaths occurred. Insurgent attacks in the Shiite south and the Kurdish north were relatively few, permitting Iraqi and Coalition Forces to concentrate their forces in the four Sunnis-majority provinces. An adverse development for such a strategy could be the danger of local militia groups wresting control over the central government in some areas, where: "Their growing authority has enabled them to control territory, confront their perceived enemies and provide patronage to their followers" [Shadid and Fainaru]. Nevertheless, hundreds of American soldiers were pulled out of Najaf and replaced by Iraqi forces to test the tactic of concentrating Coalition Forces in the Sunni Triangle to achieve stability and eventually enable American troop withdrawal. But the success of the General Assembly negotiations on organizing the new parliament and finding an acceptable compromise on the Constitution became the final determinants as to when American troop withdrawal could safely occur.

The Process of Democratization

For a nation that was the most totalitarian state in a highly autocratic region that had no word in the Arabic language for "compromise," the most fascinating development in Iraq has been its determined effort to create, from scratch, a new democratic Constitution and government. The process started enthusiastically with a high rate of participation in the January 30th elections. Only the Sunnis in their four principal provinces failed to participate, either because of a political strategy to register opposition to the proposed democracy or out of fear of retaliation by the large number of insurgents in the Sunni region. Unfortunately, the hope and promise following the encouraging January elections, and its momentum were met with months of wrangling in the creation of the new Iraqi government. The final appointments to Prime Minister Ibrahim Jafari's cabinet were not approved until the first week in May 2005 and another couple of months were spent arguing over additional Sunni appointments to the Constitutional Committee. With such a slow political process (though democracy has never been considered efficient), it is small wonder that the insurgents increased suicide bombings to further undermine confidence in the new government. The real wonder was that, despite all the delay and increased danger, the Iraqi people stubbornly became involved in the process, and the Sunnis decided to engage in the political process as their best option for the future.

After wasting much of the time available for writing the Constitution, it was surprising that the August 15th deadline was not missed by more than two weeks. The Shiite and Kurdish representatives, the vast majority of the Constitutional Committee, reached a compromise on federalism and guarantees on human rights and finessed the differences between a democratic and Islamic state, which made women's rights somewhat ambiguous, hoping to work out pragmatic solutions through later legislation. The resulting Constitution was finally approved on August 28th without action by the National Assembly or support from the Sunni committee members. Our favorite Arab observer, Amir Taheri [9/3/2005], concluded:

> The Iraqi draft is not ideal. It will not transform Iraq into the Switzerland of the Middle East overnight. The text includes articles that one could not accept without holding one's nose. But the fact remains that this is still *the most democratic constitution offered to any Muslim nation so far.* More importantly, the people of Iraq have the chance to reject it if they feel it does not reflect their wishes. That, too, is a chance that few Muslim nations have enjoyed [emphasis added].

Ironically, Sunni opposition to the proposed Constitution made the turnout for the October 15th referendum on the Constitution a huge success and did more for democratizing Iraq than anything the Coalition had done. The voter registration in some Sunni parts of Iraq soared in a long-delayed Sunni effort to finally become actively engaged in the political process [Knickmeyer and Sebti]. The mere fact of Sunni engagement in the political process, even if to vote against the Constitution, was significant for Iraq's democratic future. And if the jihadist insurgents had attempted to prevent the Sunnis from voting in the October election, as they could have been expected to do, the emerging split in the insurgency that the Coalition had been seeking would have been achieved. Just when the situation seemed headed for an all-or-nothing conclusion at the ballot box in October 2005, U.S. Ambassador Zalmay Khalilzad stepped into the process and got the Kurds and Shiites on the Constitutional Committee to agree to give the newly to be elected National Assembly an additional six months for amending the Constitution. This action gave the Sunnis strong rationale for participating in the new government.

The result of this curious political process was to make the turnout for the National Assembly election on December 15, 2005 higher than any of the previous elections. A nearly 70 percent turnout in December was greater than the 63 percent voting in the Constitution referendum and much higher than the 58 percent in the first General Assembly elections almost a year earlier. Shiite parties captured 47 percent of the 275 seats in the National Assembly, Kurds 21 percent and Sunnis 21 percent, about the same percentages as the Kurdish and Sunni population, and the balance to splinter groups. The significance of the latest Iraqi elections can be deduced from two facts: first, the Sunni leadership, learning from the January 30th elections, decided that voting was their best chance to become players in the political development of the new, post-Hussein Iraq government; and second, voting in the Sunni-populated regions of Iraq would require the promise and delivery of a cessation of insurgent violence to bring potential voters to the polls on December 15th. From the high turnout of Sunni voters and the relative lack of violence on Election Day, voters obviously understood that the Sunni leaders controlled the Iraq insurgency, including the Iraqi Wahhabis and foreign jihadists who continued to oppose free elections as anti-Islamist. Al Qaeda of Iraq and their zealous Wahhabi partners gave way to the Sunni leadership—the former Baathists and other Iraqi nationalists opposing the American occupation—presumably because of the commanding numbers in the Sunni faction and the fact that the Baathists financed the insurgency and the jihadists depended upon the Sunni-led insurgency for their own survival.

The Sunni strength suggested that they could end the insurgency in exchange for certain concessions in negotiations for a new unity government: (1) appointment of a Sunni or acceptable nonsectarian to the Interior and Defense cabinet posts to ensure broad national support for Iraqi security forces and stop harassing Sunnis, (2) reinstate lower-ranking former Baathists in politics and government jobs, and (3) amend the Constitution to strengthen the central government of Iraq and rebalance the sharing of the oil wealth. By putting an end to the insurgency on the negotiating table, together with a demonstrated ability to deliver, the Sunni leadership was finally in a position to take a giant step toward bringing peace and freedom to Iraq. Although the Sunni strategy was somewhat akin to extortion, it certainly clarified the meaning of compromise, a word previously absent from the Arab vocabulary.

The outcome of the negotiations depended on how badly the Shiites and Kurds wanted peace. One can expect, however, that the wisest Shiite, Grand Ayatollah Ali Sistani, and the ablest American diplomat in Iraq, Ambassador Zalmay Khalilzad, could be expected to bring the parties together and ensure that negotiations were given every opportunity. Placing a peace offer on the table became the strongest possible negotiating chip for this formerly totalitarian and now war-torn nation, but peace in Iraq was finally close at hand.

PHASE 5: AN UNEXPECTED MOVE TOWARD CIVIL WAR

The American policy of planting the seeds of democracy and freedom in the Middle East followed a curious and unexpected course, just the way the entire Iraq war played out, but it in fact worked, even though it proceeded like the tortoise in the proverbial race with the hare. Americans learned that patience and confidence in democracy-inspired incentives are still the best hope for long-term success in an ideological war against the black ideology of the Iraqi jihadists and al Qaeda, but the next phase in the Iraq war became even more volatile and circuitous.

The December 15th election results were not certified as final until February 10, 2006—nearly two months after the elections. Almost a week later, the 130 Shiites elected to the Iraqi parliament, officially called the Council of Representatives, assembled to select their nominee for Prime Minister in the new government. By a one vote margin, the Shiites chose to reelect Ibrahim al Jafari, a devout Shiite sectarian, over the more secular and pragmatic Abel Abdul Mahdi who was favored by the Sunnis. The vote came after Muqtada al Sadr, the firebrand leader of the aborted uprising against the Americans in the spring of 2004, had threatened civil war among the Shiites if Jafari was not chosen. Using his threat as blackmail, Muqtada al Sadr became the Shiite kingmaker by delivering 32 votes for Jafari.

In the week following the Jafari victory, the Askariya shrine of the Golden Dome Mosque in Samarra was destroyed on February 22nd by a bomb blast, presumably inspired by Zarqawi and ignited by radical Sunni Wahhabi insurgents. "This is as 9/11 in the United States" [Knickmeyer and Ibrahim] for the Shiites, according to Abdel Abdul Mahdi, one of the two vice Iraqi vice presidents and Jafari's opponent in the Shiite party election. Although Samarra's Golden Dome mosque is not as old as others in the country, it is nevertheless one of Shiite Islam's holiest shrines. Having been rebuilt most recently in 1905, its destruction provided some Shiites with a rationale to finally strike back at the Sunnis. Though restrained by Grand Ayatollah Ali Sistani from taking revenge for the mass murder of thousands of innocent Shiites for nearly three years, Shiite counterattacks finally took place with vengeance during the months following the destruction of the holy Golden Dome shrine. Hundreds of Sunnis were killed, including some connected with the insurgency and many others who were just as innocent as the Shiite casualties. Typical of the Iraq insurgency, the unexpected continued to rule events and it now appeared that elements in the insurgency had finally found a way to precipitate the civil war Zarqawi and the radical Sunni jihadists had long tried to instigate.

Sectarian Violence

The destruction of the Samarra mosque unleashed a vicious cycle of reprisal killings that had not been observed in Iraq since the March 19, 2003 Coalition invasion. Although curfews and bans on driving automobiles in the aftermath of the February 22nd bombing lessened the number of killings somewhat, the number of dead probably exceeded 1,300 in the month after the mosque's destruction—the exact number was concealed by the Shiite government's unwillingness to release official numbers—and remained over 1,000 during April 2006 in the Baghdad area alone. Large numbers of both Sunnis and Shiites had to move out of communities where they had lived peacefully as minorities for generations. Blind-folded and bound corpses, usually young men, were found all over Baghdad and its suburbs with some disfigured by torture and some beheaded. It was in many ways even crueler violence than had been inflicted by the Baathist/jihadist insurgency and more widespread, although fewer numbers of women and children—fewer innocents—were killed than in the insurgent's suicide and car bombings.

Because there were no police investigations into these killings or official prosecutions, blame cannot be unambiguously assigned. However, many believe that the 15,000-man "Mahdi Army" militia of Muqtada al Sadr was largely responsible for the Sunni deaths and violent attacks on Sunni mosques in the Sunni Triangle. Counter-killings of

Shiites were blamed on the insurgents, but the resurgence of bombings of innocent Shiites did not begin again until more than a month after the February 22nd attack. However, on March 26th, "U.S. and Iraqi special forces killed at least 16 followers of the Shiite Muslim cleric Muqtada al Sadr...in a twilight assault on what the U.S. military said was a 'terrorist cell' responsible for attacks on soldiers and civilians" [Finer and Anderson]. The U.S. military's evidence for its claim was the most direct evidence of al Sadr's involvement in the Sunni revenge murders, but it was widely disputed by Shiite allies of al Sadr in the government of Prime Minister Ibrahim al Jafari who charged that American forces had massacred a group of defenseless Shiites worshipping in a mosque. Many Shiite leaders called for President Bush to remove U.S. Ambassador Khalilzad as the primary supporter of the Sunnis and instigator of civil war. The charges and counter-charges were referred to an investigative committee chaired by President Jalal Talabani, who promised to punish everyone committing a crime. Just when the American cause looked the bleakest in three years of war, and the country appeared on the verge of civil war, the unexpected had occurred again, changing once more the unfolding politics of Iraq.

The Political Implications of Sectarian Violence

The attack on the Shiite shrine had the unexpected effect of consolidating the non-Shiite members of Iraq's new parliament. As more and more Sunnis were killed after February 22nd, the Sunnis appealed to the al Jafari government to provide more security in their neighborhoods to stop the horrible reprisal killings. But, as increasing evidence pointed to al Sadr, al Jafari's king maker and principal instigator of the reprisals, al Jafari's inability to stop the killing mounted new opposition to his reelection. Suddenly, it was not the Americans who were responsible for the lack of security and the slow recovery of the economy; it was the al Jafari government that had been in office for nearly a year and had to bear that responsibility. As a result, by the beginning of March most Sunni and Kurd opposition parties had consolidated into a 133-seat block that was resolutely opposed to the reelection of Prime Minister al Jafari.

The effectiveness of al Jafari and his government came into further question on March 16th when the Council of Representatives finally met in its formal opening session for the swearing in of the representatives elected three months earlier. Al Jafari dismayed Iraqis by suggesting that it could take another month to reach agreement on a new government, which would mean that a new government would not take office for a full four months after its election. Al Jafari's real problem was that virtually everyone in Iraq knew that the only stumbling block to the formation of the new government was his own reelection as prime minister. The downward spiral in al Jafari's popularity continued, his stubbornness increased, and his resolve stiffened.

However, the embattled prime minister didn't seem to understand that he was being taken down by his association with Muqtada al Sadr. In a March 20th article in *The Washington Post*, al Jafari devoted two paragraphs of a thirteen-paragraph statement defending the radical cleric and claiming credit for bringing al Sadr into the political process. Al Jafari's economic news was equally disheartening to his supporters, for he promised "tough and unpopular change" to bring about the country's economic rehabilitation [Jafari]. Finally, by early April members of the Shiite block in parliament began to call for his withdrawal as their candidate for prime minister. Although he refused to acquiesce in these demands, the likelihood that Ibrahim al Jafari would ever be reelected prime minister rapidly approached zero, ending his career in politics. The personal plight of Ibrahim al Jafari and the resulting difficulty in forming a new government concealed the very real progress that had been made toward the formation of a unity government. David Ignatius [4/5/2006], based on his sources in Iraq, concluded that negotiations among the various factions produced the following kind of agreement:

> Here's the framework for the unity government, as outlined by Khalilzad, who has attended nearly all of the meetings. First, the broad strokes: The Sunni leaders have accepted that the new government will operate under the

Iraqi constitution and that it will be based on the results of last December's election, both of which reflect the reality that the Shiites are Iraq's largest religious group. The Shiites, in turn, have agreed that the new government will be guided by the consensus among all factions. And they have agreed to checks that will, in theory, prevent the key security ministries from being hijacked by Shiite militia groups.

To implement this consensual approach, the Iraqi factions agreed on two bodies that weren't mentioned in the constitution. They endorsed a 19-member consultative national security council, which represents all the political factions. And they agreed on a ministerial security council, which will have the Sunni deputy prime minister as its deputy chairman. Shiite leaders have tentatively agreed that the defense minister will be a Sunni. And for the key job of interior minister, the dominant Shiite faction, known as the Supreme Council for Islamic Revolution in Iraq [what's in a name?], appears ready to accept the replacement of one of its members by an independent Shiite, perhaps Qasim Dawood, a man acceptable to most Sunni leaders.

All that remained on April 5, 2006 was for al Jafari to step down and that finally took place on April 21st, when the world learned that the Shiites had broken the impasse and Iraq had not only avoided civil war but was instead ready to form its long awaited unity government. By selecting Jawad al Maliki, ("Nouri Kamal al Maliki" as he prefers to be called), a member of the Council of Representatives from the Dawa Party, the Shiite coalition finally pulled the rug out from under al Sadr, no longer a king maker and now only an out-of-step radical Shiite cleric with disturbing ties to Iran. Indeed, part of the reason for the delay was al Sadr's reluctance to let go. It seems that he was waging his own civil war against Abdul Aziz al Hakim, the clerical leader of a rival Shiite dynasty, who had opposed Jafari, causing Sadr to dig in his heels [Finer]. But much more important than this bickering between two Shiite clerics, as costly as it might have been for so many innocent people, the Iraqis were finally ready to enter the sixth and final phase in the post-Saddam era: the development of the first freely elected, peaceful, democratic Arab Muslim government in history.

CONCLUSIONS ABOUT THE WAR

The Iraq War was not the finest hour for the U.S. military despite the brave efforts of many fine combat soldiers and a sound invasion plan that was well executed in the early combat phases. But from the moment Saddam Hussein was toppled and his statue fell in Baghdad, the lack of a post-hostilities plan and good actionable intelligence assessments, coupled with serious misunderstandings regarding the nature of the enemy, lead to a downward spiral in Coalition fortunes. Whether this confusion reflected overconfidence of military leadership, once the initial goal of the invasion was so easily realized, or simply the lack of a good plan and sound intelligence about what the troops were likely to encounter, the U.S. military did not recover its equilibrium until a political solution was forced upon the Americans by a wise Shiite cleric.

The result of American planning failures resulted in a tragic loss of life endured by the ranks of the Coalition Forces and the citizens of Iraq. Obviously, the most significant cost in human suffering during the period was the rising number of Coalition deaths and civilian casualties from insurgent attacks, the latter increasing from 35 in July of 2003 to more than ten times that number in January 2005 just before the first 2005 election. Indeed, if the increases in casualties weren't bad enough, the number of mass murders through suicide bombings actually increased immediately after the election as the militant Islamists tried to take advantage of the slow political progress. While the prospects for a stable democratic government in Iraq grew, the militants began to target the Shiite population more frequently in hope of creating civil conflict to nullify the positive political effects of the elections and the emerging democracy. The number of Coalition military casualties during the post-election period actually declined, but increasingly brutal slayings of Iraqi military personnel offset this gain. And the final test came after the Samarra mosque destruction and Iraq tottered on the verge of sectarian civil war.

Political resolution, however, came very slowly after the December 15, 2005 elections. Politicians across religious and ethnic lines came together to form a unity government. These negotiations were successful when the Sunnis finally accepted the reality of their minority position in exchange for Shiite recognition that their majority position did not mean they could govern without the consensual support of the Iraqi minority. After a slow learning process, compromise was finally a word Iraqi politicians came to understand and appreciate. How quickly the Sunni participation in the unity government could be transformed into an all-out war against the radical religious foreign and domestic jihadists was still an open question, but the Iraq War was expected to wind down, with Coalition troop levels dipping below 100,000 at the end of 2006, down from 151,000 in December 2005. In a January letter to the Wall Street Journal, Ambassador Khalilzad [2006] laid out a remarkably perceptive plan for making 2006 the turning point in fulfilling American plans to end the war.

> This will [2006] be a year of decision in Iraq. Full participation in the December national elections by all communities has created the opportunity to significantly advance our strategy for success as recently outlined by President Bush. Building on this momentum is up to the Iraqi people. However, the United States will work intensively with Iraq's leaders to make progress on all three tracks of our strategy: [1] developing democracy, [2] providing security and [3] reviving the economy. In implementing the president's strategy, we are working to support the creation of the institutions of a unified and

lasting democracy, particularly the formation of a national government and an amended constitution that can obtain broader acceptance. We are continuing to transfer control of more territory to Iraqi security forces and are seeking to exploit fissures in the insurgency. We are adjusting our military posture to emphasize focused operations on terrorists and we are making a concerted effort to improve Iraqi police, fight corruption and disband militias. We are also moving forward with our reconstruction plan and encouraging economic reform to stimulate private-sector growth.

The prospects for a stable Islamic democracy in the midst of the formerly totalitarian Arab Middle East are very promising, although ancient rivalries and ethnic enmity still run deep. The despised and ruthless dictator, Saddam Hussein, has been overthrown and faces Iraqi judgment and punishment for crimes against humanity. Even if these positive results were to be limited to Iraq, the Middle East is a much better place than before the invasion and liberation began. There are also signs that these accomplishments may prompt further movement throughout the region for the spread of democratic institutions, which could mean substantial improvement for all people of the Middle East, but the achievement of these benefits has not been without great cost.

By the time the Coalition Forces leave Iraq, 2,500 American and other Coalition young men and women will have given their lives to the cause of freedom and greater security for the world. More than 35,000 Iraqi citizens, most killed by fanatical insurgents or religious zealots, will have died in creating a democratic government for Iraq. In addition, billions of U.S. funds have been spent rebuilding crumbling Iraqi infrastructure, long neglected under Saddam.

These costs, while significant, were minute in comparison with Iraqi civilian casualties during Saddam's reign where hundreds of thousands were murdered by the regime, or in America's war in Vietnam where more than 58,000 Americans and 5 million Vietnamese died. Despite the best efforts of bin Laden and Saddam's Baathists, the Iraq War was a far cry from becoming another Vietnam, as bin Laden had hoped and many critics had so decried. Nearing the fifth anniversary of 9/11, it had become increasingly clear that Bin Laden continued to lose the war on terror and that painful but gradual American success in Iraq had become a vital step toward his ultimate defeat.

The next and concluding chapter summarizes major findings regarding the causes of the war on terror, assesses where we stand in the war today, and emphasizes the ideological nature of the war on terror in a global struggle that will likely require the dedicated effort of the next generation of Americans to complete the West's victory over radical, militant Islamism.

CHAPTER SIX

The War on Terror: Recapitulation, Prognosis, and an Unfinished Agenda

This concluding chapter answers, in turn, three questions: (1) What and who caused the war on terror? (2) Where does the war stand nearly five years after 9/11? (3) What must the United States and its Coalition do over the next generation to complete the West's victory over Bin Ladenism and radical, militant Islamism?

THE EXPLOSIVE MIXTURE OF POLITICS AND RELIGION

The answer to the question of what and who caused the war on terror requires a short summary of the events that created modern Saudi Arabia and paved the way for 9/11. Since the inception of King

THE TRIUMPH OF DEMOCRACY OVER MILITANT ISLAMISM

Abdul Aziz Ibn Saud's efforts to create an Islamic state in the Arabian Peninsula, an explosive mixture of politics and religion has marked the desert kingdom. The radical religious beliefs of the father of Wahhabi-Salafism, Ibn Abdul Wahhab (1703-1791), were central to the formation of the Kingdom of Saudi Arabia. Aware of the possible backbite of militant Islamist radicalism, Ibn Saud nevertheless created an Islamic state in which Wahhabism was the state religion. That religious tie, plus control of Mecca and Medina and the discovery of oil, gave the al Saud family the resources and legitimacy necessary to maintain absolute autocratic control over the kingdom, subject only to periodic confirmation of the family's rulings by the Ulama, senior Wahhabi clerics who function as the supreme interpreters of the most rigid and brutal form of Islamic law on earth.

When Egypt threatened Saudi regional leadership with socialistic pan-Arabism in the 1960s, the Saudis encouraged the Muslim Brotherhood to lead a religious revolt against the Egyptian government, culminating in the 1981 assassination of Nasser's successor, Anwar Sadat. The Saudi relationship with the Muslim Brotherhood had earlier led to the founding of the Islamic University in Medina in 1961 and the Brotherhood's subsequent indoctrination of Saudi universities and the broader educational system in Saudi Arabia. One of their students was Osama bin Laden who graduated from King Abdul-Aziz University in Jeddah in 1981, inspired by a radical, militant professor, Abdullah Azzam.

The question of who holds the upper hand in Saudi Arabia, the al Saud royal family or intolerant and extremist Wahhabi clerics, has been a recurring struggle in Saudi Arabia over the years. In 1979 when Islam's most sacred site, the Grand Mosque in Mecca was under seige, the al Saud family could only regain control by enlisting the support of the Wahhabi-controlled Ulama to ruthlessly suppress the militants. But the price to be paid opened the royal purse strings in support of the spread of Wahhabi-Salafism and billions of these funds found their way into the financing of al Qaeda and the global Wahhabi-Salafist movement.

Desperate to defuse the radical Wahhabis within the kingdom, the royal family seized upon the Soviet Union's invasion of Afghanistan as an Islamic rallying cause in a holy war against atheistic communism. The diversion worked for a while, but only at a very high future cost to the kingdom, for the jihadists returned home better trained in terrorist tactics and brimming over with confidence and zealotry, believing that they had defeated one of the world's nuclear-armed superpowers.

When the Iraqis invaded Kuwait in 1990 and threatened the Saudi oil fields, Osama bin Laden offered King Fahd his veteran "Afghan Arabs" to drive the Iraqi imperialists out of Kuwait and defend the Saudi oil complex. Instead, the Saudi royal family accepted assistance from the United States, allowing nearly one million foreign troops including 550,000 Americans to enter the holy land of Islam. This decision by King Fahd infuriated bin Laden and led him to call for driving the infidel Americans from Saudi Arabia and the Middle East and overthrowing the Saudi monarchy. Bin Laden's easy victory in Afghanistan over the Soviets, as well as the weak American responses to earlier terrorist attacks, led him to place his American target ("the far enemy") ahead of his Saudi one ("the near enemy"). He subsequently planned and inspired a series of attacks against American interests in the 1990s, culminating on September 11, 2001 with one of the most devastating attacks in American history, which finally drew a declaration of war from the "far enemy," the United States of America.

CURRENT STATUS OF THE WAR ON TERROR

So, where does the United States stand in its global war on terror five years after 9/11? Al Qaeda and bin Laden were quickly forced on the defensive after capturing the advantage by beginning the war with a sophisticated and highly complex terrorist attack on thousands of innocent civilians—infidels as al Qaeda viewed them—people who were working in two buildings that were the very symbols of the United

States, the Twin Towers of the World Trade Center in New York City and the Pentagon in the nation's capitol in Washington, DC.

Al Qaeda on the Defensive

Although al Qaeda got the response it sought from the United States when the West's hastily assembled military coalition intentionally drove into al Qaeda's deliberately set trap in Afghanistan, it turned out to be a trap for the Islamists, because in Afghanistan the British and American Coalition was able to utilize its high-tech weaponry, with little Western manpower and an army of paid Afghans, to rout al Qaeda and its affiliated Taliban government in less than two months in late 2001. Osama bin Laden, al Qaeda's leader, and his second in command, Ayman Al Zawahiri, the radical Muslim Brotherhood theorist, were able to narrowly escape to the more remote mountains of northwest Pakistan at great cost to themselves and their movement. The Americans, who were new at fighting terrorist organizations, instinctively launched the right offense, destroying al Qaeda's command and control center and disrupting internal communications—its eyes and ears to the outside world.

The big problem for al Qaeda in its new headquarters in the Vale of Peshawar in the Northwest Frontier Province of Pakistan was its isolation and the very rugged living conditions and limited communications in the area. Bin Laden's Afghanistan headquarters had been quite comfortable, with an extensive group of cohorts and their wives and children living and ruling "over mini-emirates of their own" [Taheri, 3/26/2005]. More important to the terrorist movement, in Afghanistan they were accessible to al Qaeda members, with relatively easy access to the headquarters for training and instructions. In their banishment to this remote area, communications were drastically reduced in number and in speed, so important in directing dynamic military operations.

The United States could easily argue that it had bin Laden exactly where it wanted him—out of sight and sound. Although he and his number two henchman managed to release a number of audio and video messages through the Qatari Arab satellite television network Al

Jazeera since their Pakistani confinement, these messages have been costly and difficult to get out in a timely fashion. An example is bin Laden's ill-timed and ineffective video attempting to influence the 2004 American presidential election. Bin Laden's audio tape on January 19, 2006 called for a truce or armistice ("hudna" in Arabic) but it actually rallied global support for the Allied efforts in Iraq and Afghanistan, the opposite of what bin Laden desired. In addition, the number of written communications, books, and pamphlets has dropped drastically, from 83 in 2001 to only one since 9/11.

As a result of bin Laden's isolation, al Qaeda has no longer been able to function as a well-structured network carrying out the orders of its commanding general and central planning staff. It has been reduced to a semi-autonomous network of isolated terrorist cells, operating virtually independently, a mixed blessing for the West. On the positive side, highly sophisticated, complex terrorist attacks, like 9/11, are less likely to occur from such a disconnected network. In addition, various parts of the network have been forced to operate with competing objectives; Zarqawi in Iraq has called for the faithful to concentrate on fighting a Middle East jihad ("the near enemy"), while bin Laden has urged al Qaeda members to create another 9/11-type attack in the United States to show the world the power of the global Islamist movement and its continued effectiveness against the hated "far enemy." On the other hand, the West's intelligence agencies now have to work harder because al Qaeda planners are more diverse and, consequently, less predictable but still just as deadly, yet their freedom to communicate, move, and operate, especially in Europe, has not been diminished. Unless the terrorist cause and its ideology are defeated, the danger in the West of a large number of innocent victims being killed or injured from future al Qaeda terrorist attacks remains high and the cost of maintaining heightened and costly security systems must be continued. Moreover, failure of the terrorist insurgency in Iraq may make the global al Qaeda network more desperate and cause it to concentrate on launching deadly new suicide strikes on the American homeland and in Europe.

But since its defeat in Afghanistan, the al Qaeda movement has mounted little offense, and significantly, there have been no successful attacks on the American homeland since 9/11. Besides rallying its forces to the cause of insurgency in Iraq, al Qaeda's only major success was on March 11, 2004 in the simultaneous bombing of four rush-hour commuter trains in Madrid that killed 191 people and injured more than 1,500. The immediate effect of the tragedy in Spain was to change the outcome of the Spanish election, bringing into power a socialist government that immediately removed Spanish forces from the Iraq coalition and a resounding victory for the terrorists by showing Western capitulation as the direct result of their violent and deadly attacks. The timing and complexity of the assaults in Spain had the earmarks of a centrally planned bin Laden operation, but the arrests of some 75 suspects, mostly Moroccan nationals, did not produce clear answers to the questions of how and by whom the attack was organized.

Similarly, the July 2005 London subway bombings were, indeed, the work of a local Islamist cell that was not well coordinated with a worldwide terrorist network. Those bombing might have been politically disruptive if the attacks had been launched during Prime Minister Blair's parliamentary re-election campaign of 2004, as the Spanish bombings were timed in conjunction with their elections. Europe may well be in more danger than the United States for future terrorist attacks because of the larger number of highly active Islamist cells in Europe than in the United States and because of Europe's large, discontented Muslim population, open borders, and a liberal EU-wide immigration policy. Although the French Muslim riots in the fall of 2005 were not necessarily part of an Islamist movement, they do indicate the deep discontent of French Muslims and their latent anger with the West. But while European Islamist movements share common ideological underpinnings derived from Saudi Wahhabi-Salafist propaganda, there are increased signs in Europe that Saudi funding may be finally drying up.

One other factor that has dampened the ability of al Qaeda to mount a vigorous offense against the United States and its Western allies has been the success of coordinated international efforts to cut off the flow of funds, especially Saudi funds, for financing terrorist operations. Bin Laden erroneously believed that it was the success of his "Afghan Arabs" that had bankrupted the Soviet Union, but the U.S.-led campaign to force the Saudis and its Muslim charities to withhold their support of radical Islamist causes has restricted the resources now available to the Islamist terrorists. Part of the reason so many foreign jihadists flocked into Iraq to join the insurgency was that the funds Saddam Hussein had stolen from the Iraqi people were among the few remaining sources of cash readily available for financing al Qaeda operations. The reported decline in the rate of new Islamist recruits for Iraq may reflect the drying up of money or a lessening of interest in the Iraqi cause by the militants. And as the United States and France apply greater pressure on Syria, which is also home to millions in Saddam's stolen funds, the insurgents in Iraq face increasing problems funding their operations and recruiting teenage jihadist suicide bombers from Saudi Arabia. If the new Iraqi government is successful in cementing the split in the Baathist and jihadist insurgencies, even that limited source of funds will no longer be available for al Qaeda. Its only remaining assets will be knowledge and understanding of terrorist strategy and tactics, the radical religious fervor, and the zeal of its members and financial supporters in Saudi Arabia.

In the aftermath of 9/11, American policy makers viewed al Qaeda as a totalitarian ideology every bit as pernicious as the fascist and communist ideologies that threatened freedom and democracy in the 20th century. Al Qaeda violently burst forth upon the world scene for a number of reasons, but primary among these was the extent and persistence of autocracy and the deficit of freedom that has existed in the Middle East since modern states and boundaries were established following the First World War. In the eyes of the Bush administration, the strategic antidote to Middle East autocracy and tyranny is freedom and democracy. To achieve the goal of freedom and democracy after 9/11, the United States pursued an offensive strategy, taking the fight to the enemy first in Afghanistan and then into the heart of the Arab-Muslim world in Iraq.

THE TRIUMPH OF DEMOCRACY OVER MILITANT ISLAMISM

America on the Offense

For nearly five years after 9/11, the United States has been on the offense, breathlessly pursuing al Qaeda with three powerful thrusts: (1) first in Afghanistan; (2) then moving against the policies and programs of its allies, such as the Russians, Pakistanis, and Saudis, that it viewed as supporting or insufficiently opposing Islamist terrorist organizations; and (3) invading Iraq and toppling Saddam Hussein who, in addition to horrendous cruelty to his own people over many years, was in fact a terrorist himself and gave aid and comfort to terrorist organizations, which might have included chemical and biological weapons of mass destruction.

The attacks against the American homeland on 9/11 forced policy makers in Washington to reassess the entire gamut of America's national security requirements since the onset of the Cold War. It also forced policy makers to understand the origins and extent of the ideology and threat from radical, militant Islamism, and to determine what Western civilization must do to counter the threat posed by al Qaeda, the self-named "World Islamic Front for Jihad against Crusaders and Jews."

As the United States mobilized its many resources in responding to the 9/11 attacks, all instruments of national policy and strategy were examined—ideological, political, economic, diplomatic, and military—and the President declared to the world that Western civilization, led by the United States, would embark upon a great and sobering generational war against a totalitarian ideology that preaches hate, intolerance and death. American policy makers recognized that they were dealing with a nihilistic form of barbarism set to destroy all advocates of freedom and democracy and that the enemy was ruthlessly intent upon controlling the Middle East and its oil wealth—nearly two-thirds of the earth's oil reserves—with a reactionary pan-Islamic Caliphate that would try to eventually control Europe and the entire world. Policy makers agreed that the enemy—radical, militant Islamists symbolized by Bin Ladenism—despised Western values and fought to replace those values with an extreme and barbaric Islamist code similar to what the Taliban violently forced upon the people of

Afghanistan. The administration's policy makers concluded that the only effective antidote to such an ideology of intolerance and hate would be an ideology of hope represented by what the militant Islamists despise most about the West—freedom and democracy as advocated by "decadent" America.

The Afghan invasion was by far the most popular of America's post 9/11 initiatives and the most visible and dramatic victory, especially in light of the Soviet Union's debacle there in the 1980s, and the U.S. military scored its quickest victory. It was America's swiftest offensive show in the war on terror. However, the profound damage that this military action did to al Qaeda's organization escaped notice when the elusive Osama bin Laden escaped capture, keeping alive his legend in the Muslim world as a great Islamic warrior defiant of the West and his global reputation as a shrewd, scheming, and evil mass murderer.

Even if bin Laden had been killed or captured in Afghanistan, militant Islamists would have continued their ideological struggle against the infidels in the United States and the West. Like bin Laden, other militant Islamists sought to install pro-Wahhabi, Taliban-like regimes throughout the Middle East, drive the United States and all Westerners out of the region, establish a Wahhabi-inspired Sunni Muslim Caliphate, and utilize the vast Middle East oil resources to proselytize their radical religion throughout the rest of the world. Killing bin Laden would not have stopped the militant Islamists, who would have gone underground until the West became less alert to terrorist risks, only to reemerge, better-organized, bitter in defeat, and seeking revenge, an even more dangerous threat to peace-loving people in both the Muslim and Western worlds. Currently isolated in Pakistan, it is increasingly evident that bin Laden has already initiated such a regrouping.

America's second thrust in the war on terror was its least visible and most unglamorous—two diplomatic incursions into (1) relations with Pakistan, Iran, Libya, and Russia to ensure that their weapons of mass destruction programs were under strict security controls and that WMD were not available to terrorists; and, (2) a series of forceful U.S. diplomatic moves with Saudi Arabia to stop the Saudis from funding al

Qaeda and proselytizing their Wahhabi-Salafist state religion around the world. Other Saudi reforms were also urged by the Bush administration, but America's first priority was to stop the spread of the ideology of Wahhabi-Salafism and the evil step-child it inspired, al Qaeda.

America's first diplomatic initiative successfully safeguarded the nuclear programs of Russia and Pakistan, forced Libya to totally abandon its nuclear weapons program, uncovered the A.Q. Khan global nuclear proliferation network, and placed Iran on notice of the consequences of any transfer of knowledge or weapons to terrorist organizations. The success of this diplomacy can be verified from the change in behavior of the first three nations, but Iran's nuclear ambitions remained disturbingly unchecked.

America's diplomacy during this entire episode was strengthened because of the new urgency and clarity with which the United States pursued its efforts. Having had three thousand innocent Americans killed using the country's own hijacked airplanes made the Bush administration realize just how many more American victims could be murdered with nuclear or biological weapons in the hands of ruthless Islamists such as bin Laden. As a consequence, separate bilateral negotiations took place with a far different and sterner tone than any prior American diplomatic discussions since the end of the Cold War. The capture of bin Laden would have reduced the legitimacy for such strong and urgent talk from American diplomats, for when American diplomats spoke to these nations the immediate threat of bin Laden still hung heavily over the negotiations.

However, the success of the first set of forceful American diplomatic negotiations with Russia, Pakistan, and Libya did not carry over to the Saudis. Despite the same challenging and provocative tone in American discussions with members of the Saudi royal family, Saudi Arabia persistently refused to acknowledge culpability for the 9/11 attacks and continued to deny knowledge of Saudi involvement in financing of al Qaeda, even as some wealthy Saudis and members of the royal family openly continued their support for bin Laden. Instead of responding positively to the American inquiries, the Saudi government terminated its previous understanding with the United States by asking it to remove its troops from Saudi soil and even hinted at severing diplomatic relations unless the United States resolved the long-standing impasse in the Israeli-Palestinian dispute. The Saudis, so accustomed to gulling the normally compliant Americans, failed to understand that their inaction and recalcitrant behavior were almost a full admission of guilt for an unsavory relationship with al Qaeda and the massive funding that had been supplied to expand the Wahhabi-Salafist faith under the cover of billions in Saudi foreign aid for many years.

In our view, it was this Saudi behavior that likely played a crucial part in formulating President Bush's decision to undertake the third thrust in the war on terror, a massive American-led allied invasion force into the heart of the Arab-Muslim world, an invasion of Iraq to depose Saddam Hussein and declare the Bush Doctrine of freedom and democracy as the antidote to "Bin Ladenism." The Saudis did not believe the American president had the "guts" or resolve to take such action but they were wrong again in their misjudgments of the second President Bush. As soon as the Saudis realized the seriousness of Bush's determination to leave no stone unturned in America's pursuit of al Qaeda and the imminent danger that al Qaeda created for the kingdom, they gradually acquiesced, providing the United States with some sensitive information it had requested, and slowed the flow of Saudi funds to al Qaeda. Saudi Arabia's demands for a resolution of the Israeli-Palestinian impasse were also tabled, but the Saudis did not cease urging the United States to reconsider its Iraq decision right up to the moment of the invasion in March 2003. Prince Bandar bin Sultan, after nearly 25 years of highly visible service representing Saudi interests in Washington, was the first Saudi 9/11 casualty of Crown Prince Abdullah after his ascendance to power in the post-Fahd era. The Saudis had gambled and for the first time in decades had lost a sweepstakes hand in its diplomatic poker game with the United States.

The strategic thrust into Iraq allowed the United States to expeditiously topple Saddam Hussein, but America did not win an easy victory because of poor postwar planning for the occupation and because of the Abu Ghraib prison disaster. The U.S. and its coalition partners overthrew two brutal regimes in Afghanistan and Iraq, liberating over 50 million people in the process, but had to persevere through several years of occupation. There were, however, no mass uprisings in the Muslim world, as predicted before the Iraq war, and no Muslim government fell or shifted support to al Qaeda. Moreover, the world witnessed positive change among countries in the region, from Libya to Lebanon and Saudi Arabia to the Gulf States. Iraqi sovereignty transferred on June 28, 2004 and the first free national elections were held in Iraq on January 30, 2005, followed by the drafting of a new Constitution in August, ratification in October, and a second successful election of permanent Council of Representatives on December 15, 2005, followed by a new democratic government in 2006.

The war in Iraq was won, not only by Allied soldiers valiantly fighting, but by bringing democracy to Iraq through these three elections and a long process of political compromise between Shiites, Sunnis, and Kurds. The U.S. quickly recovered from its disastrous occupation and the Abu Ghraib prison disaster by the success of the January 30, 2005 elections, the real turning point in the Iraq war. The first election demonstrated to the majority of Iraqis that the Western occupiers intended to turn over the government to the democratically elected representatives of the Iraqi people. The election, in the eyes of the Iraqis, transformed the occupiers into enablers of freedom. There was, however, no immediate relief for the sufferings of the Iraqi people because the insurgents recognized this attitudinal change in the Iraqi view of Coalition forces. As a consequence, the insurgents fought harder and inflicted even more pain on innocent Iraqi civilians, primarily Shiites, during much of 2005 and early 2006, while raising the kill rate among the Coalition forces for most of 2005.

Meanwhile, the drafting of the Constitution and the compromise that was reached in the final week before the ratifying election in October to permit amending the initially approved document, preserved the healing power of the democratizing process. The Sunnis finally decided that their best interests would be served by participating in the parliament, directly contrary to their decision in January. This decision put the Sunnis at odds with the foreign jihadists who were a main source of horrendous civil violence in the insurgency. Americans and other Coalition forces continued to die at a higher rate just before and after the October 15th election, but the rate of civilian casualties fell as the Iraqi insurgents withdrew their support for the foreign jihadists in the fall of 2005. Even the February 2006 destruction of the mosque with the Golden Dome in Samarra, resulting in Shiite reprisal killings of Sunnis and nearly causing a sectarian civil war, could not deter the process of negotiating a unity government. The continuing efforts of U.S. Ambassador Zalmay Khalilzad who brought the Sunnis into the government with the Shiites and Kurds were critical to the success of the democratization process. He, more than any other American representative that has been sent to Iraq, deserves the lion's share of the credit for the ultimate political compromise that brought victory.

Security responsibilities will be gradually transitioned to the new Iraqi government while U.S. forces in Iraq plan reductions from 130,000 troops in the spring of 2006 and the potential for a NATO command structure similar to Afghanistan, but expanded into a broader security regional framework called "Southeast NATO" (SENATO). The American victory in Iraq came at a time in 2006 when Americans had lost patience with the war. While such an action would have been tantamount to reestablishing America as a paper tiger, the Senate came within ten votes on November 15, 2005 of establishing a mandated timetable for the scheduled withdrawal of American troops from Iraq and President Bush's job approval ratings dropped to an all-time low in May 2006. Fortunately, the turnaround in American fortunes in Iraq had occurred precisely at the moment when most Americans had given up hope for victory.

Iraq still has a long way to go to build a stable, democratic government, but its prospects are better than anytime since Saddam Hussein came to power as president in 1979. In addition, other factors, such as Turkey's progress toward European Union membership, could serve to strengthen Western ties in the Middle East. Because Turkey is a long-standing Muslim member of NATO, its support could serve as a basis for permitting NATO to extend its collective security guarantees to traditional enemies like Iraq and Iran and eventually to the Persian Gulf states, and even Israel, through the creation of "Southeast NATO" or "SENATO" (or perhaps "Middle East NATO" or "MENATO"), consisting of Israel, the Gulf States and selected Muslim member countries. Article 5 of NATO's charter, the North Atlantic Treaty of 1949, reads: "The Parties agree that an armed attack on one...is an attack against them all..." A long-term U.S.-led NATO force in the region could have a broader mission to secure a generation of peace while protecting the Persian Gulf oil fields and providing regional security that could also extend to the Israeli-Palestinian settlement as a respected international buffer under a formal U.N. charter.

Beyond success in Iraq are the significant benefits the liberation of Iraq have served to portray the United States in a new light in the Arab-Muslim world:

- Determination of the Bush administration to track down and eliminate Osama bin Laden and the network of terrorists that hide under the umbrella of al Qaeda and Islamism.
- Reelection by the American people of its wartime president on a platform of the Bush Doctrine as evidence of America's firm commitment to those policies;
- Willingness of the Bush administration, at high political risk, to stay and fight when things weren't going well, in stark contrast with America's prior reputation in the Middle East as a "paper tiger" without backbone or strong political will; and,
- Commitment to freedom and democracy, as evidenced by the Iraqi reaction to America's willingness to cede total power to the freely elected government and abide by its decision on the nature of the government and duration of the American presence in the country.

The last attribute is the most significant because freedom and democracy represent America's ultimate antidote to Wahhabi-Bin

Ladenism. The definitive proof of the American commitment to democracy is in its willingness to abide by the decisions of the Iraqi people in determining their own future. Americans changed the subject of the war: the war was no longer seen as East versus West or Muslims versus Infidels, but instead it was seen as free people—"Societies of Freedom"—versus people enslaved by fanatical religious doctrines or totalitarian governments—"Societies of Fear"—[Sharansky]. The war was won on the grounds of a firm commitment to American values and it is those eternal values that have triumphed.

Muslim Support for Terror Wanes

The war on terror is not only being fought in Iraq; it is also being fought in the court of public opinion worldwide. Muslims do not approve killing other Muslims in support of radical Islamist doctrines that would take the faith back to the 7th century and establish a medieval totalitarian theocracy as the Taliban did in Afghanistan. The major source of information about Muslim opinion is a recent survey from the Pew Global Attitudes Project conducted in the spring of 2005, which was confirmed by subsequent public opinion polls later in the year. Its major conclusions were:

> Concerns over Islamic extremism, extensive in the West even before this month's terrorist attacks in London, are shared to a considerable degree by the publics in several predominately Muslim nations surveyed. Nearly three-quarters of Moroccans and roughly half of those in Pakistan, Turkey, and Indonesia see Islamic extremism as a threat to their countries. At the same time, most Muslim publics are expressing less support for terrorism than in the past. Confidence in Osama bin Laden has declined markedly in some countries and fewer believe suicide bombings that target civilians are justified in the defense of Islam [Pew].

This survey was conducted prior to the rise in insurgent attacks in Iraq during the summer of 2005 and we can deduce that support for bin Laden and al Qaeda's attacks on innocent Muslim civilians has deteriorated even further.

Improved public opinion polls are not the only indicator of a changing attitude in the Muslim world. At an ecumenical conference of Islamic clerics held July 4-6, 2005 in Jordan, the clerics issued a religious edict (fatwa) "forbidding the declaration of any Muslim an apostate (takfir) and limiting the issuance of religious edicts to qualified Muslim clerics in the eight schools of Islamic jurisprudence" [International Islamic Conference]. Action by the clerics, including a Grand Imam, a Grand Ayatollah, and three Grand Muftis, among other Islamic religious leaders, was directly intended to forbid Osama bin Laden and other terrorist leaders from issuing religious edicts or justifying the killing of other Muslims by declaring them apostates. It is hard to imagine a stronger or more universal Islamic renunciation of Osama bin Laden and al Qaeda's terrorist practices against fellow Muslims.

Next, the outcome of the Pakistani elections for local governments on August 18th and 25th further reflected Muslim disenchantment with Islamists and their ideology. For the first time since 2002, the gains of the radical Islamists were reversed. President Musharraf was jubilant is saying: "Local…elections have resulted in the victory of moderates and defeat of extremists everywhere in Pakistan" [Khan]. Perhaps the most promising was the showing by moderates in the North Western Frontier Province where the religious parties were the strongest and that might even promote renewed Pakistani military efforts to capture Osama bin Laden in that area. After evidence emerged that al Qaeda was responsible for the London bombings, Salam al-Marayati, the executive director of the Muslim Public Affairs Council, on September 2nd said:

> Now, we can't afford to be bystanders any more, we have to be involved in constructive intervention. So we're doing it collectively, speaking out with one voice and now telling

our children that they have to get it right, they can't be confused and can't give any credence to anybody who comes to them and says there is room for violence [Goodstein].

This action by the Council stood in sharp contrast to its denials of Islamist involvement in terrorism since 9/11/01. It represents a recognition, in the words of Sayyid M. Syeed, the secretary-general of the Islamic Society of North America, that "Muslim youth...could be indoctrinated, and in spite of their upbringing, their birth and years of living in the West, that they could be vulnerable to this kind of thing" [Ibid]. The next day in London, an Islamic member of Parliament, Shahid Malik, said "Far too many Muslims have been living in a state of denial, but now they have heard out of the horse's mouth and must come to terms with the undoubted challenge this presents" [Cowell and Van Natta].

Even in Saudi Arabia, the monarchy has led an aggressive and violent military campaign to root out al Qaeda cells in the country. Unfortunately, the royal family has followed the old Saudi practice of exporting some of the most extremist radicals to fight with foreign jihadists in Iraq against the infidel Americans. The key role of the Saudis in the foreign jihadist movement in Iraq can be measured in the body count of dead insurgents, with 61 percent coming from Saudi Arabia and less than 9 percent Iraqi [Paz]. These contradictory actions of killing al Qaeda members in Saudi Arabia while exporting terrorists to Iraq suggests that the Saudi monarchy is singularly pursuing its own self-preservation while the royal family remains split or unable to reign in powerful Wahhabi clerics. Always desirous of enhancing its position as the true defender of the Muslim faith, the Saudi response to the 2006 Danish cartoon controversy was also disturbing. Dr. Ali H. Alyami, the Washington, DC-based Executive Director of the Center for Democracy and Human Rights in Saudi Arabia remarked [2/21/2006]:

"Knowing that Muslims will rise against anyone who defames their Prophet or its religion, the Saudi ruling dynasty saw a unique opportunity to stimulate a global protest against the Danish cartoons while deflecting the impact of other events. Well before the cartoon controversy broke into violent demonstrations, King Abdullah of Saudi Arabia called a summit meeting of the Organization of Islamic Conference (OIC) that met in Mecca December 7, 2005 ostensibly to discuss religious extremism and the image of Islam with the leaders of the world's 57 Muslim nations.

On February 9th Hassan M. Fattah reported in the New York Times ("At Mecca Meeting, Cartoon Outrage Crystallized") that heads of Muslim states, including extremist Iranian President Ahmadinejad, spent much of the conference discussing the infamous cartoons and the anti-Islam campaign they were perceived to represent. The Mecca conference served as the spark that activated violent reactions to the four-month-old cartoons and eclipsed other events. "It was no big deal [the cartoons] until the Islamic Conference, when the OIC took a stance against it," said Muhammad el-Sayed Said, deputy director of the Ahram Center for Political and Strategic Studies in Cairo."

The monarchy seemed to smoothly navigate King Fahd's death, which was reported on August 1, 2005, but it is possible the King might have died as early as May 2005, permitting sufficient time for the ruling al-Sauds to peacefully work out difficult succession issues within the royal family. Prince Sultan was chosen as Abdullah's successor as Crown Prince. However, reports from Fahd's funeral indicated that Sultan, who is in his early 80s and in poor health with apparent stomach cancer, may not outlive Abdullah, so the current succession plan is at best a temporary situation. King Abdullah, who is a year or two older than Prince Sultan, ordered that senior ministers currently in office would remain in place. The King continued as commander of the fiercely loyal, tribal-oriented Saudi Arabian National Guard (SANG) and the Crown Prince remained in charge of the conventional armed forces as Minister of Defense and Aviation. Prince Nayef, probably the most dedicated Wahhabi supporter in the senior ranks of government, continued as Interior Minister, charged with internal security and spearheading the domestic campaign against al Qaeda. He may still have a chance to succeed Abdullah if Sultan succumbs first.

Meanwhile, Prince Turki bin Faisal, (son of former King Faisal), who was formerly ambassador to Great Britain, was chosen by Abdullah as the replacement for Prince Bandar bin Sultan (son of the Crown Prince) as ambassador to the United States in Washington, DC. In the final analysis, the al-Saud family remains deeply divided over the degree of Wahhabi influence in the Saudi government that can be tolerated, even as the state vigorously defends itself against its ideological offspring, al Qaeda. It is a balancing act unlike any other and the eventual outcome is anyone's guess.

American Support for Iraq War Wanes

Paradoxically, while America appeared to be winning the war for the hearts and minds of Muslims in the battle against Bin Ladenism and al Qaeda, a majority of the American public seemed to have lost confidence in President Bush and his ability to lead the country to victory in the war in Iraq. Bush's overall job approval rating had dropped to 29 percent by May 2006. His handling of the war in Iraq was at 38 percent in September 2005 and went even lower to 36 percent in April 2006, the lowest level since the war started in 2003, after it had risen near the end of 2005 following four urgently needed presidential addresses on the Iraq war [Froomkin].

Wartime leadership is the sole responsibility of the nation's chief executive, as Lincoln demonstrated during the American Civil War, and as Napoleon had earlier observed. On wartime leadership, Napoleon said that a nation's morale is three times more important than its physical assets. What he meant was that failure to attend to the morale of a nation in wartime—failure to articulate a clear strategy and demonstrate progress—is the greatest possible failure of political leadership. To be successful, wartime leaders must explain and re-explain what's at stake, as Lincoln did during the Civil War with his call for universal freedom as the basis for the American system of government. Lincoln enlarged the meaning of the war as the central front in the worldwide struggle for human liberty and freedom, a goal no less true today in Iraq and the broader Middle East. But the responsibility to carry that message rests solely with the president.

Unfortunately, by the spring of 2006 a majority of Americans—liberals and conservatives alike—came to believe that the United States was "bogged down" in Iraq and that President Bush had misled the country about the reasons for going to war. Simply stated, the Bush administration has done an extremely poor job explaining the Iraq invasion as an integral part of its strategy in the war on terror. That deficiency came back to haunt the president in 2006 as he faced increased political pressure to pull American troops out of Iraq, especially as a prelude to the bitter fall congressional elections. Understanding the Iraq invasion in the context of "killing two birds with one stone"—eliminating a despicable dictator who supported terrorism and getting the Saudis to stop funding al Qaeda—was a reasonable and valid reason for the invasion and a sound strategy for winning the war on terror but the president consistently hesitated to address the Saudi problem. Bush came closest to this analysis in his four December 2005 addresses in which he tried to link the Iraq war more broadly to the war on terror and militant Islamists but avoided addressing the Saudis and the broader problems there.

President Bush also suffered from not appearing to be a strong CEO in his second term, despite his press clippings and Harvard MBA. The Hurricane Katrina tragedy that devastated New Orleans and the slow federal response further diminished his national standing in early September. His problem has been: "Loyalty counts far more for this CEO than performance—an attitude that is deadly in managing any enterprise" [Ignatius, 9/7/2005], not that all American presidents have performed like Jack Welch. Just as we argued in Chapter 5, the president should have accepted Secretary Donald Rumsfeld's resignation after the Abu Ghraib prison scandal for all of the management difficulties in the Iraq war, but he instead rewarded Rumsfeld's impeccable loyalty. In addition to fully reporting to the nation on all his reasons for the Iraq invasion, President Bush must exercise leadership and executive responsibility far more boldly to recover the respect of the American public for his policies, many of which provide excellent guidance for winning the war on terror.

The problems the president faced in 2005 and early 2006 revealed that Americans had become increasingly impatient with sustaining military fatalities in a continuing struggle without understanding why a victory in Iraq is possible and so important and why defeat is not an option. Not only would defeat vindicate Saddam Hussein's original plan for taking his nation's defense underground, it is al Qaeda and Osama bin Laden, through his henchman Abu Musab al Zarqawi, who would be the principal benefactor of Hussein's strategy. The United States could not afford to let Iraq become a victory for al Qaeda like the Soviet Union defeat in Afghanistan and a repeat of previous American retreats from al Qaeda aggression. Most Americans agreed that the U.S. must stay the course to win the war on terror and came to that conclusion as they better understood the reasons for the invasion and the essential purpose for winning in Iraq.

CEMENTING VICTORY

Achieving victory over a relatively small radical religious terrorist group is not a surprising feat for the world's only superpower. Felled by his own hubris and megalomania, the biggest strategic error bin Laden made was to believe that the shortest and best route to conquering the Muslim world was to take on the infidel West and its leader, America, the "paper tiger." That bin Laden lost in his misjudgment is not surprising. However, what is surprising is the way the United States responded to being challenged by a fanatical religious organization, al Qaeda. The United States responded in kind by generally staying true to its basic values and whenever it strayed from those values, as it did

THE TRIUMPH OF DEMOCRACY OVER MILITANT ISLAMISM

in the disastrous Abu Ghraib prison scandal, it paid a high price. When the United States was not true to its values, it suffered loss of respect and diminished progress in spreading freedom. Moreover, America's unfortunate failures also jeopardized making its citizens more secure, the overriding objective of American foreign policy in the first five years of the Bush administration's global war on terror.

But America's fundamental resilience gave it new knowledge and determination from its encounter with evil and persistent terrorism. It learned that American citizens cannot be safe in the modern world, even with its technologies for mass destruction, unless those types of weapons are finally brought under absolute and total control by the world community. These weapons almost created parity between big nations, even superpowers, and small groups of zealots who are fearless in their determination to defeat superpowers, regardless of the consequences to their members or to other people anywhere on the globe.

The world after 9/11 had changed dramatically, and the United States decided to begin its new mission by resolutely pursuing and eliminating the terrorist organization that had killed so many of its innocent citizens and sent shock waves throughout its land and the entire world. With the initial part of its mission virtually accomplished nearly four years after invading Iraq, America's next priority is to lead the world in overhauling the United Nations and reinvigorating NATO so together they can effectively manage the new world order of the 21st century and ensure lasting security, freedom, and opportunity for all people, everywhere.

Back to Multilateralism

The Bush policies of unilateralism and preemption/prevention were adopted in the immediacy and demanding aftermath of the 9/11 moment. The United States believed that al Qaeda could strike again quickly after 9/11 and that the United States had to mount a rapid offense to keep the militant Islamists on the defensive, so al Qaeda could not strike again until better homeland security arrangements were in place and working. The strategy proved effective, but

America's aggressive unilateralism could have been conducted more diplomatically and the United States government may not have understood just how much of a deterrent its Afghan offensive had been in disrupting al Qaeda's operations. In addition, the diplomatic difficulties the United States encountered in persuading the Saudis to cut off the flow of funds to al Qaeda magnified American concerns of another imminent attack. Because the threat from al Qaeda seemed so severe in the immediate aftermath of 9/11, the American president's war council advisors continued to believe that offensive speed was of the essence for an effective defense of American and Western security. Under such circumstances, U.S. policy makers realized that multilateral action through either the United Nations or NATO against the terrorists could not possibly be undertaken quickly enough to meet the speedy schedule that the Bush administration had outlined for an effective offense.

The important conclusion from this review of the Bush post-9/11 policy is that it was the special circumstance of the moment, together with the heightened concern about American security, which led to the unilateral approach of the first Bush term. Those times are now past and the immediate dangers of another imminent al Qaeda attack are somewhat diminished, which of course doesn't mean that another attack still couldn't happen, but the probability of such an attack has been lowered. As a consequence, when the Bush administration issued its revised national security strategy on March 16, 2006, it was a vastly larger and different state paper that the one issued in September 2002. The word "unilateral" only appeared once in the new strategy document and that was a reference to the dispute between China and Taiwan [Bush]. The United States now had a different set of near-term objectives:

> 1. Bring all WMD under absolute control to prevent al Qaeda or any other terrorist groups from killing innocent persons or extorting nations for concessions or tribute;
> 2. Bring freedom and democracy to the remaining third of world still enslaved in tyranny and autocracy, especially the Middle East; and

3. Overhaul and reinvigorate institutions such as the United Nations and NATO to improve their effectiveness in the new post-9/11 world.

These goals were essentially multilateral by nature and could be much better accomplished by broad multilateral efforts through existing channels than the previous, urgent, and time-specific Bush policy of acting unilaterally outside the well-established multilateral framework.

A new style of foreign policy, as well as a new secretary of state, Condoleezza Rice, emerged early in 2005 in the second Bush term. Although many observers credited their criticism of President Bush's "abrupt and arrogant" actions for the administration's change in style, the real reason was a change in circumstances. There was no longer an urgent and tight timeframe for reducing imminent security risks and a different set of goals were being sought that could only be achieved through multilateral cooperation. In his second term, President Bush has the luxury to use diplomacy, and America's traditional set of trading inducements to bargain with other nations to gain broad acceptance of America's national security policy objectives. The objectives of this new and friendlier diplomatic and multilateral initiative were:

1. Achieve a permanent peace treaty between Israel and a new sovereign and independent state of Palestine, Secretary Rice's number one priority, even though it was set back by the Hamas political victory in the January 2006 elections;
2. Create a permanent and iron-clad system of controlling nuclear, biological, and chemical weapons to prevent terrorist organizations and sovereign states like North Korea and Iran from extorting other nations, conceptually the most difficult and complex objective.
3. Reform the United Nations to make it more representative of the 21st century balance of world power

and a more effective instrument for peace, human rights, and the relief of human suffering.

4. Work with the Europeans to reinvigorate NATO and its southern flank as a newly structured security organization prepared to face the 21st century threat of radical, militant Islam along the Mediterranean Basin, Middle East, and Central Asia.

5. Initiate a reopening of the Kyoto Treaty so that the United States could indicate a willingness to participate in a worldwide effort to reduce dependence on fossil fuels and combat global warming.

Except for the first goal, the Israeli-Palestine peace process, which is now problematic, accomplishing the other goals may take longer than the remaining time President Bush has in office. However, each of these long-term goals can be further broken into concrete steps that can be taken during the remainder of the Bush term in office to advance progress toward their eventual accomplishment. Establishing such a set of American foreign policy goals clearly differentiates the unilateral and preemptive stage of the administration's global war on terror and the subsequent phases that require broad and well-coordinated multilateral efforts. In addition, all of the goals are in some way related to fighting terrorism and improving political conditions, primarily in the Arab-Muslim world. Undertaking such an agenda would represent a diplomatic way of calling an end to the unilateral and preemptive phase of the global war on terror, without fully renouncing that sovereign right, should the United States ever again be faced with an imminent national security risk that, in its view, requires independent and unilateral action.

Lessons Learned About Using Military Options

The most controversial aspect of American actions under President Bush was its willingness to employ military force to achieve its strategic objectives. The American use of massive military force in 1990-1991 and again after 9/11 represented a seismic policy shift in the post-

Vietnam era. Although the United States used military force in Somalia, the Balkans, and as peacekeeping troops in Haiti and other trouble spots around the world in the 1990s, these engagements were lower-risk operations of limited duration. In Afghanistan and Iraq, American troops were employed in fighting that was as intense as in Vietnam, but this time without high casualty rates even though the risks were equally great, especially with the severity and intensity of the Iraqi Baathist-Islamist insurgency. Several lessons were learned.

First, the vast majority of the American people supported the President's aggressive use of military force in the global war on terror against the enemy, al Qaeda. In its initial attack on innocent Americans, al Qaeda had invited retribution, and the causes of justice and national security required the type of search-and-destroy operations that only the deployment of strong and well-trained military forces could accomplish. America's political will for fighting a war against radical, militant Islamists was as strong as it had been in the nearly 50-year Cold War struggle against the Soviet Union and communism before the tragic and unfortunate Vietnam experience sapped American willpower for over a generation. America's rapid victory in Afghanistan buoyed support for U.S. military intervention and made it possible for President Bush to continue the pursuit of its policies into Iraq, even though the administration unfortunately failed to present a cogent case for the linkage of the Iraq war to the overall goals of the global war on terror.

Second, American support of military action has very definite limits, as President Bush learned after a quick victory conquering Iraq and deposing Saddam Hussein. The slippery slide into a growing war of fierce insurgency and undetermined duration raised many issues, some reminiscent of failing public support for the Vietnam War just as bin Laden had predicted. In the run-up to the 2004 American presidential election, the more the evidence suggested that the American occupation might slip into a Vietnam-type quagmire, the stronger the case for withdrawal became. However, even during the bitter 2004 presidential election, a majority of Americans seemed to understand that the United States could not abandon Iraq without conceding a major victory to Osama bin Laden and his militant Islamists. Even amidst all the criticism of the administration, both at home and abroad, Americans and a growing number of Europeans came to understand the ultimate stakes involved in the Iraq war and the broader war on terror. And despite disappointment with the results on the ground in Iraq and the lack of a clear-cut victory, the American public reelected President Bush in November 2004, indicating that a majority had retained a sufficiently strong political will to continue the fight, ostensibly for as long as it would take to win.

Third, advocates of the use of military force should heed an important lesson. Never commit too few American troops to an aggressive military action far from home that the United States can't win with minimum military casualties in a reasonable period of time. Americans have reached an understanding that they will support a war against radical, militant Islamists if needed, but they do not have the patience of Job over the continued use of military force with no apparent end in sight. It is for this reason that war advocates must be prepared to fight smarter wars when they commit American forces to military action in the future.

Fourth, Americans also received a rudimentary education in what is required to fight a better and smarter war. Although improvements can be made in having larger numbers of trained soldiers available before entering an engagement, which probably means paying better salaries to obtain larger enrollments in the voluntary army (or reinstating the draft), the principal deficits in the Iraq war were in contingency planning, the quality of intelligence information about the enemy, and the poor training and deplorable leadership in U.S. Army Reserve units. The planning, leadership, and training deficiencies are more easily remedied because professional military officers know how to plan for battlefield contingencies and Americans have generally been good at training, planning, and adapting to the uncertainties of fighting.

The fundamental lesson that was learned in Iraq is that civilian leadership in the Pentagon and military hierarchy must require field commanders (i.e., Central Command in the case of Iraq) to develop broad contingency plans for post-combat operations that are continually updated during the battle phase and allow enough time for such detailed and comprehensive planning to occur. Ironically, in the Iraq War the Pentagon had on the shelf a nearly finished plan for the occupation of Iraq that had been prepared by General Franks' predecessor, General Anthony Zinni, but the Pentagon apparently rejected the Zinni plan because "its assumptions were too negative" [Packer, 119]. Cheney and Rumsfeld even refused to allow Franks to discuss his plans with Zinni. Moreover, implementation of the post-combat plan should rest solely with the military commander responsible for field operations until the administration's objectives are achieved.

The intelligence deficiency plagued the American military establishment from before 9/11 through the entire period of the global war on terror and is the most serious systemic problem that exists today. The failures are many and well-documented: (1) poor intelligence led to the lack of advance warning of the 9/11 attack; (2) major failures in assessing the WMD threat in Iraq; (3) lack of knowledge of Iran's pre-war clandestine organizing Iraqi Shiites; (4) inability to alert the American military of the impending Baathist-Islamist insurgency; and (5) lack of understanding the nature and origin of the Iraqi insurgency operations during the occupation phase. Although George Friedman's [2004] skepticism about how much can ever be learned and predicted from any intelligence apparatus is understandable, the United States must improve its intelligence gathering and analysis functions as comprehensively and as quickly as possible. It has to do far better, and the recently mandated reorganization of intelligence assets under new leadership is a necessary first step in repairing America's overlapping and dysfunctional intelligence apparatus with 15 separate and competing agencies. The plan for implementing the best of the commissions' recommendations and periodically reassessing the progress of the reforms, with periodic corrections as needed, is a step in the right direction.

Regardless of how long it takes to repair U.S. intelligence capabilities, America's global war on terror has led to placing the military option back on the table as one of the tools that policy makers can again employ in the conduct of American foreign policy and the defense of U.S. national security interests. Americans and the rest of the world are aware that this significant change in American policy resulted from bin Laden's mocking his American infidel enemy as a "paper tiger."

Bin Laden's derision backfired and the ultimate availability of America's military option is once again an effective foreign policy tool, but it must be used sparingly, as President Theodore Roosevelt recommended at the start of the 20th century: "Speak softly and carry a big stick." For if conditions necessitate, such as radical, militant Islamists creating civil war and chaos in Saudi Arabia, for example, the United States must be prepared to defend its vital interests in the region with all of its resources, including rapid military intervention with overwhelming force.

The Carrot of Freedom and Democracy

Fortunately, the primary antidote that the Bush Doctrine wisely proposed for defeating radical, militant Islamism is freedom and democratization, and it should not normally require the use of military force. The preferred American approach to the promotion of democracy has been to play a supporting role as the United States did with Corazon Aquino when Ferdinand Marcos was eased out of the Philippines. Political freedom has its own energy for conquering fear and oppression, and as more Muslims and other enslaved peoples around the world become aware that they too can independently obtain their own human rights and freedom, the likelihood of the need for American military intervention will diminish. Saddam Hussein's insidious strength as an ironclad ruler and ruthless dictator made him and his regime an exception to the general rule that despots cannot contain the instinctive human desire for freedom. Perhaps even in Iraq, Saddam's days would eventually have been numbered if tyranny's circle could have been effectively broken elsewhere in the Middle East. But that was not possible, and by starting with the toughest case and the people with the most to gain from being liberated, the American-led intervention in Iraq has made the dream of freedom and democracy more accessible and more attainable than it has ever been in the history of the Middle East. Truly, the seed of democracy spread quickly throughout the region since the Afghanistan elections in October 2004 and the elections in Palestine and Iraq in 2005 and 2006.

By the spring of 2005 Arabs were shouting "kifaya" in the streets of Cairo and Beirut, meaning "enough" in Arabic. Charles Krauthammer [3/4/2005] wrote in *The Washington Post:* "The ice is breaking, the region is changing—remarkable, unexpected, hugely significant progress, with hope of an Arab spring. We are at the dawn of a glorious, delicate, revolutionary moment in the Middle East." Democracies around the world started to get on the bandwagon, working with the United States, as the French did with Lebanon and Syria and the Germans with Iran, rather than working against American interests. The Bush policy was not the sole factor in creating the movement toward democracy, but by putting democracy into Iraq and the heart of the Arab-Muslim world, and by turning power over to the people with free elections, the region is now riding the worldwide trend toward democracy. For as President Bush said in Brussels [2/21/2006]: "...the United States is **the** beacon of liberty in the world...and we have a solemn responsibility to promote freedom...for we owe it to these people to help them be set free" [emphasis added].

Some have argued that the Hamas victory in the January 2006 Palestine elections was a set back for President Bush's democratization policy as a remedy for Islamic extremism and terrorism, but that remains to be seen as the pressures increase on a former terrorist organization that must now govern the emerging but impoverished state of Palestine. History has shown that governing responsibilities can profoundly change the nature of initially unstable radical organizations. Financial pressure exerted by the United States and the European Union pushed Hamas to recognize the state of Israel and its right to exist, as well as past peace agreements between Israel and the Palestinians. Pressure also came from Israel, which committed to define its own state boundaries unilaterally, an action that could eventually bring Hamas to the bargaining table.

As we have seen in Iraq, the process by which democracy ultimately evolves can do strange and unpredictable things to the participating parties. Clancy Chassay [2006] points out that "a growing schism [is developing] between reform-minded Islamists like Hamas and its parent group the Muslim Brotherhood, who seek to Islamize their societies through the democratic process, and those, such as al Qaeda, who refuse the democratic political system altogether, attempting to force a radical transformation through the use of violence." By joining the political fray, Hamas has directly spurned al Qaeda's demands that it reject the hated infidel democratic process.

America's foreign policy may not need to aggressively promote democracy for this is one political movement that has proved to be self-promotional, as the rapid spread of freedom and democracy throughout Eastern Europe demonstrated after the fall of the Iron Curtain. American foreign policy, and for that matter, the foreign policies of all major democracies in the developed world, now need to nurture the forces of freedom and democracy by providing technical and economic assistance to these emerging governments and by being patient with the development of the fragile and complex process of bringing power to the people. Human mistakes will be made as a natural part of development and learning, but the Western world should be reluctant to intervene unless cruel and inhuman treatment becomes a real prospect for a very large number of people, as it was in Iraq. Having an effective international organization to manage this process will be of tremendous benefit to put pressure on autocrats and assist in the process of giving birth to freedom, which is a strong reason for giving reform of the United Nations highest priority.

The United States is in a position to make the tragedy of 9/11 a profound stepping stone for the betterment of all humankind. Continuing its resolute response and emphasizing American values as the antidote to terrorism could provide the most appropriate memorial to the innocent victims of 9/11 and their families.

The paradox of the United States is that it has always started its global struggles by overestimating the strength of its enemies, and it has concluded its struggles by accomplishing far more than could reasonably have been expected or imagined at the outset. The fifth year in the war against al Qaeda and radical, militant Islamists has not proven to be an exception to this American paradox. America's victory over al Qaeda can easily be sustained and strengthened by following a more popular and cooperative multilateral plan, as long as the United States continues to be vigilant and prepared to use all available options—ideological, political, diplomatic, economic, and military—as the need arises.

SEEDS OF HOPE—ROOTS OF CHANGE

In the longer-term, how will the United States continue to build its lead in the global war on terror and ultimately triumph over al Qaeda and other extremist terrorist organizations over the next generation? Osama bin Laden and his al Qaeda cronies may well be dead and buried by the end of President Bush's term in office, but that does not mean total victory over the militant Islamists will have been achieved.

Reform of Islam Needed
The history of Islam reveals periodic movements of radicalism dating back to the 13th and 14th centuries when Ibn Taymiyah (1263-1328) reacted to the Mongol victory over the Arabs by blaming negative developments in the faith since the era of the Prophet. Ibn Taymiyah, like Ibn Abdul Wahhab, called for a return "to the fundamentals of the Quran" and "the habits and religious practice of the Prophet Muhammad, which were recorded for posterity by his companions and family and are regarded as the ideal Islamic norm" [Armstrong, 104 and 202]. Ibn Abdul Wahhab made much the same suggestion in the 18th century, but his radical view was kept alive by King Abdul Aziz Ibn Saud's official endorsement of Wahhabism in establishing the Saudi monarchy early in the 20th century.

Both Ibn Taymiyah and Ibn Abdul Wahhab looked to the past when the condition of the Arabs looked bleak and they were radical reactionaries in the fullest sense. This backward view of battling the challenges of modernity is the root of contemporary radical, militant Islamism. Tom Friedman [11/27/01] observed shortly after 9/11:

> Christianity and Judaism struggled with this issue [modernity] for centuries, but a similar internal struggle within Islam to reexamine its texts and articulate a path for how one can accept pluralism and modernity and still be a passionate, devout Muslim has not surfaced in any serious way.

The reformation of Christianity, fueled by the latest 16th century technology of the printing press, forever changed the way Western nations viewed the relationship between church and state and redefined the political rights of humankind, but there has been no similar reformation of Islam.

Most mainstream Muslims around the world were intimidated into silence due to the events of 9/11 and its aftermath, but signs of a Muslim reformation began to emerge in 2005. The new Bush Doctrine was predicated upon the belief that the genie of freedom had been released to the world, especially with satellite television and the internet providing the means for people to communicate their thoughts and ideas and break down the walls of rigid, autocratic regimes. The movement toward freedom and democratization provides an environment for the destruction of radical, militant Islamism in a multi-generational war of ideology, but it can only go so far. The movement must also bring about reform and modernization of Islam that can only come from within the faith itself, and it will likely require several generations.

There are some hopeful signs. Gamal Banna, the 85-year-old brother of Hassan Banna who founded the Muslim Brotherhood in 1928, "has created a stir in Egypt recently" by arguing that "Islam allows for freedom of thought and evolution. Reform requires an open mind... Change is the greatest priority" [Williams]. In the article, Banna also challenges the commentary attributed to the prophet

Mohammed, much of which Banna believes "was invented and even falsified in the earliest centuries of Islam by self-styled jurists." Just as the Protestant Reformation called into question the authority of the Roman Catholic Church, mainstream Muslims must learn to challenge the monopoly that Sunni and Shiite clerics have had on their interpretations of the Koran. However, that challenge must be made by mainstream Muslims as a by-product of democratic political freedom that is now emerging in the Middle East. Support of autocratic governments in the region by Islamic clerics has been largely based on their concern that political freedom will lead to exactly this sort of challenge of clerical authority. Freedom is always opposed by special interests that have something to lose in the process of spreading freedom into the political arena and other aspects of life.

Even though the West cannot participate directly in the religious issues surrounding the battle for the soul of Islam, the West's penetrating ideology of freedom and democracy represents compelling ideas that the West needs to strongly promote in its war of words and ideas. One way to start might be to translate the works of Thomas Jefferson, Alexander Hamilton and Abraham Lincoln into Arabic and distribute the documents freely and widely throughout the Arab-Muslim world, showing how Islam and democracy are compatible and why freedom belongs to all people of the world. In addition, "Voice of America" needs a stronger and more compelling voice—for Al Jazeera, Al Arabiya, and hundreds of Islamist web sites on the internet have outpaced U.S. information efforts, and mainstream Islam has been largely silent on the root cause of today's radical, militant Islamist terrorism that has been derived and nurtured from the dominant Wahhabi-Salafist religious creed practiced in Saudi Arabia.

A Generation of Peace

To secure ultimate victory and a generation of peace, the American people must learn patience and its leaders must use all of the instruments of American national security policy—ideological, political, diplomatic, economic, and military—to implement comprehensive solutions to one of the world's long-neglected regions, the Middle East, and build the framework for a generation of peace so that today's suicide bombers can outgrow their militancy through hope for a better future and jobs to support their families. To do this, the United States must partner with Arab-Muslim forces of moderation and implement long-term policies and strategies that will create a generation of peace and put in place the economic and political framework needed as a cornerstone for open and pluralistic societies.

Historically, American foreign policy almost never looks good in the short term and it is often difficult to grasp the historical perspective of unfolding events that frequently conflict. But when considered in the longer perspective of history and over many years, the United States has done a far better job implementing its foreign policy than other countries and it has had resounding success in the process, restoring Western Europe and rebuilding Japan after World War II, and now the Middle East. And a simple fact remains: The United States is the principal exponent of decency and equality in the world today and its goals are to give to all people the same opportunity for life, liberty, and the pursuit of happiness that is inscribed in the "self evident truths" of its own Declaration of Independence.

But how does the world secure peace and justice in the 21st century and how does the United States convince the world that its major goal is truly to enhance human freedom, dignity, and tolerance for people of all faiths? In the twelve months following 9/11, the Bush administration formulated a new national security strategy that is now unfolding in the Middle East as al Qaeda and the Islamists are on the run and scattered, with funding drying up, recruiting down, and the number and effectiveness of its attacks declining.

Where are we today? To start, it is clear that Christians, Jews, and Muslims are all children of the same God and the same father, Abraham. Together, they make up over half the people on the planet. They must learn to live together in peace, but some would say that organized religion is the problem and not the solution, and that mainstream Muslims, Christians, and Jews have abdicated moral responsibility by failing to find solutions to the world's vexing problems of autocracy, poverty, and war. Others would say that Christianity has abdicated responsibility in containing the excesses of freedom, ceding its moral compass to groups like the Muslim Brotherhood and its theoretician Sayyid Qutb who said that the modern world had lost its way and can only be brought back to its moorings through rigid Islamic law that condemns modernization and nonbelievers.

Where are the courageous and towering Christian voices of people like Dietrich Bonhoeffer (1906-1945), Paul Tillich (1886-1965), and Reinhold Niebuhr (1892-1971) today? In NAZI Germany Bonhoeffer and Tillich witnessed the acquiescence of established churches to Hitler's National Socialism and it was Niebuhr who wrote during the dark days of World War II, "For democracy is [merely] a method of finding proximate solutions for insoluble problems" [Niebuhr].

Perhaps we have reached new middle ground that predates both Christianity and Islam and involves a shift in global ethics based on a rediscovery of Plato and Aristotle as described by Stanley Hauerwas at the Duke University School of Divinity: Ethics based on character and virtue on the model of Aristotle [Hauerwas and Pinches]. Plato and Aristotle viewed virtue as being fundamentally heroic, especially in the actions required to defend a democratic Greek city-state by force of arms. Aristotle addressed what is "best," in the broadest sense, for human beings and noted that ethical inquiry seeks to resolve disagreements that arise over the fundamental human goal of determining what is "best" for humankind. Aristotle's search was for the "highest good" and as Plato argued in The Republic, the best type of "good" is one that is desirable both in and of itself and also for the sake of what it achieves.

Bin Laden implausibly argues that to achieve the ultimate good that he envisions, he must destroy the enemies of true Islam and kill or convert all nonbelievers. Because the struggle bin Laden has embarked upon is fundamentally ideological in nature, and because bin Laden's message echoes widely throughout the Muslim world, especially the Arab-Muslim world, the West must prepare itself and its future leaders, not only with practical knowledge, but also with the tools of ancient virtue and ethics and an appreciation for the long-term nature of the struggle and the very hard work that lies ahead.

Buttressed with knowledge and tempered with hard experience in Afghanistan and Iraq, we have witnessed that freedom and democracy are true antidotes to Bin Ladenism and we should remain confident that the West and its values will triumph over militant Islamism and its message of hate and death.

Light Some Candles
We must go into the world with a pragmatic message of confidence and hope based on Western values and do all in our power to light candles of knowledge and peace to shine into the darkness of the demonic forces that have been released upon the world, to enlighten the darkness of terrorism, the darkness of Islamist fundamentalism, the darkness of radical, militant Islamism.

The momentum that has built since September 11, 2001 reveals that ideologies of hate will ultimately disappear and that true peace will come to regions of the world like the Middle East when autocracy ends, justice prevails, economic opportunities are provided, and national security issues are resolved by planting and nourishing seeds of hope and roots of change. And we must implement a new national strategy to lessen our increasingly onerous dependence on imported oil as we demonstrate to the world that the "Law of Democracy" is as enduring and eternal as the "Law of Gravity."

APPENDIX A

Chronology of Key Events

610—Prophet Mohammed's Divine Revelations started

632—Death of Prophet Mohammed

1187—Saladin (Iraqi Kurd) defeated Crusaders and recaptured Jerusalem

1300—Beginning of Ottoman Empire

1683—Islam's conquest of Europe halted at gates of Vienna

1703—Birth of Ibn Abdul Wahhab, founder of Wahhabi-Salafist movement

1744—Wahhab-al Saud agreement and marriage pact (approximate date)

1792—Death of Ibn Abdul Wahhab

1798—France (Napoleon) invaded Egypt, occupied Palestine

1801—Wahhabis destroyed holy Shiite shrines in Iraq (Karbala and Najaf)

1871—Ottomans took control of al Hasa province in eastern Arabian Peninsula

1891—Al Saud family exiled to Kuwait by Rashidi family

1902—Abdul Aziz ibn Saud took control of Riyadh, brought Al Saud family back into Saudi Arabia

1912—Ikhwan founded, grew quickly based on Wahhabism, provided support to Abdul Aziz ibn Saud

1913—Al Hasa Province taken from the Ottomans by Ibn Saud

1922—End of Ottoman Caliphate; Ibn Saud assumed title "Sultan of Najd"

1924—Mecca recaptured by Abdul Aziz Ibn Saud

1925—Medina recaptured by Ibn Saud, Ikhwan revolt began

1926—Abdul Aziz Ibn Saud proclaimed "King of the Hijaz" in the Grand Mosque of Mecca

1928-30—Ikhwan revolt defeated by Abdul Aziz Ibn Saud, leaders beheaded in public

1932—Abdul Aziz Ibn Saud proclaimed King, country unified under the name Kingdom of Saudi Arabia

1933—Saud, eldest son of King Abdul Aziz Ibn Saud, named Crown Prince

Oil concession granted to Standard Oil of California (SOCAL)

1938—Oil discovered, production started under ARAMCO (Arabian American Oil Company)

1953—Death of King Abdul Aziz Ibn Saud, succeeded by son Saud; son Faisal named Crown Prince

1957—Birth of Osama bin Laden

1960—Saudi Arabia founding member of OPEC (Organization of Petroleum Exporting Countries)

1964—King Saud deposed by royal family in favor of his brother Prince Faisal

1967—Arab-Israeli War ("Six-Day War")

1972—Saudi Arabia acquired 20 percent of ARAMCO from American oil companies

1973—Arab-Israeli War ("Yom Kippur War"), Saudi Arabia led oil boycott, oil prices quadrupled

1975—King Faisal assassinated by nephew, succeeded by brother Khaled

1979—Saudi Arabia severed diplomatic relations with Egypt after Egypt made peace with Israel
Wahhabi/Muslim Brotherhood extremists seized Grand Mosque in Mecca

Saudi government regained control, publicly executed 60 extremists

Shah of Iran overthrown by Shiite cleric Ayatollah Khomeini

Soviet Union launched invasion of Afghanistan

1980—Saudi Arabia acquired full control of ARAMCO

Iran-Iraq War (1980-1988) started

1981—Saudi Arabia founding member of Gulf Cooperation Council (GCC)

Osama bin Laden completed university in Jeddah

1982—King Khaled died of heart attack; succeeded by brother, Crown Prince Fahd

1986—King Fahd assumed the title "Custodian of the Two Holy Mosques"

1987—Saudi Arabia resumed diplomatic relations with Egypt, severed since 1979

1990—Iraq invaded Kuwait

Saudi Arabia condemned Iraqi invasion of Kuwait

Nearly one million foreign troops in Saudi Arabia including 550,000 Americans

U.N. imposed trade sanctions on Iraq

1991—U.S. & coalition forces launched air war against Iraq in January, rapidly liberated Kuwait

Cease-fire announced in February

U.N. Security Council specified conditions for lifting sanctions and destruction of Iraq's WMD

1992—King Fahd proclaimed new "Basic Law," responsibilities of the ruler, Consultative Council (Majlis)

1993—King Fahd divided Saudi Arabia into 13 administrative regions

1993—Saudi Consultative Council inaugurated with chairman and 60 members chosen by the King

Iraq refused to remove missiles in defiance of cease-fire agreement and U.N. sanctions

Allied warplanes and warships attacked Iraqi missile sites and nuclear facility near Baghdad

U.S. fired 24 cruise missiles at Iraq headquarters for assassination attempt on first President Bush

1994—Osama Bin Laden stripped of Saudi nationality, King Fahd ill

Iraqi troops moved toward Kuwait, pulled back, U.S. dispatched carrier group, 54,000 troops & warplanes

1995—King Fahd had stroke(s); day-to-day operation of country transferred to Crown Prince Abdullah

1996—U.N. allowed Iraq to make limited oil sales under corrupt oil for food program

1996—Bomb exploded at American al Khobar military complex near Dhahran killing 19, wounding 300

1997—King Fahd increased number of Consultative Council from 60 to 90

    Iraq refused to disclose details of banned weapons programs, U.N. imposed new restrictions for inspections

    U.S. & British military buildup in the Persian Gulf

    U.N. Security Council condemned Iraq's actions as "flagrant violation" of U.N. resolutions

    U.S. & British planes bombed Iraq for Saddam Hussein's defiance of U.N. weapons inspectors

    Air strikes halted after four days; Iraq cut off all cooperation with U.N. weapons inspectors

1998—Iraq Liberation Act of 1998, H.R. 4655, signed into law by President Clinton

1999—Twenty Saudi women attended a session of the Consultative Council for the first time

2000—Amnesty International described Saudi Arabia's treatment of women as "untenable"

    Hans Blix assumed post of executive chairman of U.N. weapons inspectors for Iraq

2001—British workers arrested in Riyadh after series of bomb attacks, British & American national killed

Saudi Arabia, Iran signed agreement to combat terrorism, drug-trafficking, organized crime

September 11th—15 of 19 hijackers in attacks on New York and Washington, DC were Saudis

Bin Laden taunted "infidel" Bush over Sept. 11 attacks

U.S. pressured Saudi Arabia to reform, cut off funding for terrorism; Saudis uneasy over U.S. ties

King Fahd stated terrorism prohibited by Islam

Saudi government issued identity cards to women

Taliban overthrown in Afghanistan; bin Laden escaped into Pakistan

2002—New Saudi criminal justice system banned torture and provided right to legal representation

Bin Laden said on al Jazeera, "battle has moved inside the United States"

Saudi investors withdrew billions from U.S. in protest of lawsuit filed by relatives of 9/11

Saudi border crossing with Iraq reopened for first time since Iraq 1990 invasion of Kuwait

Saudi foreign minister said U.S. cannot use Saudi facilities to attack Iraq, even if approved by U.N.

U.N. Security Council modified U.N. sanctions against Iraq to speed delivery of food and medicine

President Bush stated world leaders must enforce U.N. resolutions against Iraq or U.S. acts alone

U.N. Security Council voted 15-0 for a resolution to disarm Iraq

Stated goal of U.S. government: regime change in Iraq

Iraq released garbled 12,000-page document on its weapons programs

2003—U.S. and coalition partners invade Iraq

U.S. agreed to withdraw troops from Saudi Arabia, ending military presence since 1991 Gulf War

March—U.S. and coalition forces invaded Iraq

Suicide bombers killed 35 people at housing compounds for Westerners in Riyadh

More than 300 Saudi intellectuals, women and men, signed petition for political reform

Government said elections for municipal councils would be held within a year, first elections ever

Police broke up rally in Riyadh calling for political reform, 270 people arrested

Suicide attack by al-Qaeda militants on residential compound in Riyadh, 17 dead, many injured

King granted powers to Consultative Council to propose legislation without king's permission

2004—Saudi Arabia stated it would negotiate substantial reduction of Iraq's debt

Stampede at Hajj pilgrimage, 251 dead

Attacks near Riyadh, car bomb at security HQ killed four, wounded 148, group linked to al-Qaeda

Attack at Yanbu petrochemical site killed five; attack and hostage-taking in al Khobar, 22 killed

Bin Laden offered truce to Europeans for withdrawing troops from Muslim nations

Three gun attacks in Riyadh in one week, two Americans, one BBC cameraman dead

American engineer abducted and beheaded, security forces killed local al-Qaeda leader

Amnesty offered for Saudi militants with limited effect

Attack on U.S. consulate in Jeddah, five staff members and four attackers killed

Two car bombs exploded in central Riyadh; security forces killed seven suspects in raid

2005—Palestinian and Iraqi elections (January)

Saudi municipal elections for half the seats, king appointed other half, women could not vote

Saudi Consultative Council increased to 120 members

Saudi Arabia confirmed killing 15 Islamist extremists including al Qaeda leader for Saudi Arabia

Syrian forces completed withdrawal from Lebanon

New democratically elected Iraqi government formed

Crown Prince Abdullah and President Bush met in Crawford, Texas

Saudi King Fahd died; Abdullah crowned new King; Sultan Crown Prince

Iraqi referendum on Constitution (October 15) and election for new National Assembly (December 15)

Oil peaked at all-time high of $70 per barrel following Hurricane Katrina

2006—Oil surged to $68 per barrel in January & $75 per barrel in April 2006

Doha "Declaration of Democracy & Reform" signed by Arab democrats in Doha, Qatar

NATO charter in Afghanistan broadened

Bin Laden surfaced after a one-year absence with audio tape offering truce ("hudna" armistice)

New Iraqi government formed

U.S. troops reductions planned & implemented for Iraq & Afghanistan

APPENDIX B

Glossary of Arabic Terms

Al-Azhar. World's oldest university, located in Cairo, Egypt.

Al Qaeda. Arabic for "the base," also called "World Islamic Front for Jihad Against Jews and Crusaders;" goal is to establish fundamentalist Islamic regimes and restore Sunni Caliphate.

Ayatollah. High-ranking Shiite Muslim leader.

Bedouin. Arabic for "desert dweller," term generally applied to nomadic Arab groups.

Bin. Arabic for "son of."

Bint. Arabic for "daughter of."

Caliph. From Arabic word "khalifa" for successor to the prophet Muhammad, "Commander of the Faithful;" ultimate religious and political authority of Sunni Muslim empires; last Caliph was unseated by Ataturk in 1924.

Emir. Muslim title of nobility or high office.

Fatwa. Pronouncement or ruling by Muslim religious leader.

Hadith. Sayings and recorded experiences of the Prophet Mohammed; a source of Muslim doctrine that supplements the Koran.

Hajj. Annual Muslim pilgrimage to Mecca; one of the five pillars of Islam.

Hamas. "Islamic Resistance Movement," Arabic for "courage;" radical Palestinian Islamist movement tied to Muslim Brotherhood; goal of Hamas is an Islamic theocracy in territory of Israel, West Bank and Gaza strip; designated as a terrorist group by U.S. government; won political victory in 2006 elections.

Hegira. Mohammed's departure from Mecca for Medina in the year 622, marking the start of the Muslim calendar.

Hezbollah. In Arabic, "party of God;" Iranian-sponsored Shiite terrorist organization operating against Israel and the West from Lebanon; designated as a terrorist group by U.S. government.

Ibn. Arabic for "son of."

Ikhwan. Wahhabi religious militia; loyal Bedouin tribesmen organized by Ibn Saud into Wahhabi Ikhwan army, precursor of al Qaeda; main military force that played key role in establishing Saudi rule over the Arabian Peninsula.

Imam. Muslim religious leader.

Infidel. One who doubts or rejects Islam or a particular doctrine, system, or principle.

Islam. Arabic for "submission to the will of God;" the religion of Islam.

Islamic. Of or pertaining to the religion, people and culture of Islam.

Islamism (Islamist). Political Islam espoused by militant Islamists; political ideology of Muslim fundamentalists; belief that Islam is both a religion and a political system that governs (through Sharia) all religious, legal, economic and social aspects of life.

Jihad. Arabic for "striving in the way of God;" violent and personal struggle in defense of Islam.

Kaaba. Most sacred shrine of Islam, located in Mecca, believed to have been erected by the Prophet Abraham.

Kafir. A person who rejects God and the Islamic faith; an infidel.

Koran. Holy text of Islam revealed to Mohammed.

Levant. Imprecise geographical area of the Middle East incorporating Israel, Jordan, Lebanon, Palestine Syria and parts of Egypt; French Mandates of 1920 under the League of Nations were called the "Levant States" of Syria and Lebanon.

Madrassa. Muslim school for instruction in the Koran and Islamic law.

Maghreb. Islamic lands of North Africa that include Algeria, Libya, Morocco and Tunisia.

Majlis ("Majlis al Shura"). Saudi Arabian consultative council; Bedouin assembly.

Mecca. City in western Saudi Arabia, birthplace of the Prophet Mohammed about 571; location of Grand Mosque and Kaaba, holiest Muslim site; destination for annual Muslim pilgrimage; non-Muslims prohibited from entering Mecca.

Medina. City in western Saudi Arabia, second holiest city of Islam after Mecca; site of Mosque of the Prophet; non-Muslims prohibited from entering Medina.

Muezzin. Individual who calls faithful to prayer at local mosque five times a day.

Mufti. Muslim scholar who issues fatwas.

Mujahadeen. Muslim who wages violent jihad in perceived defense of Islam.

Muslim. One who practices the religion of Islam.

Muslim Brotherhood. In Arabic "al-Ikhwan al-Muslimun;" secret, militant radical Islamist society active in 70 countries with links to terrorism; founded in Egypt in late 1920s by Hassan al-Banna (1905-1949); not to be confused with Wahhabi Ikhwan army in Saudi Arabia.

Muttawa. Religious police in Saudi Arabia who ensure strict adherence to established Sharia codes of Wahhabi conduct; offenders may be detained indefinitely and put to death.

Ottoman Empire. Muslim empire headed by Sultan and Sunni Caliph in Istanbul; Ottoman Empire included modern Turkey, Middle East, North Africa, south-eastern Europe eastward to Caucasus; Ottoman Empire dissolved at end of World War I following defeat by the Allies.

Ramadan. Ninth month of the Muslim calendar dedicated to fasting during daylight hours.

Salafist (Salafism.) "Companions of the Prophet;" Wahhabis and other Sunni Muslim fundamentalists who seek to return to the perceived purity of the early days of Islam following the death of Mohammed; Wahhabis are Salafists but not all Salafists are Wahhabis.

Shamar Confederation. Extensive Bedouin tribe that ranges from northern Saudi Arabia to western Iraq, eastern Syria and eastern Jordan; family of King Abdullah of Saudi Arabia are members of Shamar; many Wahhabi insurgents fighting Americans in Iraq are members of the Shamar Confederation

Sharia. Islamic law, "path to the watering hole" in Arabic; religious code encompassing religious rituals, politics, economics, banking, business, legal and social issues.

Shiite (Shia, Shiism). Follower of one of two major Islamic sects, about 10-15 percent of all Muslims; Shiites believe authority and leadership was passed from Mohammed to his descendants.

Sudairi Seven. Seven sons of King Abdul Aziz Ibn Saud from favorite wife, Hassa bint Sudairi; powerful Saudi royal family; defacto royal family board of directors.

Sufi (Sufism). Islamic mysticism; highly spiritual form of Islam.

Sultan. Political leader of a Muslim state; e.g.; Sultan of Oman, Sultan of Brunei.

Sunni. Largest Islamic sect, about 85-90 percent of all Muslims; Sunnis believe spiritual authority and leadership derive from consensus of the Muslim community.

Sunni Triangle. Area west and north of Baghdad occupied by Iraqi Wahhabis and members of the Sunni Shamar tribal confederation; center of Iraqi insurgent activity against American forces.

Sunnah. Deeds, sayings and teachings of Mohammed.

Takfir. Under Islamic law (Sharia), the practice of declaring individual Muslims or groups of people nonbelievers in God (kafir).

Takfir Wal Hijra. Most brutally violent Islamist terrorist operation in world; extreme extension of Saudi Arabian Wahhabi-Salafist doctrine. Zawahiri and Zarqawi are Takfiris.

Taliban. Arabic for "student;" militant Wahhabi-Salafist group that ruled Afghanistan from 1996-2001; implemented Islamic law (Sharia) under reign of terror; overthrown by American military forces following al Qaeda attacks against the United States on 9/11/2001.

Ulama. Learned Muslim men, legal scholars; elders of a Muslim community.

Ummah. Worldwide Muslim community of believers that forms the heart of Islam.

Wahhabi (Wahhabism). "Companions of the Prophet," followers of the teachings of Ibn Abdul Wahhab; Wahhabis prefer to call themselves "Salafists."

Wahhabi-Bin Ladenism. Ideology of al Qaeda derived from the state religion of Saudi Arabia.

Wahhabi-Salafism. Fanatical Sunni Muslim doctrine zealously promoted by Saudi Arabian missionaries worldwide.

World Trade Organization (WTO). Established in 1995, the WTO consists of 149 nations and is the sole international organization that deals with the rules of trade between nations.

Zakat. Alms tax, donation to charity; one of the five pillars of Islam.

APPENDIX C

About the Authors

Colonel B. Wayne Quist. Author of several publications and articles in the field of radical, militant Islamism, national security policy, and American history, and coauthored *Winning the War on Terror* with David F. Drake in 2005. He has been featured as a popular speaker on the ideology of al Qaeda and recently lectured at the Nobel Peace Prize Forum. He has a B.A. degree from St. Olaf College plus advanced degrees from the University of Southern California and The National War College in Washington, D.C., specializing in the Middle East. He retired from the Air Force as a full colonel (O-6) with 3,500 flying hours as a navigator and AWACS mission commander. While serving in Washington, DC, he worked in the Pentagon, later directed the Air Force AWACS program, and led the first deployment of AWACS into Saudi Arabia in 1980 following the Iranian revolution. After leaving the Air Force, he headed a Fortune 500 company's operations from Brussels, Belgium and is currently a partner with an investment banking firm specializing in the sale and recapitalization of privately held companies.

Dr. David F. Drake. Has written and spoken extensively on health economics, finance, and regulation, and coauthored *Winning the War on Terror* in 2005 with B. Wayne Quist. For the past 13 years he has written about health economics, political economics, foreign affairs, and the detective stories of Georges Simenon and Agatha Christie. He has authored several articles on health economics and national health insurance topics and published *Reforming the Health Care Market: An Interpretative Economic History* with Georgetown University Press in 1994. He recently completed a manuscript on healthcare reform, *Mandate for 21st Century America: Universal Health Insurance,* and completed *The World's Greatest Detective: Hercule Poirot or Jules Maigret* for publication. Dr. Drake received his doctorate in business administration from the University of Chicago Graduate School of Business, where he subsequently taught, full and part time, for 20 years. Dr. Drake retired in 1992 after 25 years with the American Hospital Association, serving as Senior Vice President and Secretary-Treasurer.

BIBLIOGRAPHY

Abdullah bin Abdul Aziz ibn Saud, Crown Prince, "Press Release of May 3, 2004," Riyadh, Saudi Arabia: Saudi Press Agency, May 3, 2004.

Alexiev, Alex, "Wahhabism: State-Sponsored Extremism Worldwide," *Testimony before U.S. Senate Committee on Terrorism, Technology and Homeland Security*, June 26, 2003, http://www.centerforsecuritypolicy.org/index.jsp?section=static&page=alexievtestimony.

Alyami, Dr. Ali H. and B. Wayne Quist, "The Saudi Role in the Cartoon Controversy," February 21, 2006, www.cdhr.info.

Anderson, John Lee, *The Fall of Baghdad*, New York: Penguin Press, 2004.

Armstrong, Karen, *Islam, A Short History*, New York: Random House, Inc., Modern Library Edition, 2000.

Benoit, Bertrand, "EU Body Shelves Report on Anti-Semitism," *Financial Times*, November 21, 2003.

Bergen, Peter L., *Holy War, Inc: Inside the Secret World of Osama bin Laden*: London: Orion Books, 2002.

___, "The Al Qaeda Connection, Try Riyadh, Not Baghdad," December 18, 2002, www.thenation.com.

Berman, Paul, "The Philosopher of Islamic Terror," *New York Times*, March 23, 2003.

Bodansky, Yossef, *Bin Laden: The Man Who Declared War on America*, New York: Random House, Inc., 2001.

Bremer, L. Paul III, "The Right Call," *Wall Street Journal*, January 12, 2005.

Bremmer, Ian, and Hawes, Crispin, "An Insatiable Thirst for Oil," *National Interest*, Fall 2003. http://www.inthenationalinterest.com/Articles/October2004/October2004Bremmer.html.

British Broadcasting Corporation, "News: Saudi Prince Gets Libel Damages," December 6, 2004, http//www:BBC.co.uk/2/hi/uk/-news/4072219.stm.

Broad, William J., and Sanger, David E., "As Nuclear Secrets Emerge, More Are Suspected," *New York Times*, December 26, 2004.

Buruma, Ian, "An Islamic Democracy for Iraq?" *New York Times*, December 5, 2004.

Burns, John F. and Glanz, James, "Iraqi Shiites Win, But Margin Less Than Projection," *New York Times*, February 14, 2005.

Bush, George W., "The National Security Strategy of United States of America," Office of the President, March 16, 2006, http://www.whitehouse.gov/nsc/2006/#.

___, "President Discusses American and European Alliance in Belgium," the White House, Office of the Press Secretary, Concert Noble, Brussels, Belgium, February 21, 2005, http://www.whitehouse.gov/news/releases/2005/02/20050221.html.

___, "The National Security Strategy of the United States of America," Office of the President, September 17, 2002, http://www.whitehouse.gov/nsc/print/nssall.html.

___. "President Bush Delivers Graduation Speech at West Point," June 1, 2002, http://www.whitehouse.gov/news/releases/2002/06/print/20020601-3.html.

___, "President Delivers State of Union Address," Washington, DC, January 29, 2002, http://www. whitehouse.gov/news/releases/2002/01/print/20020129-11.html.

___, "Address to a Joint Session of Congress," Washington, DC, September 20, 2001, http://www. whitehouse.gov/newsrelease/2001/09/print/20010920-8.html.

Campo-Flores, Arian, "The Most Dangerous Gang in America," *Newsweek,* March 28, 2006, http://www.msnbc.msn.com/id/7244879/site/newsweek/.

Central Intelligence Agency, *The World Fact Book,* Washington, DC: Government Printing Office, 2006.

Chassay, Clancy, "The Gun of the Ballot Box? Hamas or Al Qaeda?" *Counterpunch,* April 1-2, 2006, http://www.counterpunch.org/chassay040120006.html.

Clarke, Richard A., *Against All Enemies: Inside America's War on Terror,* New York: Free Press, 2004.

CNN.com, "Terrorist acts of bin Laden 'totally banned'" Friday, March 11, 2005, http://www.cnn.com/2005/WORLD/europe/03/10/spain.fatwa.osama.ap/.

CNS News, "More Mosques in France Falling Under Sway of Radicals," www.CNSNews.com, Paris, June 30, 2004.

Cohen, Richard, "Intolerance Swaddled in Faith," *Washington Post*, May 1, 2003.

Colson, Chuck, "Evangelizing for Evil in Our Prisons: Radical Islamists Seek to Turn Criminals into Terrorists," *Wall Street Journal*, June 24, 2002.

Copeland, Libby, "Prison Revolt" *Washington Post*, Page C01, May 10, 2004.

Cordesman, Anthony H., "The Best Defense Is a Good Offense," *New York Times*, December 27, 2004.

Cowell, Alan, and Van Natta, Don, Jr., "Top Muslims in Britain Reject Call to Violence," New York Times, September 3, 2005.

Daalder, Ivo H., and Lindsay, James M., *American Unbound, The Bush Revolution in Foreign Policy*, Washington, DC: Brookings Institution Press, 2003.

Emerson, Stephen, *Terrorists Among Us: Jihad In America*, PBS Documentary, Washington, DC: 1994, updated 2001.

Engel, Richard, *A Fist in the Hornet's Nest: On the Ground in Baghdad before, during and after the War*, New York: Hyperion, 2004.

Fainaru, Steve, "Elation, Reflection for GIs Going Home," *Washington Post*, February 6, 2005.

Fandy, Mamoun, "Avoiding the Next Generation of al Qaeda," Statement to the third public hearing of The National Commission on Terrorist Attacks Upon the United States, July 9, 2003.

FBI Most Wanted Poster, "Ayman al Zawahiri," Washington, DC: 2005.

Ferguson, Niall, "The Last Iraqi Insurgency," *New York Times*, April 18, 2004.

___, "The End of Europe?," American Enterprise Institute Bradley Lecture, March 1, 2004, http://www.aei.org/news/filter.,newsID.20045/news_detail.asp.

Filkins, Dexter, "Suddenly, It's 'America Who,'" *New York Times*, February 6, 2005.

___, "Insurgents Vowing to Kill Iraqis Who Brave the Polls on Sunday," *New York Times*, January 26, 2005.

Finer, Jonathan, and Anderson, John Ward, "16 Sadr Loyalist Killed in Assault," *Washington Post*, March 27, 2006.

Finer, Jonathan, "At Heart of Iraqi Impasse, a Family Feud," *Washington Post*, April 19, 2006.

Franks, Tommy, *American Soldier*, New York: HarperCollins Publishers, 2004.

Freeh, Louis J., *My FBI: Bringing Down the Mafia, Investigating Bill Clinton, and Fighting the War on Terror*, New York: St. Martin's Press, 2005.

Friedman, George, *America's Secret War, Inside the Hidden Worldwide Struggle between America and Its Enemies*, New York: Doubleday, 2004.

Friedman, Thomas L., "A Day to Remember," *New York Times*, February 2, 2005.

___, "The Real War," *New York Times*, November 27, 2001.

Froomkin, Dan, "Is Bush Vulnerable on Iraq?" Washington Post, August 5, 2005, http://www. washingtonpost.com/wp-dyn/content/blog/2005/08/0500917_pf.ht.

Gaddis, John Lewis, "Grand Strategy in the Second Term," *Foreign Affairs*, January/February 2005, http://www.foreign affairs.org/20050101/john-lewis-gaddis/grand-strategy-in-the-second-term.html.

___, *Surprise, Security, and the American Experience*, Cambridge, MA: President and Fellows of Harvard College, 2004.

Gold, Dore, *Hatred's Kingdom: How Saudi Arabia Supports the New Global Terrorism*, Washington, DC: Regency Publishing, Inc., 2003.

Goodstein, Laurie, "Muslim Leaders Confront Terror Threat within Islam," *New York Times*, September 2, 2005.

Gordon, Michael R., and Trainor, Bernard E., "Dash to Baghdad Left Top U.S. Generals Divided," *New York Times*, March 13, 2006.

___, "Even as U.S. Invaded, Hussein Saw Iraqi Unrest as Top Threat," *New York Times*, March 12, 2006.

Halper, Stefan, and Clarke, Jonathan, *America Alone, The Neo-Conservatives and the Global Order*, Cambridge, U.K.: Cambridge University Press, 2004.

Hartford Seminary, Institute for Religious Research in Connecticut, "Mosque in America," a part of "Faith Communities Today," April 2001.

Hauerwas, Stanley and Pinches, Charles, *Christians Among the Virtues. Theological Conversations with Ancient and Modern Ethics*, South Bend: University of Notre Dame Press, 1998.

Ignatieff, Michael, "The Uncommitted," *New York Times*, January 30, 2005.

Ignatius, David, "Let the Iraqis Bargain," *Washington Post*, April 5, 2006.

___, "A CEO's Weakness," *Washington Post*, September 7, 2005.

International Islamic Conference, "True Islam and its Role in Modern Society," July 4-6, 2005, http://mac.abc.se/home/onesr/ez/cim/Muslim.Clerics.Ag.takfir.htiml.

International Energy Agency (IEA), *World Energy Outlook*, Paris: IEA, 2006.

Jacoby, Mary and Brink, Graham, "Saudi Form of Islam Wars with Moderates," *St. Petersburg Times*, March 11, 2003.

Jafari, Ibrahim al, "My Vision for Iraq," *Washington Post*, March 20, 2006.

Joscelyn, Thomas, "The Pope of Terrorism," *The Weekly Standard*, July 25, 2005.

Kagan, Robert, *Of Paradise and Power, America and Europe in the New World Order*, New York: Alfred A. Knopf, 2003.

Kaiser, Robert G., "Enormous Wealth Spilled into American Coffers," *Washington Post*, Page A17, February 11, 2002.

Kaplin, Lee, "The Saudi Fifth Column on Our Nation's Campuses," *FrontPage Magazine.com*, April 5, 2004, http://www.frontpagemag.com/articles/ReadArticle. asp?ID=12833.

Keiler, Jonathan F., "Who Won the Battle of Fallujah?" *The Naval Institute: Proceedings*, January 2005, http://www.military.com/Content/MoreContent1?file=NI_0105_Fallu-jah-P1.

Khaled al Faisal bin Abdul Aziz, Prince, "Open Letter to the People of Saudi Arabia," *Ain-Al-Yaqee, Weekly Arab Political Magazine*, July 16, 2004.

Khaled bin Sultan bin Abdul Aziz, Prince and General, *Desert Warrior: A Personal View of the Gulf War by the Joint Forces Commander*, New York: HarperCollins, 1995.

Khalilzad, Zalmay, "The Challenge Before Us," *Wall Street Journal*, January 12. 2006.

Khan, Asfraf, "Voters reverse Islamist' rise in Pakistani politics," *Christian Science Monitor*, September 6, 2005, http://www.csmonitor.com/2005/0906/p04s02-wosc.html.

Knickmeyer Ellen, and Ibrahim, K.I., "Bombing Shatters Mosque in Iraq," *Washington Post*, February 23, 2006.

Koh, Harold Hongju, "Preserving American Values: The Challenge at Home and Abroad," *The Age of Terror*, ed. by Strobe Talbott and Nayan Chandra, New York: Basic Books, 2001.

Krauthammer, Charles, "The Road to Damascus," *Washington Post*, March 4, 2005, http://www. washingtonpost.com/wp-dyn/articles/A5695-2005Mar3. html.

Kyle, Senator Jon, Statement Before Senate Judiciary Subcommittee on Technology, Terrorism and Homeland Security, United States Senate, Washington, DC: July 2003.

Levitt, Matthew, "Subversion from Within: Saudi Funding of Islamic Extremist Groups Undermining U.S. Interests and the War on Terror from within the United States," *Testimony before the Senate Judiciary Subcommittee on Terrorism, Technology, and Homeland Security, Washington Institute for Near East Policy*, Washington, DC: September 10, 2003.

Lewis, Bernard, *The Crisis of Islam: Holy War and Unholy Terror*, New York: Modern Library, 2003.

Lindsey, Gene, *Saudi Arabia*, New York: Hippocrene Books, 1991.

Lippman, Thomas, "King Fahd, Man of Maddening Contradictions," *Washington Post*, August 1, 2005.

___, "The Crisis Within—In Saudi Arabia, Rebellion, and Reform Seize Center Stage," *Washington Post*, June 13, 2004, http://www.washingtonpost.com/wp-dyn/articles/A35988-2004Jun11.html.

___, *Inside the Mirage: America's Fragile Partnership with Saudi Arabia*, Boulder, CO: Westview Press, 2003.

___, *"Comments"on Saudi—U.S. Relations*, Washington DC: School of the Advanced International Studies (SAIS), Johns Hopkins University, November 7, 2003, http://www.saudi-us-relations.org/newsletter/saudi-relations-interest-12-16.html.

Long, David E., *The Kingdom of Saudi Arabia*, Gainesville: University Press of Florida: 1997.

Mann, James, *Rise of the Vulcans, The History of Bush's War Cabinet*, New York: Penguin Group (USA), Inc., 2004.

McPhee, Michele, "Eastie gang linked to al Qaeda," *Boston Herald*, January 5, 2005, http://news.bostonherald.com/localRegional/view.bg?articleid=61903.

Mintz, John, and Farah, Douglas, "In Search Of Friends Among the Foes; U.S. Hopes to Work With Diverse Group," *Washington Post*, Page A01, September 11, 2004.

Mintz, John, and Vistica, Gregory L., "Muslim Troops' Loyalty a Delicate Question," *Washington Post*, November 2, 2003.

Moss, Michael, "Many Actions Tied to Delay in Armor for Troops in Iraq," *New York Times*, March 7, 2005.

Munif, Abdul Rahman, *Cities of Salt*, translated from Arabic to English by Peter Theroux, New York: Cape Cod Scriveners Company, 1987.

Murawiec, Laurent, "The Wacky World of French Intellectuals," *Middle East Quarterly*, Spring 2002, www.meforum.org/article/37/.

Niebuhr, Reinhold, *The Children of Light and the Children of Darkness*, New York: Charles Scribner's Sons, 1944.

Nordling, Rod, Masland, Tom, and Dickey, Christopher, "Unmasking the Insurgents," *Newsweek*, February 5, 2005.

Packer, George, *The Assassins' Gate: America in Iraq*, New York: Farrar, Straus & Giroux, 2005.

Pas, Reuven, "Arab volunteers killing in Iraq: An Analysis," *Global Research in International Affairs*, Volume 3, Number 1 (March 2005), www.e-prism.org.

Pew Global Attitudes Project, "Islamic Extremism: Common Concerns for Muslim and Western Publics," July 2005.

Pipes, Daniel, "The evil isn't Islam," *New York Post*, July 30, 2002, http://danielpipes.org/ article/437.

Podhoretz, Norman, "Who is Lying About Iraq?" *Commentary*, December 2005, pp. 27-33.

___, "World War IV: How It Started, What It Means, and Why We Have to Win," *Commentary*, September, 2004, pp. 17-54.

Posner, Gerald, *Why America Slept: The Failure to Prevent 9/11*, New York: Random House, 2003.

Qayash, Rafat, "Lessons from Afghanistan's presidential election," *Afghanistan's Development Network*, November 18, 2004, http://www.afgha.com/?af=printnews &sid=46964.

Qusti, Raid, "Saudi Arabia is a Male-Dominated Country," *Arab News*, September 17, 2003.

___, "Criticism of the Saudi Custom Forbidding Women to Show Their Faces in Public," *Arab News*, September 3, 2003.

Ricchiardi, Sherry, "Missed Signals," *American Journalism Review*, August/September, 2004, http://www.ajr.org/article_printable.asp?id=3716.

Ricks, Thomas E., "Briefing Depicted Saudis as Enemies; Invasion Urged to Pentagon Board, *Washington Post*, August 6, 2002.

Rivilin, Paul, and Even, Shmuel, "Political Stability in Arab States: Economic Causes and Consequences," *Memorandum 74*, The Jaffe Center for Strategic Studies, Tel Aviv University, December 2004, http://www.tau.ac.il/jcss/memorandum/memo74.pdf.

Saudi Ministry of Culture and Information, *The Saudi Arabia Information Resource*, Riyadh, Arabia: Kingdom of Saudi Arabia, 2004.

Schumer, Senator Chuck, "Press Release," May 14, 2003. http://schumer.senate.gov/ Schumer Website/pressroom/press_releases/PR01704.html.

Schwartz, Stephen, "Interview," *Frontpagemag.com*, December 13, 2004, http://www.frontpagemag.Com/ articles/ReadArticle.asp?ID=16283.

___, *Two Faces of Islam: The House of Saud from Tradition to Terror*, New York: Doubleday, 2002.

Scowcroft, Brent, "Don't Attack Iraq," *Wall Street Journal*, August 16, 2002.

Shadid, Anthony, and Struck, Doug, "Top Shiite Welcomes Overtures by Sunnis," *Washington Post*, February 6, 2005.

Sharansky, Natan with Dermer, Ron, *The Case For Democracy: The Power of Freedom To Overcome Tyranny and Fear*, New York: Public Affairs, 2004.

Stille, Alexander, "Experts Can Help Rebuild A Country," *New York Times*, July 19, 2003.

Stothard, Peter, *Thirty Days: Tony Blair and the Test of History*, New York: HarperCollins Publishers, 2003.

Sullivan, Andrew, "Atrocities in Plain Sight, Book Review of *The Abu Ghraib Investigations* and *Torture and Truth*," *New York Times*, January 23, 2005.

Taheri, Amir, "Sunnis and Iraq Constitution," *Arab News*, September 3, 2005.

___ "King Fahd Put His Nation on Path to Modernization," *Arab News*, August 2, 2005.

___, "Losing Battle for Islamists," *Arab News*, March 26, 2005, http://arabnews.com/services/print/print.asp?artid=61079&d=26&m+3&y=2005&hl= Losi....

___, "Iraq on the Road to Democracy," *Arab News*, February 19, 2005.

Taspinar, Omer, "Europe's Muslim Street," *Foreign Policy*, March 2003, http://www.brookings.edu/views/op-ed/fellows/taspinar20030301.html.

Tavernise, Sabrina, and Filkins, Dexter, "Local Insurgents Tell of Clashes with Al Qaeda's Forces in Iraq, New York Times, January 12, 2006.

United Nations, *Arab Human Development Report*, New York: United Nations, 2002.

U.S. Department of Energy, *Department of Energy Strategic Plan: Protecting National Energy and Economic Security with Advanced Science and Technology and Ensuring Environmental Cleanup*, Washington DC: Government Printing Office, September 30, 2003, http://www.doe.gov/engine/content.do?BT_CODE=ABOUTDOE.

U.S. Department of State, *Country Reports on Human Rights Practices 2003 Saudi Arabia*, Washington, DC: Government Printing Office, February 25, 2004.

Walker, Martin (editor), *The Iraq War, As Witnessed by the Correspondents and Photographers of United Press International*, Washington, DC: Brassey's, Inc., 2004.

Williams, Daniel, "Aging Egyptian Says 'Religion Allows Freedom of Thought,'" *Washington Post*, March 7, 2005, http//:www.washingtonpost.com/wp-dyn/articles/ A12340-2005Mar6.html.

Woodward, Bob, *Plan of Attack*, New York: Simon & Schuster, 2004.

___, *Bush at War*, New York, Simon & Schuster, 2003.

Wyatt, Caroline, "Liberty, Equality and the Headscarf (France)" by Caroline Wyatt, BBC Paris Correspondent, December 20, 2003, http://www.mabonline.net/activities/nat_events/national hijabprotest/humanrights.htm.

Yergin, Daniel, *Shattered Peace: The Origins of the Cold War and the National Security State*, Boston: Houghton Mifflin Company, 1977.

Zakaria, Fareed, "High Hopes Hard Facts," *Newsweek*, January 31, 2005.

INDEX

A
Abbas, President Mahmoud 171, 179
Abdul Aziz ibn Saud, King 5, 12, 22-4, 26, 27, 29-31, 37, 38, 45-7, 51, 55, 59, 61, 72, 81, 114, 115, 131-3, 235, 265, 272, 273, 282, 285, 314
Abdullah bin Abdul Aziz ibn Saud Crown Prince, King 26, 30, 34, 50-3, 54, 65, 81, 93, 132, 152, 244, 251, 252, 275, 280, 285, 290
Abu Ghraib Prison 7, 202-4
Adams, Secretary of State and President John Quincy 157-9
    Monroe Doctrine 157
Afghanistan 6, 11, 20, 35, 40, 47-9, 58, 59, 62, 65, 67, 69, 71, 77, 82, 97, 118-20, 123, 128-30, 138, 141-7, 150, 152-4, 162, 163, 166, 176-8, 182, 183, 185, 188, 196, 198, 200, 236, 237, 238, 240-2, 245, 246, 248, 254, 259, 263, 270, 274, 277, 280, 286, 300
    Soviet Union invasion 1979 47, 48, 49, 58, 62, 65, 69, 71, 102, 118, 123, 129, 144, 236, 240, 242, 254, 274
    Coalition invasion 2001 166, 182, 183, 237, 245
    Elections of 2004 145, 176, 177
Afghan Arabs 15, 49, 58, 66, 68, 71, 236, 240
Ahmad, General Mahmoud 141

Ahmed bin Salman bin Abdul Aziz, Prince 129
Akbar, Sergeant Hasan 104
Al Arabiya 89, 267
Al Jazeera 89, 110, 202, 217, 267, 277
Al Qaeda [see also Qaeda] 5, 6, 8, 9, 11, 12, 15, 16, 19, 20-2, 44, 54,
   55, 57, 58, 59, 63, 65-72, 76-80, 83, 84, 95, 99-102, 107-9, 111, 113,
   116, 119-21, 123, 124, 125, 128, 129, 130, 132, 138-44, 150-4, 162-
   7, 170, 175, 177-9, 182-4, 192, 198, 200, 202, 208, 212, 216, 219,
   224, 225, 235-45, 247, 249, 250, 252-4, 255, 256, 259, 264, 265,
   268, 278, 279, 280, 281, 282, 286, 288, 291, 292, 294, 299, 302
Allawi, Prime Minister Ayad 211, 218
Al Waleed ibn Talal ibn Abdul Aziz, Prince 134
Alyami, Dr. Ali H. 180, 250, 290
American Muslim Council 100
Anderson, John Lee 227, 261, 290
Anti-Semitism 17, 109, 110, 124, 134, 290
Aquino, President Corazon 161, 262
Arab American Oil Company [ARAMCO] 29, 38, 131, 273, 274
Arab-Israeli War 35, 38, 62, 63, 66, 75, 76, 115, 131, 273
    Six Day War 63, 66, 75, 273
    Yom Kippur War 35, 38, 62, 76, 115, 131, 273
Arab League 33, 46, 84, 87
Arab Oil Embargo 31, 35, 38, 61, 115, 116
Arabian Gulf [Persian Gulf] 11, 17, 21, 27, 32, 33, 34, 35-7, 39, 57,
   61, 67, 84, 87, 96, 101, 114, 115, 123, 135, 143, 151, 187, 189, 247,
   276
Arafat, President Yasser 63, 64, 171, 179, 182
Aristotle 269
Armitage, Undersecretary Richard 141, 142, 146, 161
Armstrong, Karen 265, 290
Askariya Golden Dome Shrine [see Samarra] 225
Assad, President Hafez al 168, 179
Atta, Mohammed 78
Ataturk, Kemal 83, 113, 282
Australia 143, 171, 187, 195

Ayyiri, Yusuf al 84
Azzam, Abdullah 62-8, 235

B
Baathist Party 83, 87, 165, 178, 179, 186, 192-4, 198-200, 207-9, 211, 212, 214-16, 219, 220, 224, 226, 233, 240, 259, 261
Baghdad, Iraq 17, 52, 105, 174, 178, 187-9, 191-6, 198, 201, 202, 206, 207, 221, 226, 230, 275, 286, 290, 291, 293, 295
Bahrain 28, 29, 38, 94, 152, 172, 180
Bandar bin Sultan bin Abdul Aziz al Saud, Prince 53, 54, 128, 129, 132, 134, 166, 244, 252
Balkans 106, 119, 220, 259
Banna, Gamal 266
Banna, Hassan al 19, 72, 284
Basra, Iraq 189
Bedouin 5, 15, 20, 22, 23, 26, 27, 28, 37, 39, 42, 52, 82, 93, 127, 213, 281, 282, 284, 285
Beirut, Lebanon 117, 179, 263
Benedict, Ruth 196, 197
Benoit, Bertrand 110, 290
Bergen, Peter 54, 63, 291
Berlin, Germany 65, 105, 118, 124, 136
Berman, Paul 291
Bin Laden, Osama [see also Osama bin Laden] 5, 9, 11, 15, 18, 19, 49, 55, 59, 61, 62, 64-72, 74, 75-7, 111, 116, 118, 121, 122, 124, 129, 130, 134, 138, 142, 144, 153, 159, 182, 184, 212, 219, 235, 236, 237, 242, 247-49, 254, 260, 265, 273, 274, 275, 291
Bin Ladenism 5, 6, 10, 12, 48, 57, 59, 79, 80, 94, 112, 116, 122, 161, 181, 234, 241, 244, 262, 270, 286
Blackwell, Robert 146
Blair, Prime Minister Tony 171, 172, 183, 239, 301
Bonn, Germany 107, 108, 145
Bosnia 119, 137, 143, 175
Bremer, Paul 199, 210, 214, 291
Bremmer, Ian 37, 291

British 17, 18, 28, 29, 30, 39, 85, 91, 106, 109, 142, 143, 171, 173, 183, 189, 193, 195, 197, 205, 212, 237, 276, 291
Broad, William J. 291
Burns, John F. 216, 291
Buruma, Ian 291
Bush, President George H. W. 35, 49, 137, 275
    Grand Alliance 35, 49, 137, 170
    New World Order 137
Bush, President George W. 6-7, 11-12, 51-2, 112, 120, 132, 136, 139-41, 144-7, 149, 150, 154-85, 187, 200, 204-5, 208, 214, 227, 231, 240, 243-4, 246-247, 252-60, 262-3, 265, 266-7, 277, 278, 280, 291-3, 295, 299, 303
    Addresses: 9/20/2001, Declaration of War on Terror 139, 144, 292
        1/29/2002, "Axis-of-Evil" Speech 147, 149, 162, 292
        6/1/2002, West Point Graduation Speech 154, 292
        9/12/2002 U.N. General Assembly Speech 163
    Bush Doctrine 6, 7, 11, 12, 52, 112, 136, 139, 141, 145-6, 150, 154-5, 158-63, 166-7, 171, 173, 178, 181-4, 244, 247, 255-257, 262, 263, 266, 267
    Democratization 154-6, 158-9, 160-1, 167, 175-8, 184, 240, 247, 256, 263
    Job Ratings 166, 167, 246, 252
    National Security Strategy of United States of America 156, 157, 256, 267, 291-2

C

Cairo, Egypt 64, 66, 68, 76, 84, 133, 251, 263, 281
Caliph, Caliphate 18, 55, 59, 64, 69, 70, 77, 84, 113, 241, 242, 272, 281, 282, 284
Campo-Flores, Arian 99, 292
Canada 34, 171,
Carter, President Jimmy 35, 36, 115, 117, 122, 146
    Carter Doctrine 35, 115
    Camp David Agreement 120

Center for Democracy and Human Rights in Saudi Arabia 180, 250, 290
Central Intelligence Agency [CIA] 31, 81, 89, 90, 113, 117-20, 131, 143, 150-1, 168, 186-7, 194, 198, 204, 210, 292
Chechnya 105, 109, 142
Cheney, Vice President Richard 140, 165, 166, 261
China 27, 33, 34, 41, 56, 93, 141, 150, 173, 182, 256
Chirac, President Jacques 183
Churchill, Prime Minister Winston 17, 30, 195
Clarke, Jonathan 161, 295
Clarke, Richard A. 102, 292
Clinton, President Bill 119, 120, 124, 133, 167, 171, 175, 276, 294
Cohen, Richard 57, 293
Coalition 35, 77, 88, 112, 148-9, 156, 166, 170-4, 182-4, 188, 190-3, 195, 198-9, 201, 202, 205-10, 212-14, 216-21, 223, 226, 229-34, 237, 239, 245-6, 275, 278
Cold War 11, 36, 38, 48, 50, 75, 86, 136-8, 148-9, 154-5, 157, 159, 170, 182, 241, 243, 259, 303
Colson, Chuck 99, 293
Copeland, Libby 204, 293
Cordesman, Anthony H. 293
Council on American-Islamic Relations [CAIR] 130
Crusades 59, 60, 108

D
Daalder, Ivo H. 146, 293
Damascus, Syria 17, 63, 297
Dermer, Ron 248, 301
Dhahran, Saudi Arabia 30, 120, 276
Dickey, Christopher 299
Doha, Qatar 151, 152, 172, 180, 237, 280

E
Egypt 23, 30, 46, 48, 62, 64, 66, 67-8, 72-73, 75, 77, 80, 83, 87-9, 105, 131, 179, 180, 235, 266, 272, 273, 274, 281, 283, 284

Eisenhower, President and General Dwight D. 30, 195
Engel, Richard 206, 293
European Union [EU] 83,105, 106, 110, 112, 113, 114, 170, 246, 263
Even, Samuel 300

F

Fahd bin Abdul Aziz ibn Saud, King 26, 47, 48, 49, 50, 51, 52, 65, 69, 107, 110, 129, 133, 236, 244, 251, 274-7, 280, 298, 302
Fahd bin Turki bin Saud al Kabir, Prince 130, 132
Fainaru, Steve 217, 221, 293
Faisal bin Abdul Aziz ibn Saud, King 31, 37, 46, 47, 53, 62, 75, 129, 131, 252, 273
Faisal, Turki bin, Ambassador 65, 129, 252
Fallujah, Iraq 7, 207, 212-14, 297
    April 2004 Assault 207
    Round II, November 2004 7, 212-14
Fandy, Mamoun 75, 294
Farah, Douglas 72, 299
Ferguson, Niall 106, 197, 212, 294
Filkens, Dexter 216, 217, 219, 294, 302
First Gulf War 88, 100, 101, 115, 119, 124, 136, 143, 165-6, 170, 172, 188-91, 193, 197-8
First World War 17, 18, 22, 29, 84, 85, 113, 176, 197, 240
Franks, General Tommy 189-90, 196, 206, 261, 294
Friedman, George 142, 145, 150-52, 163, 191, 261, 294
Friedman, Thomas L. 11, 52, 152, 180, 266, 295

G

Gaddis, John Lewis 157, 159, 160, 161, 295
Garner, U.S. Army Lieutenant General Jay 197, 198, 199
Geneva Convention 204, 205
Germany 17, 105-9, 111-12, 118, 131, 144-5, 169, 173, 183, 269
Giuliani, Mayor Rudolf 134
Glanz, James 216, 291
Gold, Dore 18, 47, 72, 295

Grand Mosque 47, 61, 62, 235, 272, 273, 284
Graner, Specialist Charles 204
Great Britain [United Kingdom] 23, 105, 106, 143, 157, 173, 252
Greece 110
Guantanamo Bay, Cuba 59, 202, 205
Gulf War [see also First Gulf War] 88, 100, 101, 115, 119, 124, 136, 143, 165-6, 170, 172, 188-90, 191, 193, 197-8
Gulling 6, 28, 81, 113, 115, 127, 131, 133, 135, 152, 166, 167, 244

H
Hadley, Stephen 146
Haiti 137, 175, 259
Hajj 27, 103, 279, 282
Halper, Stefan 161, 295
Hamas 63, 80, 83, 125, 171, 181, 182, 257, 263, 264, 282, 292
Hakim, Abdul Aziz al 229
Hauerwas, Stanley 269, 296
Hawes, Crispin 37, 291
Hezbollah 117, 282
Hormuz, Straits of 27, 32
Howard, Prime Minister John 171
Hussein, Qusay 188, 200
Hussein, Saddam 35, 49, 50, 56, 77, 83, 87-8, 115, 124, 137, 153, 164-9, 171, 172, 181-3, 187-202, 205, 208-10, 212, 214-15, 219, 230, 232-3, 240-1, 244, 246, 254, 259, 262, 276
Hussein, Uday 188, 200
Husseini, Hajj Amin al 86

I
Ignatieff, Michael 215, 296
Ignatius, David 228, 253, 296
Ikhwan army 21-3, 47-8, 52, 55, 72, 123, 272, 282, 284
India 16, 33, 105, 143, 150, 151
Indonesia 17, 50, 105, 248
International Energy Agency [IEA] 33, 296

International Islamic Relief Organization [IIRO] 130
Iran 16, 21, 28, 32, 34, 35, 39, 56, 69, 83-4, 105, 123-4, 132, 141-4, 147, 150, 154, 165, 174, 181, 215, 217, 229, 242, 243, 247, 251, 257, 261, 263, 274, 277, 282
    Iranian Shiite Revolution, 1979 37, 117, 122, 123, 288
    Iran-Iraq war 35, 123-4, 274
    Shah of Iran 35, 39, 47, 54, 55, 62, 69, 115, 132, 134, 181, 274
Iranian Shiite Ayatollahs 83, 87, 117, 124, 215
Iraq 7, 8, 12, 17, 20, 21, 28, 34, 35, 40, 49-50, 52, 56, 59, 69, 77, 83, 87-8, 97, 101, 104-5, 107, 109-12, 118, 123-4, 128, 136-7, 143-4, 147, 149, 152-4, 157, 163-75, 178-81, 183-233, 236, 238, 239-41, 244-50, 252-5, 259-64, 270-2, 274-280, 285-6, 291, 294-7, 299-303
    Casualties 2003-2006 195, 200, 226, 230-2, 246, 260
    Kuwait invasion, 1990 49, 124, 137
    Elections of 2005 7, 12, 40-1, 176, 178-82, 184, 201, 206, 214-25, 227-31, 238-9, 245-7, 249, 257, 263, 279, 280
Iraq Liberation Act of 1998 167, 276
Islam 5, 6, 8-13, 15-23, 25-33, 35, 37, 39-41, 43-5, 47-51, 53, 55-85, 87-91, 93-113, 115, 116-19, 121-39, 141, 143, 145, 147-51, 153, 155, 157, 159-61, 163-5, 167, 169-71, 173-81, 183-4, 193, 199, 201, 205, 215-17, 219-20, 222, 224-5, 229-30, 232-43, 247-51, 253, 255, 258-71, 277, 280-91, 293, 295-303
Islamist jihad [jihad, jihadist] 6, 9, 15-16, 48-9, 58, 63, 65-6, 71, 73, 75, 77, 79-80, 83-4, 89, 97, 99-100, 109, 118-19, 122, 129, 134, 183, 186, 192, 193, 198, 200, 202, 207-8, 211-12, 214-15, 219-20, 223-26, 231, 236, 238, 240-1, 246, 250, 281, 283-284, 293
Islamic law or Sharia 19, 40, 43, 60, 63-4, 73, 82, 97, 113, 283, 284-6, 310, 315
Islamic Society of North America 130, 250
Islamists 9, 10, 12, 19, 58, 60, 62, 65-7, 78, 82-3, 97-9, 109, 112, 117, 122, 133, 174, 181, 230, 237, 241-3, 249, 253, 255, 259-60, 262, 264-5, 268, 283, 293, 302
Israel 18, 33, 35, 38, 46, 52, 57, 62-3, 66, 70, 75-6, 81, 84-6, 89-90, 108-10, 115, 118, 120, 131-4, 150, 152-3, 165, 167-8, 170-1, 174, 179, 182, 193, 244, 247, 257-8, 263, 273, 282-3

Israeli-Palestinian conflict [see also Arab-Israeli War] 108, 182
Italy 94, 105, 111-12, 171, 173

J
Jafari, Prime Minister Ibrahim al 201, 222, 225, 227-30, 296
Japan 33, 34, 113, 144, 171, 182, 196, 197, 268
Jeddah, Saudi Arabia 61, 62, 64, 75, 235, 274, 279
Jews 60, 64, 66, 84-86, 89-90, 97, 107-10, 127, 241, 268, 281
Jihad, jihadist [see also Islamist jihad] 6, 9, 15-16, 48-9, 58, 63, 65-6, 71, 73, 75, 77, 79-80, 83-4, 89, 97, 99-100, 109, 118-19, 122, 129, 134, 183, 186, 192, 193, 198, 200, 202, 207-8, 211-12, 214-15, 219-20, 223-6, 231, 236, 238, 240-1, 246, 250, 281, 283-4, 293
Jordan 29, 46, 52, 61, 63-4, 69-70, 77-8, 83, 87, 105, 152, 193, 209, 211, 249, 283, 285

K
Kagan, Robert 169, 296
Kaiser, Robert G. 94, 296
Khaldun, Ibn 55
Kaplin, Lee 133, 297
Karachi, Pakistan 120,
Karbala, Iraq 123, 190, 193, 272
Karpinski, General Janis 203-4
Karzai, President Hamid 145, 176-7
Kennan, George 138-9, 140, 161,
Kenya 120
Kerry, Senator John 204, 208
Khaled al Faisal ibn Abdul Aziz al Saud, Prince 297
Khaled bin Abdul Aziz ibn Saud, King 47, 50, 273-4
Khaled bin Sultan bin Abdul Aziz al Saud, Prince and General 22, 53, 103, 297
Khaled Sheik Mohammed 102
Khan, Dr. A.Q. 150, 243, 249, 297,
Khomeini, Ayatollah 39, 47, 69, 117, 274
Koh, Harold Hongju 137, 297

Koran 16, 19, 23, 28, 40, 43, 58, 60, 68, 73, 79, 82, 95-6, 98, 108-9, 111, 267, 282-3
Korea, North 147-8, 150, 257
Korea, South 33-4, 144, 171
Kosovo 119, 137, 175
Krauthammer, Charles 263, 297
Kurds 143, 197, 211, 215, 217-8, 220, 223-4, 245-6
Kuwait 22, 24, 28-9, 35, 49, 54, 104, 115, 117, 124, 136-7, 152, 172, 174, 180, 188-9, 192, 210, 236, 272, 274-5, 277
    Iraq invasion [see also Gulf War, First Gulf War], 1990 115, 124, 136-7, 188-9, 236, 274-5, 277
Kyl, Senator John 125, 298

L
Lebanon 29, 90, 105, 116-7, 179-80, 245, 263, 280, 282-3
Lewis, Bernard 80, 298
Libya 83, 118, 150, 174, 180, 242, 243, 245, 283
Libyan terrorists 118
Lincoln, President Abraham 252-3, 267
Lindsay, James M. 146, 293
Lippman, Thomas 37-8, 47, 56, 298
Long, David E. 27, 298

M
Madrid, Spain 110-11, 239
Mahdi, Vice President Abel Abdul 225
Majlis [Majlis Al Shura] 42, 275, 284
Maliki, Prime Minister Jawad al [Nouri Kamal al] 229
Malaysia 17
Mann, James 140-1, 147, 161, 166, 299
Masland, Tom 299
Mawdudi, Sayyid 19
McKinley, President William 157
McPhee, Michele 99, 299
McVeigh, Timothy 101-03

Mecca, Saudi Arabia 10, 16, 20, 22-3, 26-7, 47, 51-2, 55-6, 61-2, 75, 103, 165, 235, 251, 272-3, 282-4
Medina, Saudi Arabia 16, 20, 22-3, 26-7, 52, 55, 61-2, 75, 165, 235, 272, 282, 284
Mexico 93
Mintz, John 72, 101, 299
Mir, Mushaf Ali 129
Mohammed 16, 19, 21, 23, 27, 40, 42, 83, 98, 123, 126, 267, 271, 282-6
Morocco 105-6, 283
Moss, Michael 209-10, 299
Moussaoui, Zacharias 99
Mubarak, President Hosni 88, 179
Munif, Abdul 127, 299
Murawiec, Laurent 113, 299
Musharraf, President Pervez 141-2, 150-1, 249
Muslim 9-10, 12, 15, 17-23, 26-8, 32, 35, 37, 39-40, 43, 47-8, 50, 55, 58-60, 63-4, 68-70, 72-4, 76-86, 89-91, 96-101, 103-14, 117-27, 130, 134-5, 137, 142, 145, 148, 150, 152-4, 161, 163-5, 170-1, 174-6, 178, 180-1, 184, 200, 202, 206-7, 209, 213, 215, 217-8, 220, 222, 227, 230, 239-40, 242, 244-52, 254, 258, 262-4, 266-9, 279, 281-6
Muslim Brotherhood [Brotherhood] 19, 41, 46-8, 59, 61-4, 66, 68, 71-3, 75-6, 79-80, 97, 112, 125, 128, 131, 133, 235, 266, 269, 273, 282, 284
Muslim World League 76, 130
Muttawa 40, 44, 284

N
Nasser, Gamal Abdel 46, 48, 73, 75, 235
Nayef bin Abdul Aziz ibn Saud, Prince 40, 50-1, 53-4, 81, 252
National Front for the Liberation of Iraq 193
Neo-conservatives 146, 152
Netherlands 105, 111, 145
Nixon, President Richard M. 39, 146, 203
    Twin Pillar Persian Gulf Policy 39
Nordland, Rod 183, 194, 207

North Atlantic Treaty Organization [NATO] 55, 83, 86, 113-4, 143, 145-6, 149, 166, 178, 182, 246-7, 255-8, 280

O

Oil 10-11, 15-16, 23, 26-40, 45-7, 49-50, 52, 54-6, 59, 61-2, 69-70, 72, 76, 80-7, 91, 94-5, 113-16, 120, 123-4, 127-9, 131-2, 135, 137, 153, 162, 164-5, 168-9, 174-5, 187-9, 192, 198, 206, 224, 235-6, 241-2, 247,270, 273, 275, 280

Oman 105, 152

Organization of Petroleum Exporting Countries [OPEC] 31, 35-7, 46, 48-9, 55, 57-60

Osama bin Laden [see also Bin Laden] 9-12, 15, 18-9, 21, 48-9, 55, 57-72, 74-9, 80, 83, 94, 97, 104, 111-12, 116, 118-25, 128-30, 133-4, 138,142-4, 148, 155, 159-63, 173, 181-2, 184, 200, 202, 205, 212, 219, 233-9, 240-4, 247-9, 252, 254, 259-60, 262, 265, 269-70, 273-5, 277, 279-80, 286

Ottoman Empire 17-18, 20-22, 29, 39, 82-5, 105, 109, 113, 197, 271-2, 284

P

Pakistan 64-5, 67, 105-6, 120

Palestine 65, 152, 174, 180, 258, 263, 272, 283

Palestine Liberation Organization [PLO] 63, 125, 171

Paris, France 33, 66, 68, 108, 112

Pentagon 10, 100, 120-1, 124, 138, 164, 186, 188, 196-8, 203-4, 207-10, 237, 260-1, 288

Perle, Richard 146

Persian Gulf [Arabian Gulf] 11, 17, 21, 27, 32-7, 39, 57, 61, 67, 84, 87, 96, 101, 114-5, 123, 135, 143, 151, 187, 189, 247, 276

Philby, Harry St. John 29-30

Philippines 17, 50, 102, 161, 262

Pinches, Charles 269, 296

Podhoretz, Norman 161-2, 169, 300

Posner, Gerald 128-30, 300

Powell, Secretary of State and General Colin 141, 144, 146, 172-3, 190
    Powell Doctrine 137, 190
Putin, Prime Minister Vladimir 142

Q
Qaddafi, President Muammar al 118
Qaeda, al 9, 11-12, 15-6, 19-22, 44, 54, 57-9, 63, 65-72, 76-80, 83-4, 95, 99-102, 107-9, 111, 113, 116, 119-21, 123-5, 128-30, 132, 138-44, 150-4, 162-7, 170, 175, 177-9, 182-4, 192, 198, 200, 202, 208, 212, 216, 219-20, 224-5, 235-45, 247, 249-50, 252-6, 259, 264-5, 268, 278-82, 286, 288
Qatar 151-2, 172, 180, 237, 280
Qusti, Raid 44, 300
Qutb, Mohammed 64, 75
Qutb, Sayyid 41, 64, 66, 68, 72-6, 79-80, 125, 128, 269

R
Rahman, Sheik Omar Abdul 64, 78
Reagan, President Ronald 35, 48, 117-8, 139-40, 146, 155, 161, 176
Ricchiardi, Sherry 202, 300
Rice, Secretary of State Condoleezza 146, 257
Riyadh, Saudi Arabia 21-2, 24-5, 29-30, 39, 42, 44, 51, 61, 81, 120, 272, 276, 278-9
Rivilin, Paul 87, 300
Roosevelt, President Franklin D. 12, 30, 38, 114-5, 131, 141, 159, 170
    Roosevelt-Abdul Aziz ibn Saud Meeting, 1945 12, 30, 38, 114-5, 131
Roosevelt, President Theodore 262
Rumaylah Oil Fields (Iraq) 189
Rumsfeld, Secretary of Defense Donald 140, 163, 166, 185, 189, 192-3, 196, 204-5
Russia 34, 93, 137, 142, 146, 150-1, 154, 168-9, 173, 182-3, 241-3
Rwanda 137

S

Sadat, President Anwar 46, 48, 65-7, 235
Sadr, Muqtada al 200-1, 225-30
Sanger, David E. 150, 291
Saladin 17, 85, 271
Salafi or Salafism [see also Wahhabism] 10-11, 19-23, 26, 28, 39-40, 47-50, 57, 59-60, 64, 69, 71-2, 76-77, 79-83, 85, 89-90, 94-7, 99, 103-4, 106, 108-11, 124-25, 127, 131-2, 164, 173, 211, 235, 239, 243-4, 267, 271, 285
Samarra 225-6, 231, 246
Saud, Muhammad bin 20
Saudi-American relations 33, 116, 135
Saudi Arabia 11, 15-16, 18-23, 26-35, 37-41, 43-50, 52-3, 55, 57, 59, 61, 64, 66-7, 69-72, 74-6, 80-3, 87-8, 90-1, 93-7, 100-1, 103-4, 107-8, 110-1, 113-6, 119-20, 122-31, 133-5, 137, 149-50, 152-4, 159, 163-5, 172-5, 179-80, 183, 186, 193, 200, 212, 219, 234-6, 240, 242-5, 250-2, 262, 267, 272-80, 284-6, 288
    Basic Law 38, 42, 275
    Consultative Council 27-31, 35, 42, 275
    Kingdom 15, 20-3, 26, 43-5, 47-9, 55, 57, 61-2, 82, 95, 127, 286
    Majlis 42, 275, 284
    Ulama 42-3, 47-8, 51-2, 235, 286
Schlesinger, Secretary James 204
Schroeder, Chancellor Gerhard 169, 183
Schumer, Senator Charles 126, 301
Schwartz, Stephen 109, 301
Schwarzkopf, General Norman 103
Scowcroft, General Brent 174, 301
September 11, 2001 [9/11] 8, 10-11, 15, 33-5, 37, 53, 57, 59, 70, 75, 78, 81-2, 89, 94-5, 99, 104, 107, 111, 116, 118-9, 121-2, 124-5, 128-9, 131-2, 134-5, 139-40, 142, 144, 146, 151, 153-4, 162, 166, 169, 171, 173, 177, 182, 184, 196, 202, 225, 233-4, 236, 238-44, 250, 255-8, 261, 264, 266, 268, 270, 277, 286

Shadid, Anthony 218, 221, 301
Shah of Iran, 35, 39, 47, 54-5, 62, 69, 115, 132, 134, 180, 181, 274
Shamar Confederation 52, 211, 219, 285-6
Sharansky, Natan 248, 301
Sharia, Islamic Law 19, 40, 43, 60, 63, 64, 73, 82, 97, 113, 283-6
Shiite 21-3, 28, 35, 37, 39-40, 47, 62, 77, 83-4, 87, 117, 120, 122-4, 134, 143, 165, 189-90, 194, 197-201, 211-12, 214-231, 245-6, 261, 267, 272, 274, 281-2, 285
    Minority in Saudi Arabia 40, 123
    Majority in Iraq, Iran 12, 123, 165, 181, 194, 201, 214, 216, 231
Shultz, Secretary George P. 161, 176
Sistani, Grand Ayatollah Ali al 83, 201, 214-5, 224, 226
Somalia 116, 119, 209, 259
Soviet Union 48-50, 58, 62-3, 65, 69, 71, 86-7, 103, 118, 123-4, 129, 134, 136-8, 140, 142, 159, 240, 242, 254, 259
Soviet Union invasion, 1979 48, 58 65, 236, 254, 274
Spain 16, 46, 51, 85, 110-12, 122, 171, 173, 239
Standard Oil of California [SOCAL] 29, 273
Stille, Alexander 197, 301
Stothard, Peter 183, 301
Struck, Doug 218, 301
Sudairi, Hassa bint Ahmad 50, 285
    Sudairi Seven 50-2, 285
Sudan 63, 66-8, 78, 119-20
Sufi 22-3, 40, 285
Sullivan, Andrew 205, 301
Sultan bin Abdul Aziz ibn Saud, Crown Prince, 50-4, 132, 251-2, 280
Sultan bin Faisal bin Turki, Prince 129
Sunni 15, 18-20, 39, 47, 55, 59,64, 69, 77, 80, 82-4, 90, 124, 145, 165, 178, 186, 193-4, 196-200, 202, 207, 211-2, 214-29, 231, 242, 245-6, 267, 281-2, 284-6
Sunni Triangle (Iraq) 52, 178, 191, 193, 198, 200, 207, 211, 213, 221, 226, 286
Sweden 105, 112

Syria 46, 48, 52, 61-2, 75, 80, 83, 87, 105, 128, 131, 133, 165, 168, 179-80, 193, 212, 240, 263, 280, 283, 285

T
Taheri, Amir 49, 218, 222, 237, 302
Tajikistan 137, 141-3
Takfir wal Hijra 69, 71, 77-8, 211, 226
Taliban 11, 20, 40, 55, 69, 82-3, 97, 118, 130, 142-5, 147, 149, 152, 166, 177-8, 182, 215, 237, 241-2, 248, 277, 286
Tanzania 120
Taspinar, Omer 111, 302
Taymiyah, Ibn 19, 265
Tehran, Iran 117, 142, 180
Tikrit, Iraq 201
Treaty of Versailles 197
Truman, President Harry 38, 138-9, 141, 170
    Truman Doctrine or Containment Policy 136-9, 158
    Point Four Program 38
Tunisia 106, 283
Turabi, Hassan 63, 66-8
Turkey 70, 83-4, 86, 105-7, 113-4, 145, 165, 172, 176, 246, 248, 284
Turkmenistan 137, 141-2

U
Ukraine 171, 179
Ulama 42-3, 47-8, 51-2, 235, 286
United Arab Emirates 149, 180
United Arab Republic 172
United Kingdom [UK] 105-6, 183
United Nations [UN] 149, 157, 163, 168, 173, 176, 182, 209, 255-7, 264, 275-7, 302
    General Assembly 163
    Resolution 172-3, 183
    Security Council 172-3, 182-3, 276-8

United States [US] 11, 12, 15, 26-7, 30-41, 46, 48-50, 53-7, 59, 65, 67-70, 72, 74-8, 81, 84, 86-91, 93-5, 97-105, 107-8, 110, 112-7, 119-22, 124, 128-45, 148-54, 156-76, 180, 182-6, 188-92, 196-8, 200-5, 207-10, 213, 216-7, 220, 223, 225, 231-2, 234, 236-47, 252-6, 258-68, 273, 276-80, 282, 286
USS Cole 99, 120
Uzbekistan 137

V

Van Gogh, Theo 111
Vienna, Austria 80, 94, 116, 122, 286
Vietnam 116, 119, 198, 203, 209, 232-3, 259
Vistica, Gregory L. 101, 299

W

Wahhab, Sheikh Muhammad Ibn Abdul 19-20, 22, 235, 265, 271, 286
Wahhabism or Salafism 10-11, 15-6, 18-23, 26, 28, 30-1, 39-40, 42-44, 46-57, 59-60, 62, 64, 69, 71-3, 75-77, 79-83, 85, 89-91, 93-104, 106-14, 119, 123-5, 127-8, 130-2, 135, 150, 152, 164-5, 173, 175, 186, 207, 211, 213-4, 216, 219-20, 224-5, 235, 239 242-43, 250, 252, 265, 272-3, 282, 284-6
    Wahhabi Bin Ladenism 80, 94, 116, 122, 286
Walker, Martin 187, 195, 303
Weinberger, Secretary Caspar 117
Williams, Daniel 266, 303
Wilson, President Woodrow 158-61
Wolfowitz, Undersecretary of Defense Paul 139, 146, 157, 161, 166, 208
    Defense Planning Guidance Proposal of 140, 157
Woodward, Bob 143, 166, 172-3, 187, 190, 303
Woolsey, R. James 119
World Assembly of Muslim Youth 130
World Trade Center 10, 64, 78, 99, 119-21, 124, 138, 237
    Bombing, 1993 64, 78, 119-20

Twin Towers, 9/11, 2001 10, 99, 121, 124, 138, 237
World Trade Organization [WTO] 175, 287
Wyatt, Caroline 112, 303

Y
Yergin, Daniel 138, 303
Yemen 61, 116, 120, 122, 151-2

Z
Zahedi, Ardeshir 134,
Zakaria, Fareed 196, 303
Zakheim, Dov 146
Zarqawi, Abu Musab al 69, 77, 200, 202, 211-3, 219, 225-6 238, 254, 286
Zawahiri, Ayman al 63-4, 66-8, 71, 77-8, 237, 286
Zinni, General Anthony 261
Zoellick, Robert 146
Zubaydah, Abu 129-30